Routledge Revivals

The Autonomous Child

Originally published in 1986, this book's focal point is a field study which asks whether the social childrearing context of daycare transmits to young children values different from those within America's dominant value tradition of individualism. Daycare critics were concerned that this social childrearing within daycare would weaken the family and promote collectivist rather than individualistic values, and thereby threaten the social continuity of America's values. Through participant observation four daycare teachers' interactions as they emphasize children's individual learning experiences and children's social learning experiences are examined. By focusing on the actions and words of daycare teachers and their children in their daily activities over time, this field study provides a conceptual model for an initial understanding of the relationship of daycare to the continuity of America's values.

The Autonomous Child

Day Care and the Transmission of Values

Carol Speekman Klass

Routledge
Taylor & Francis Group

First published in 1986
by The Falmer Press

This edition first published in 2023 by Routledge
4 Park Square, Milton Park, Abingdon, Oxon, OX14 4RN

and by Routledge
605 Third Avenue, New York, NY 10017

Routledge is an imprint of the Taylor & Francis Group, an informa business

Publisher's Note
The publisher has gone to great lengths to ensure the quality of this reprint but points out that some imperfections in the original copies may be apparent.

Disclaimer
The publisher has made every effort to trace copyright holders and welcomes correspondence from those they have been unable to contact.

A Library of Congress record exists under ISBN: 1850001154

ISBN: 978-1-032-42561-0 (hbk)
ISBN: 978-1-003-36329-3 (ebk)
ISBN: 978-1-032-42574-0 (pbk)

Book DOI 10.4324/9781003363293

The Autonomous Child

For Denny, Greg and Ben

Was it not then that I acquired all that now sustains me? And I gained so much and so quickly that during the rest of my life I did not acquire a hundredth part of it. From myself as a five year old to myself as I now am there is only one step. The distance between myself as an infant and myself at five years is tremendous.

Leo Tolstoy, 1905

The Autonomous Child

Day Care and the Transmission of Values

Carol Speekman Klass
Illinois Department of
Children and Family Services

The analysis and interpretation in this book do not represent the official policy of the Illinois Department of Children and Family Services.

The Falmer Press
(A member of the Taylor & Francis Group)
London, New York and Philadelphia

UK The Falmer Press, Falmer House, Barcombe, Lewes, East Sussex. BN8 5DL.

USA The Falmer Press, Taylor & Francis Inc., 242 Cherry Street, Philadelphia. PA 19106-1906.

First published in 1986

Library of Congress Cataloging-in-Publication Data

Klass, Carol Speekman.
The autonomous child.

1. Day care centers — United States. 2. Child rearing — United States. 3. Socialization. I. Title.
HV854.K57 1986 362.7'12'0973 86-13424
ISBN 1-85000-114-5
ISBN 1-85000-115-4 (pbk.)

Cover photograph by Kitty Daly
Jacket designed by Caroline Archer

Typeset in 11/13 Caledonia by
Imago Publishing Ltd, Thame, Oxon

Printed in Great Britain by Taylor & Francis (Printers) Ltd, Basingstoke.

Contents

List of Figures

Acknowledgements

My greatest indebtedness is to the Rosehill Day Care Center staff, who must remain anonymous. Their willingness in having me observe, their patience in answering my questions and thoughtfulness in discussing their teaching made possible the field study reported in this book.

Dorothea Gray Pflug, my long-time mentor, colleague and friend, has been part of this project since its initial conceptualization. I am grateful for her wisdom, and unswerving support and encouragement.

This study was originally written as a dissertation at Washington University, in St. Louis, Missouri. I would like to thank members of my Committee, Marilyn Cohn, Alan Tom and Arthur Wirth. Harold Berlak's perspective challenged me to penetrate the meaning of observations beyond the immediate context of my field study. As I prepared this project for publication, Louis Smith's suggestions and critical reading were invaluable.

I thank friends Nancy Neumeyer and David Thiel for their careful editing of this manuscript.

My husband, Dennis Eugene Klass, has offered his experience, his wisdom, his humor and his love during the entire life of this project. And our teenage sons, Greg and Ben, provided companionship, joy and humor, even amidst the sometimes untidy particularities of our life together.

New Preface to the Reissue of 2023

I am enormously pleased that this book is being reissued nearly 40 years after I wrote it. Unfortunately, four decades later the cultural battles that led me to write it continue, and we are still not close to meeting the challenge of providing quality care to young children. I hope the reissue of this book will be of some use to those working on that issue.

In 1971, Congress passed the Comprehensive Child Development Act (CDA). The bill would have used federal funding to help poor and working parents secure quality childcare for their young children. Richard Nixon had, in a 1969 message to Congress, called for "a national commitment to providing all American children an opportunity for healthful and stimulating development during the first five years of life." After Congress passed the CDA, however, Nixon came under pressure from the right to veto it. It was the height of the Cold War, and some conservatives considered government supported childcare to be a threat to American values, and even a step toward communism. They characterized universal day care and other elements of the CDA as the state's attempt to take on a job that properly belonged to parents and as the socialization of childhood. Nixon paid attention to those voices. In his veto statement, he wrote that "good public policy requires that we enhance rather than diminish both parental authority and parental involvement with children—particularly in those decisive early years when social attitudes and a conscience are formed, and religious and moral principles are first inculcated."

I began the research that resulted in *Autonomous Child: Day Care and the Transmission of Values* in the aftermath of the CDA's failure. Those who opposed government support of early childcare believed that it represented a threat to traditional values, including the dominant value of American individualism. I set out to test that premise through the close observation of daycare teachers' interactions with the children they cared for.

What I found was that those childcare providers transmitted to children many of the same values that opponents of universal childcare held dear. As I wrote in the introduction to the original, "daycare centers, in their daily operations, actually emphasize individual more than social or collectivist values and experiences." It turns out that in the transmission of cultural values, the medium is not the message. Though children were being cared for together, the values that caregivers were sharing with them corresponded to traditional American individualism.

In a sense this is unsurprising. Government funding of early childcare does not turn daycare providers into agents of the state. Daycare providers are members of our community and share in our community's culture and cultural values. But that fact was and remains important to document. Universal early childcare is not a threat to our shared values.

In the decades since I wrote this book, it has only become more difficult for especially poor and working families to secure quality childcare for their young children. Since the mid-70s, according to the Department of Labor, the rate of labor force participation for women with children under three has nearly doubled. The supply of affordable early childcare has not kept up with demand. Low-income families with young children regularly spend a third of their income on childcare—if they are lucky enough to find it. A 2020 study by the Center for American Progress found that over half our families live in childcare deserts, where demand for childcare outstrips supply.

And yet, when President Biden proposed additional federal spending on childcare in the American Rescue Plan, politicians like Senator Marsha Blackburn trotted out the same tired comparisons to the Soviet Union, as if the government's efforts to help working families care for their children was a threat to our market economy and individual freedoms. Old tropes, it seems, die hard. I hope the reissue of my study will be of some use to those who continue to argue against those tropes and to fight for sensible child-care policies.

A few words about method. The years since this book was published have seen major advances in the data sciences and empirical methods. I hope, however, that empirical psychology does not lose touch with its interpretive roots, or with the case-study method employed in this book. As I argue in Appendix B, our study of the mind should include the study of meaning, and of what gives meaning to our shared lives. Empirical psychology should search not only for knowledge, but also for understanding. I believe that in the human sciences especially, one cannot take the observer out of the equation. In writing this book, I sought to be transparent about the perspective I brought to my observations, the reasons for the questions I asked, and my role in the answers I received. I hope that in doing so I provide readers the tools to judge for themselves how to interpret and use my data and conclusions.

Lastly, a word of thanks again to the individual caregivers who were the subject of this study, and to the many wonderful people who spend their careers caring for young children. Though we all know the value of the work they do, our society and economy continue to undervalue these amazing people. I remain grateful for their dedication to helping families raise their children with intelligence, love and joy.

Carol Speekman Klass

1 Introduction

> Pam arrives and opens the center at 6.30 a.m. By the time she has the lights on and the heat turned up, two 3 year-olds have arrived. Children's arrival patterns during this first hour seem quite ritualistic: as the parents sign in at the entry, children put their coats in their cubbies and then go to the choice shelf, get a toy and take it to a front table. By 7.30, 25 children, the cook and a second teacher have arrived. Six children eat breakfast at the front table and the other children play with table toys at the front table area. A soft hum of voices and a calm atmosphere pervades throughout the room.
>
> Jesse calls out 'Give it back' to Kay who holds Lego in her hand. Pam says to Jesse: 'Use an inside voice please Jesse'. Jessie replies, 'But it was my choice first'. Pam then says to Kay: 'You need to get your own choice Kay. . . .'
>
> Later in the day, I asked Pam what was her rationale for telling Kay to get her own choice. Pam replied: 'We always have enough materials for everyone. A child should have the chance to use materials in her own way. . . .'
>
> (Field notes from Rosehill Child Center, September 1980)

Many Americans wince at the thought of very small children going from the bed to a child care institution for breakfast while their parents go to work. Similarly, people are concerned about the values and practices that very young children will learn through day care experiences. In the teacher-child exchange above, some parents would prefer that their child develop skills in sharing toys; whereas, other parents would be pleased that their child's right to his own toy was protected.

Traditionally the family has functioned as transmitter to young children of our society's values, attitudes and patterns of relating. The American family ideal is that childrearing of the very young is the responsiblity of the family, especially the mother. When people outside the family are involved in childrearing, the question of the very continuity of our society's value tradition is called into question. Day care exists within this tension of social and familial childrearing.

This book discusses a field study which asks whether the social childrearing context of day care transmits to young children values different from those within our society's dominant value tradition of individualism. It is hoped that this book will yield insight into the larger public issue regarding the socialization of our society's young children at a time of major cultural transition — from primarily exclusive familial childrearing of very young children to supplementary out-of-home childrearing for many of our society's young children.

The Book's Origin

In describing this book's origin I am accepting the tradition of those field workers who acknowledge the reciprocal relation between one's personal history and one's research process (Mills, 1959; Powdermaker, 1966; Rabinow, 1977; Reinharz, 1979; Whyte, 1943).

The conception of this book evolved from several aspects of my personal and professional life. Since the early seventies, I have been interested both in out-of-home childrearing for our society's young children, and in our society's relative emphasis on the individual and the social. Both of these interests are rooted in my experiences in the sixties.

In the mid-1960s, I was one of the legions of young adults involved in organizational work within the civil rights and peace movement. Community building and social reform occurred in multiple arenas and many of us, with little understanding of the complexities and contradictions of America's social-political structure, embraced the 1960s as the beginning of an era of social justice and reform.

In the late 1960s, when our own children were infant and toddler age, my husband and I lived in university housing for three years. With other families, we experienced many of the advantages of extended family living, such as shared meals and shared child care. Meanwhile, some of our close friends chose to live in communes and in turn challenged our decision to maintain a nuclear family.

When we moved to a suburban single family dwelling in 1971, we attempted to provide community ties beyond our nuclear family and thereby regain aspects of the social networking of our previous experiences. For example, we began a sitter cooperative. Concurrently, in reading popular journals and through our children's schools, our own work, and our personal social relations, we repeatedly met people immersed in the search for personal meaning through participation in the human potential movement.

If my personal context was tilted toward the social in the sixties, the ambience of the seventies seemed tilted toward the individual. The celebration of the self seemed to reign: in the media, superheroes captured children's imaginations; everyday jargon expressed 'do your own thing' or 'whatever turns you on'; best seller lists contained a preponderance of books on personal fitness, achieving individual success and hedonistic sexuality; and self-directed creative learning was championed in alternative 'free' schools throughout the country.

With the shifting emphasis on the valuing of the individual and the social in the 1960s and 1970s, I gradually became interested in this individual-social value tension within my professional field, early education and developmental theory. I had read several reports on early education in collectivist societies. Then I began teaching child development courses and training employed early childhood educators. At this time I met an early childhood educator who had just returned from visiting a variety of Chinese child care centers. We had extended conversations and this friendship led to expanded readings on child care in other countries. Looking outside the particularities of American early education and developmental theory expanded my own perspective, especially with regard to valuing of the individual and the social. As I stated in my application to graduate school: 'I have many questions concerning the interaction of cultural values, developmental theory, and educational practice. . . . Does our early childhood theory reflect Western values more than it reflects the nature of the young child? Dramatically different behavior seems to follow different expectations.'

During the 1960s, I studied child psychology and early childhood education and worked in several teaching and research positions. I was able to obtain family child care for our own young children, and was not aware of issues involved in institutional day care. Day care was not discussed, either in my early education graduate work or in my personal life. Then in the 1970s, I began training early educators employed in a variety of contexts: preschools, Head Start centers and day care centers.

I was astounded that I knew next to nothing about day care in spite of my study of early childhood education and use of-out-of home child care for our own children. Once I did become involved in day care, I realized that in our society, day care is a social-political issue — that with our society's familial ideal of maternal childrearing, day care is considered a stigmatized service for deficient families. I investigated colleges in the metropolitan area and discovered that day care was not a topic in curriculum. In my work with preschool teachers, I recurrently encountered their disapproval of the use of day care. At the same time, I saw the number of working mothers increasing each year and new day care centers emerging in neighborhoods of all social classes. I became intrigued with the tensions involved in our society's day care practices and policy.

Rationale for the Book

Significance of the Day Care Context

Over the past two decades, the structure of the American family has been changing dramatically. Two factors are involved in this changing family structure: an increase in single parenting and an increase in married mothers in the workforce. Between 1970 and 1980 the number of households headed by only one parent doubled (Winn, 1983). In 1982, almost half of American women with children under 6 years of age were working (Hewitt, 1982). Many families use a second income to maintain a desired standard of living. Though the American family ideal always has been that childrearing of infants, toddlers, and preschoolers is a family responsibility, only 11 per cent of American families fit our romanticized ideal of a 'breadwinning' father and a 'homemaking' mother with resident children (Washington and Oyemade, 1985).

With these changes in family structure, families of all social classes increasingly need supplementary out-of-home child care for their young children. In response to this need, the number of day care centers is expanding throughout the nation. As day care centers become more pervasive social institutions in our society and surrogate childrearing of our nation's very young children increases, this social institution and its practice becomes a significant context and problem for understanding and evaluation.

Further support for the significance of day care research is found in theoretical and clinical psychology, which gives evidence that the very early years prior to a child's entry into elementary school are the crucial formative years for the child's development of self and internalization of society's values and practices (Chodorow, 1978; Erikson, 1950; Freud, 1960; Poster, 1978; Sullivan, 1953). Traditionally the family has been the social base for this psychic structure formation. The young child's development of self and internalization of society's values and practices are organized within the love and authority patterns of parent-child relations. In these relations, interpersonal schemas (parent and child) are internalized as intrapersonal schemas (ego ideal and superego). Through the infant and young child's experience with *significant others*, s/he takes on a concept of individual self (self as distinct from others) and social self (self in relation to others). Correspondingly, the specific manifestations and emphases of the individual and social self that the child acquires reflect the behaviors, attitudes and values of the *significant others* in her/his life. As increasing numbers of young children spend eight to ten hours, five days a week, in day care centers, day care teachers also become significant others in the young child's development. Parents of day care children are no longer the exclusive source of identification; the social-emotional context of childrearing has expanded. The power of children's relationship to their day care teachers can be seen when day care children's interaction patterns and lack thereof mirror their teachers' interactions with each other. One of the findings of my day care field study is that the observed day care teachers do not coordinate their schooling acts but rather, function independently from other day care teachers with whom they share space. This same pattern can be seen as several dozen children choose their own toys and play independently within the same space for several hours each day.

There has been an accompanying surge of research on day care as the number of these centers has expanded. Most of this research has centered on the developmental outcomes of the day care experience; that is, the focus has been on how child care outside the home has affected the child's development in the emotional, social, physical, and intellectual domains. Current social science studies tend to demonstrate that given a 'high quality center', the effects on the children of being in day care are 'positive' in the developmental areas (Etaugh, 1980). These day care studies are limited in that their focus is exclusively on developmental outcomes of day care, with little or no attention to the actual day care experience itself. By giving little or no information regarding the settings or the events taking place within day care, the question of what it was in the day care experience that influenced these reported developmental outcomes is left unanswered. Bronfenbrenner (1979) calls attention to these omissions. He claims that the children's relationships with others and their daily activities within the setting are the most significant features for behavior and development, and these features rarely are even mentioned in day care research. In contrast to the research efforts focusing on developmental outcomes of day care, the field study discussed in this book looks at what day care children and teachers are doing in their day to day activity.

Significance of the Individual-Social Focus

The child's manifestations and emphases of individual self and social self reflect the behavior, beliefs, attitudes and values of significant others in the young child's life. For the day care child, these significant others are parents and day care teachers. In other words, parents and day care teachers are the vehicles of social and cultural reproduction of the larger society's values and practices.

In America[1] a dominant value orientation is individualism. The complex dynamic of behavior, belief, attitudes and values within in this tradition has been a central component of our society's education (Bronfenbrenner, 1979; Cagan, 1978). At the same time, the stance that 'all men are created equal' and a tradition of social reform also is embedded in our history and is reflected in education, most clearly exemplified by John Dewey.

> In social situations the young have to refer their way of acting to what others are doing and make it fit it. This directs their action to a common result, and gives an understanding common to the participants. For all *mean* the same thing, even when performing different acts. This common understanding of the means and ends of action is the essence of social control. It is indirect, or emotional and intellectual, not direct or personal. Moreover it is intrinsic to the disposition of the person, not external and coercive. To achieve this internal control through identity of interest and understanding is the business of education. (Dewey, 1966, pp. 39–40)

As early as in Dewey's 1929 essay *Individualism Old and New*, social theorists have argued that twentieth-century changes call for a refocusing on this individual-social value tension, from stress on the individual toward more emphasis on the social.

The last time comprehensive child care legislation received bipartisan support was the 1971 Child Development Act. This Bill was vetoed by President Nixon with the following statement:

> . . . for the federal government to plunge headlong financially into supporting child development would commit the vast moral authority of the National Government to the side of communal approaches against the family-centered approach. (Quoted in Joffe, 1977, p. xi)

With Nixon's veto, critics proclaimed that universal day care would lead to ' . . . an intolerable degree of social control going beyond acceptable limits for a democratic individualistic society' (Steinfels, 1973, p. 195).

When Nixon and other day care critics claim that day care weakens both the family and our society's 'democratic individualistic' value tradition, the issue of the meaning and purpose of childrearing is raised. Within America's traditional childrearing process, the family has functioned as the primary vehicle for the reproduction of our society's values and practices. When people outside the family are involved in childrearing, our devotion to the family surfaces. For out-of-home child care is seen as a threat not only to family life but to the very continuity of our society's values and patterns of relating.

We have ample evidence that a dominant value tradition in America is individualism (deTocqueville, 1835; Dewey, 1929; Lipset, 1967; Lukes, 1973; Wood, 1972). Day care critics imply that children in day care centers will experience some kind of collectivist valuing that is detrimental to this American tradition. Given Americans' ambivalence regarding day care as weakening the family and America's individualistic value tradition, it is important to ask if, in fact, existing day care centers are transmitting collectivist values — if America's dominant values are being threatened.

The argument of this book is that day care centers, in their daily operations, actually emphasize individual more than social or collectivist values and experience. In other words, the values within the day care experience are congruent with the values experienced by children reared exclusively in nuclear families. The book's field study addresses the question of social reproduction by using participant observation research procedures. In participant observation the internal operations of the day care process are captured. By viewing children's day by day experiences and their teachers' orientation to the individual and the social, we can begin to understand whether, in fact, America's values are being threatened in day care.

The Field Study

The Problem

The question around which the field study was formulated is: 'How are four day care teachers similar and different in terms of their emphasis on children's individual and social experiences'. Specifically, I am interested in discovering what constitutes individual experiences and social experiences for children in day care. To do this I observed in depth how four day care teachers arranged the physical environment, and how they interacted with children and with each other. In addition, I observed the children's actions that the teachers allowed or encouraged. By focusing on the actions and words of day care children and their teachers in their daily activities over time, this field study provides a conceptual model for an initial understanding of whether day care does threaten the continuity of our society's values. The heart of the task I have set for myself is *not* to generalize from my observation of four teachers to all teachers in all day care centers. Rather, the task I have set is to think through the issues of the transmission of values in day care as that care actually occurs in the day to day lives of children and teachers.

The study examines both teaching method and the teacher's emphasis of (i) children's individual experiences; and (ii) children's social experiences. In individual experience, the teaching method involves children in their own task (for example, the child either working with material or with a teacher). The teacher's emphasis is somewhat more complex and has four components: first, independent action (for example, children choosing and putting away their own materials); second, individual accomplishment (for example, children successfully completing a puzzle); a third, individual rights (for example, children's prerogative to have their own space for their belongings); and fourth, self esteem (for example, children's sense of self worth being enhanced through frequent teacher praise). These components of individual experiences are represented in figure 1.

In social experience, the teaching method involves children in tasks with other children (for example, activities involving spontaneous groupings or teacher directed group activities). The teacher's emphasis has five components: conversation (for example, children and teachers converse together as they eat lunch); helping (for example, fastening

Figure 1: Children's Individual Experiences

Teaching Method

Children involved in their own tasks:

Child and material (for example, child strings beads).

Child and teacher (for example, teacher assists child in counting spoons).

Teacher's Emphasis

Independent action (for example, children choose and then put away their own materials).

Individual accomplishment (for example, children successfully complete a puzzle).

Individual rights (for example, children have the prerogative to have their own space for their belongings).

Self esteem (for example, children's sense of self worth is enhanced through frequent teacher praise).

Figure 2: Children's Social Experiences

Teaching Method

Children interacting with each other:

Activities involving children's spontaneous groupings (for example, children role play characters in a restaurant).

Activities that are teacher directed (for example, teacher and children prepare taco salad).

Teacher's Emphasis

Conversation (for example, children and teachers converse together as they eat lunch).

Helping action (for example, children fasten each other's clothing.

Sharing action (for example, children alternate in use of tricycle).

Combined efforts (for example, children jointly construct block building).

Empathy (for example, children recognize the feelings of another person).

each other's clothing); sharing (for example, children alternating the use of a tricycle); combined efforts (for example, children jointly constructing a block building); and empathy (for example, children recognizing the feelings of another person). These components of social experiences are depicted in figure 2.

These definitions separate the terms individual and social in order to achieve conceptual clarity. Yet it is assumed in this study that in any individual's action and in social practice, the individual and the social are never completely divided but rather, are reflexively intertwined. A person is never either an individual or a social being; rather individual and social are complementary, mutually dependent aspects of being human. Social psychological theory and research give clear evidence of this reciprocal unity of the individual and the social (Damon, 1983; Erikson, 1950; Freud, 1962; Mead, 1962; Piaget and Inhelder, 1969). The individual self arises out of social interaction with significant others in the child's early years. Just as the individual self is a consequence of social relations, so too, the individuation of self from other makes possible the child's development of social skills and values. It is only when children recognize themselves as separate persons that they are able to take into consideration the perspective of other persons. For example, when a 2-year-old holds his cereal box with a picture facing himself and asks: 'What's this mommy?', he is demonstrating that he cannot see himself as separate from others. The small child assumes his mother can see the cereal box picture as it appears to him. He cannot take her perspective.

Given this complementary nature of the individual and the social, it was expected that day care teachers would provide for both children's individual and social experiencing. And in fact, in the observed center, children daily did engage in individual and social activities. The field study's question relates directly to the teachers' priorities in their emphasis of the individual and the social. I began this study with what Malinowski (1922) terms a 'foreshadowed problem', that the teachers studied would lean toward an emphasis on the individual; for my experiences gave recurrent evidence of the pervasiveness of our culture's dominant value tradition of individualism.

Research Procedure

The participant observation approach of this study attempts to document the daily happenings within day care and the meaning of those happenings from the perspective of the day care teacher.

The setting

The setting for this study is a day care center, Rosehill Child Care Center, housed in a church in Elton, a middle class suburb of an American midwestern metropolitan area. The center is heterogeneous in terms of race and social class. Approximately 20 per cent of the children are black, and the annual parent income ranges from under $8000 (30 per cent), to between $8000 and $15,000 (20 per cent), to between $15,000 and $40,000 (50 per cent). There are fifty-four 3 and 4-year-olds enrolled. The center staff consists of one female director, four female headteachers, one male headteacher, and three female assistant teachers. With the exception of one black assistant, all teachers are white.[2]

There were several reasons for choosing this setting. First, both the director of a local community college early childhood education program, and the director of the metropolitan day care association had given the center high evaluations. Second, much of the research on day care takes place in university-based laboratory centers, centers of high quality but with resources non-representative of most day care centers in this country. In choosing a non-profit community-based center, I hoped that my findings might be generalizable to typical day care settings.

A third reason was the heterogeneity of the child population. I knew that among most people in our society day care has a 'relief image' as a benevolent institution for the poor; yet the need and demand for day care in middle and upper-middle class families is increasing at an accelerating rate each year. Given my study's focus on individual and social values in social relations, I thought a heterogeneous population would allow for examination of how children from varied family environments are socialized to the same process.

The last factor had to do with opportunity and accessibility. Six months before the study, I had an interview with the center's Director. At that time, I explained my intent to study the socialization process of children as they enter their first schooling experience, and to look at similarities and differences among teachers' schooling acts. The Director was very enthusiastic about my plans and agreed to bring my research request to the center's board of directors and to the staff. The board of directors and the staff agreed to my request. In our conversations, the Director stated that I could have access to all parts of the daily happenings in the center as long as the specific teachers were in agreement.

Data collection

Once I began work at the center, I met individually with the teachers who were subjects in my study. I explained that I wanted to focus on individual and social learning experiences of the children during the course of their day at Rosehill. I told each teacher that after an initial observation phase, I would observe their work for four days each week for at least one month, and would be interested in their views of ongoing events, and therefore, often would spend time talking to them during some of their free time. My observations extended from the third week of August through the second week of February.

I gathered data from four sources: on site observation in the center, spontaneous informal conversations with the teachers and children during my observation visits, formal taped interviews with each of the four teachers studied, and documents, which were written records, letters and memos.

On site observations

The first phase of my observation lasted approximately four weeks, and the purpose was familiarization. I arrived with the first few children, shortly before 7.00 a.m. and left after the children were settled for naps. Then I returned for the last two to three hours of the day, until the center closed at 6.00 p.m..

During this first month, both teachers and children became acquainted with my role as participant observer and largely came to accept my presence as a natural part of the environment.[3] Similarly, this was the time when I became acquainted with the fifty-four children and the teachers' structuring of the day, their activity schedule and use of materials and space within these activity periods. When possible I engaged in informal conversations with teachers to both establish rapport and to check the accuracy of my observations. From the outset, I spent most of my time recording notes; however, I always engaged in any spontaneous conversation initiated by children or teachers. In maintaining a low profile, I attempted to let the 'language of my behavior' be the primary basis for the staff's acceptance of my presence. During these weeks in late summer/early fall, there often was a shortage of staff such that during several days, I actively participated: I ate lunch with a group of children, assisted teachers in helping children 'get settled' for naps, and supervised playground activity when needed.

Beginning in mid-September, I spent four days each week for four to five weeks with one teacher and her children, until mid-February, when I had completed observations and interviews with all four teachers. My choices of what to observe and record were organized around several factors. First, during each observation period of a teacher, I remained near her and tried to record her observed behavior for all activity segments. Whenever possible, I recorded verbatim comments of teacher-child interactions. Second, in order to gain an understanding of the totality of the schooling process, I recorded activity scans of all observed child action every thirty minutes; that is, I noted how many children were in specific areas and what the nature of that activity at a given time was (see appendix A). These activity scans were done during early care, activity period, and late care. A third basis for choice of focus stems from my initial interest in children's social experiences. As much as possible, I tried to record any observed child to child interaction, especially when involving extended play sequences and, in addition, any related teacher action. Given my initial foresight that teachers would lean toward an individual emphasis, I attempted to compensate for any bias by documenting children's social interaction and the role of their teachers' in that action. Obviously one person cannot observe and record all child and teacher action; hence, I visited each teacher daily for several weeks in order to obtain a representative sample of recurring salient events — what Geertz (1973) terms a 'thick description'. In writing notes, I tried to describe events as objectively as possible in a narrative fashion. I wrote interpretative comments on the back side of the paper.

In order to determine whether the patterns I was seeing were unique to this center, I made a dozen observation visits to other day care centers. In the following year, I also conducted intensive half day observations in over fifty preschool, day care and Head Start centers in the mid-west. These half-day observations were part of my position as a CDA Representative for the Child Development Associate (CDA) National Credentialing Program, through Bank Street College of Education. From these observations in varied early education centers and those initial dozen day care observations, I was able to judge tentatively that my data were representative of day care and other early education settings.

Informal and formal conversations

From the outset of this study, I stressed with each teacher that I was not only interested in understanding the ongoing events within the center, but also, in understanding what meaning each teacher thought was contained within the event. In order to gain teacher understanding of events, I engaged in spontaneous conversations with them throughout the day as opportunities emerged. In these conversations I asked questions about their own action, their understanding of observed child action, or their reactions to specific events occurring in the center that day. Though I usually initiated these exchanges, occasionally a teacher would begin sharing with me spontaneously. Notes were taken as soon after these conversations as possible. I engaged in twenty-five to thirty of these conversations with each teacher.

For three of the four teachers I taped formal interviews. The fourth teacher said she would not be comfortable if I tape recorded our interviews; thus I wrote notes as we talked together. These conversations were partially structured in that I had a prepared focus with questions based on my observation of the immediate context. My questions were open-ended and the direction of the conversations often emerged from the comments of the teachers. I had several purposes in these exchanges: to gain biographical data, to gain the teacher's perception of individual children in her group, to understand the meanings the teacher attributed to ongoing happenings, and to understand the teacher's rationale underlying her own action and decision making.

Documents

In addition to my observations, I also obtained many written records and memos. The Director was very conscientious in ensuring that I received copies of the few notes she sent to parents and the few memos given the staff. Other types of written materials included a brochure, Rosehill's annual budget, schedule of staff rotation, children's application forms, and arrival/departure parent sign up sheets.

The Field Study in Context

This book's focal point is a field study of day care which asks whether young children's experiences in day care are congruent with our society's dominant value tradition of individualism. Before discussing the findings of this research, I will locate this study within the broader structural context of two social institutions of childrearing, namely, day care and the family. Day care always has existed within the tensions of social and familial childrearing. Chapter 2 explores the issues embedded in this tension through an examination of the nature of the family and day care in America from an historical perspective. This discussion can add understanding to the social and historical meaning of the day care teachers' actions in this field study. In this unity of the historical and the sociological, I am following Mills (1959) challenge:

> The sociological imagination enables us to grasp history and biography and the relations between the two within society. That is its task and its promise. (p. 6)

Day care critics, most notably President Nixon in his 1971 veto of the Child Development Act, claim that day care will weaken America's individualistic value tradition. Chapters 3 and 4 depict at a micro-level how four day care .teachers' actions lean toward an emphasis on children's individual experiences more so than social. In Chapter 5, I move beyond this field study to first examine America's tradition of individualism from an historical perspective and then ask how these teachers' actions are reflective of this dominant value tradition.[4] In an exploratory heuristic manner, it is hoped that the understandings reached through this process can provide a concrete basis for a fundamental question: what values and practices do we as early childhood educators and as a society give or want to give to our children.

Notes

1 Readers outside the United States may find the use of the term 'America' as referring to only one country of the many on the American continents, to be either parochial or chauvinistic. The term as self-reference, exemplified in

patriotic songs such as 'God Bless America' or slogans such as 'The American Dream', makes any other term bulky or foreign sounding to 'Americans' themselves, that is, to the citizens of the United States. Because so much of this book revolves around central values in the United States, the choice of the term 'America' has a symbolic content that other terms lack.

2 At Rosehill, children and adults address each other by first names. In this book, I have followed this form of identification, for to have given formal pseudonyms to teachers would have portrayed a quality of relationship different from the Rosehill pattern.

3 Though I attempted to maintain a 'low profile' at Rosehill and remain focused on unveiling teacher understandings, it also is a given that I represented more power, status and knowledge than did the teachers, and my participant field work no doubt led to many unintended consequences. A conversation with Barb in December was a stark reminder of these issues. Barb told me that during the previous night she had had a dream, in which she became terrified when her car broke down on the highway, for she didn't know what to do. Barb continued: 'But then you stopped by, and I said to myself: "Carol knows how to fix a car, for she always knows all the answers."' (Some of the unintended consequences and pitfalls of this form of research are addressed in Walker's recent provocative essay: 'Three good reasons for not doing case studies in curriculum research' (1983)).

4 The social science perspective of this book takes its direction primarily from the interpretive social science tradition; however, my approach also integrated aspects of the positivist and critical social science perspective. A discussion of this book's theoretical orientation can be found in appendix B.

2 *Social and Familial Childrearing: Day Care in Context*

To understand day care in context is to understand how day care is related to family life, and the broader social, political and economic forces at work in America. Exploring these interconnections from an historical perspective clarifies the tension between social and familial childrearing in America and provides the broader structural context of this day care study.

The Family

Historical Context of the Modern Family

Historically the structure of the family is intertwined with the social structure, especially the economy. The family and the economy can be seen as a single integrated system in the sense that the form of family relationships is connected to society's means of production (Chodorow, 1978; Poster, 1978; Young and Wilmott, 1973; Zaretsky, 1973). A brief overview of changes in family structure as related to changes in the economic system will provide the context and highlight relevant issues for an analysis of the modern family.

Young and Wilmott (1973) identify three periods in the evolution of the modern family structure. The first period encompasses the sixteenth and seventeenth century agrarian period before industrialization. Families were units of production as men, women, and children worked together in the home and field. For both peasants and aristocrats of this period, privacy was non-existent and childhood was not seen as a separate stage in life (Aries, 1962).

A different family pattern within the working class emerged during the early industrial period of the late eighteenth century in England and the nineteenth century in Europe and America. Peasants flooded the cities and formed a working class. Production took place in the factories, where typically the entire family had to work; factory wages became the economic basis of the working class family. Conception of the work process was separated from implementation. Operations were separated and assigned to different workers, work became alienated labor (Braverman, 1974). In addition to this alienation, workers experienced fragmentation of their previous community life in their villages.

The third period in changing family patterns, that of the middle class family structure, started in the nineteenth century. By the end of the nineteenth century, skilled workers achieved a sufficient wage to allow mothers to stay at home with their children (Poster, 1978). A proportion of the working class began to live in the family structure developed by the middle class. Freud considered this middle class family to be the universal family form, and it is so considered by many today. The private sphere of the family became a source for personal identity and fulfillment as work became increasingly alienating. Family relations consisted of strict sex-role and age differentiation as children were barred from employment and required to attend school. In this way childhood was legitimized as a separate stage in life. At the same time, women took on familial roles as providers of a refuge and as caretakers of children. As their familial role became idealized they were isolated from socialized production (Zaretsky, 1973).

Concomitant with the explosive growth of industrial capitalism at the turn of the century was the large immigration which expanded the ranks of the poor in large urban slums. At the same time that middle class workers retreated into the private realm of the family, progressive social reformers developed an array of services for immigrant families. A new coterie of professional experts — teachers, social workers, probation officers — provided services to socialize immigrants to the middle class family ideal. America's liberal political tradition of equal rights for all individuals was preserved through providing equality of opportunity to children through public schooling. The new helping professions of the progressive era had common features related to the American ideology of the family. First was their focus on the *child* as the avenue for resolving social inequities. Their goal was to 'uplift' the future generations through assisting individual children (for example, through casework). Second, their focus was on the micro-environment of the *family* as the determining factor in how a child develops. And third, in giving primacy to assisting *individual* children, the reform movement ignored possibilities of collective action to change the social structural conditions in which social inequities and poverty are embedded.

The decade of the 1920s was a period of professionalization of preschool work and tremendous growth in the field of child development (Greenblatt, 1977). From their inception, preschools placed heavy emphasis on parent education. Popular journals and radio programs became vehicles for stressing maternal childrearing and for popularizing the psychology of Freud and Watson, two theoretical perspectives that often conflicted, but both stressed the importance of the early years; women's role in the home continued to be idealized.

The post World War II years through the 1950s were characterized by increased prosperity. An unprecedented number of working class families now could afford homes and could adopt life styles typical of the traditional familial ideal, an ideal reinforced by several popular social movements. Psychology stressing individual development and the crucial significance of mother-infant bonding became widely circulated in popular women's magazines and in child rearing manuals. Newly-developed mass media romanticized the nuclear family organization in advertising and programming. Families of all social classes 'tuned in' to programs like 'Father Knows Best' and 'Ozzie and Harriet', glorifying the joys of domesticity.

The mass movement of working class families to suburbia, continuing after the 1950s, has seen families seeking refuge and a place for personal fulfillment within the home. Personal fulfillment has been distinguished by subjectivity, the search for personal meaning (Zaretsky, 1973). Paradoxically, as subjectivity has increased, it has become predetermined and standardized via the advertising industry and mass media. Again family and economy are intertwined; for in their pursuit of subjective experiences, families expand personal life through predetermined forms of consumption (for example, self help manuals, labor saving machines, pre-packaged leisure activities like spectator sports or video recorders).

The Family as the Base for Psychic Structure Formation

An historical understanding of the modern family clarifies our society's valuing of the family as provider of refuge from alienated work, as the setting for individual personal fulfillment, and as the foundation of young children's development. American ambivalence toward day care has been based on an underlying belief that the family is the primary and ideal agent of childrearing. The following discussion utilizes a psychoanalytic framework to grasp the meaning of familial childrearing.

Psychoanalytic theory points to the very early years prior to the child's entry into elementary school as the crucial formative years of the child's development of self and internalization of society's values and practices (Chodorow, 1978; Erikson, 1950; Freud, 1962; Poster, 1978). It is the children's early relationship with parents that is crucial. Using Freudian theory as a frame of reference, Poster (1978) and Chodorow (1978) argue that the uniqueness of the family as a social institution is within its role as mediator of individual psychic structure and social structure. By this they mean the children's self identity and internalization of society's rules, values and hierarchies of authority emerge within their very early relationships with their parents.

Poster claims that the family is not a unitary phenomenon; rather, throughout history, different family structures have involved distinctly different emotional patterns of relating. To understand the modern family we need to examine the everyday relations of young children and their parents, for it is within the everyday interactional process of childrearing that children's self-hood and internalization of societal values and practices are organized. The family thus becomes the social base for the child's psychic structure formation. Poster postulates that the child's psyche is organized by love and authority patterns within parent child relations. These daily patterns, once established within the context of children's psychosexual stages, lead them to internalize hierarchies of sex and role expectations.

Poster claims that the modern family arose from the middle class nuclear family, and he follows Freud in analyzing this family structure. The middle class is distinguished by a new degree of emotional intimacy between parents and children. With the separation of the public sphere from the family's private sphere, families are isolated from society and children's dependency is heightened. The very young child's sources of identification are severely restricted; often the child's own parents are the main available adult models.

The traditional middle class family has been characterized by orderliness, cleanliness, constant maternal attention, regularity in feeding, and rigorous toilet training. Rigid feeding schedules, early toilet training, and restriction of sexuality result in the young child's exchange of bodily gratification for parental, especially maternal, affection. The exchange between the child's body and parental love becomes the psychic context of the young child's daily life. This intense relationship leads to deep ambivalence. Poster notes:

> . . . the important result of the child's drama of ambivalence was that it internalized deeply a pattern of rules which summed up its authority-love relation with its parents. The secret of the bourgeois family structure was that, without conscious intention

> on the part of the parents, it played with intense feelings of love and hate which the child felt both for its body and for its parents in such a way that parental rules became internalized on the strength of both feelings. Love (as ego ideal) and hate (as super-ego) both worked to foster the attitudes of bourgeois respectability. (p. 175)

It is within the everyday childrearing process that interpersonal schemas (parent and child) are internalized as intrapersonal schemas (ego ideal and super ego) as the child moves through developmental stages.

Chodorow (1978) demonstrates how the sex-role differentiation of males and females reproduces an asymmetry of psychic structures and of parenting practices, an asymmetry that perpetuates our society's sexual division of labor and status. Within this primary bonding, the omnipotent mother has complete control of giving and withholding gratification to her infant. Mother thus is the significant other from whom the selfhood of both male and female children emerge. In contrast, father's work and masculine activities are removed from the child's home, a distancing that has dramatic implications as the infant child matures and establishes sex-gender identification. The boy must attempt to develop a masculine gender identification and learn masculine roles in normally father-remote families, without a continuous and ongoing personal relationship with his father. Hence the boy gains a sense of what it is to be masculine through identification with cultural images of masculinity, through repression of that which is feminine in himself, and through a devaluing of the feminine (as that which threatens his selfhood). The boy tends to identify with a gender role. The girl's identification processes, however, are embedded in an ongoing relationship with the mother; they are particularistic and affective. As a result of this differential identification process for boys and girls, sons develop with their nurturant and affiliative capacities repressed. They are equipped to participate in the impersonal world of work. In contrast, daughters develop with a psychological capacity and need to mother. Thus, the traditional family reproduces the psychic structure necessary to the maintenance of a sexually stratified society.[1]

While the daily interactional process of familial childrearing is one of the most concrete of human activities, Freudian theory upon which Poster and Chodorow build is among the most abstract reflections on human development. Psychoanalytic theory provides generalizations which help to organize and relate concrete childrearing experiences and uncover their significance. Yet the specific interactions of childrearing are subtle and ever changing, and they are extremely hard to depict.

While Poster argues that family analysis must go beyond theory to analyze also routine everyday life within the family and the family's relation to society 'with an ethnographer's sense of the mundane' (p. 156), neither Poster nor Chodorow depict this daily life.

In their examination of psychoanalytic theory, Poster and Chodorow provide valuable interpretive lenses for discussing the childrearing process. An examination of alternative childrearing strategies may further illuminate ways in which childrearing interactions contribute to the development of psychic structures. Chodorow claims that communal alternatives would be preferable to familial childrearing; and Poster suggests that the childrearing methods of the kibbutz would be more desirable. Studies of existing collective childrearing arrangements, such as those found in Israel's kibbutz, China or the Soviet Union, demonstrate that these young children do have greater experiences in empathy, cooperation, and social responsibility than their American counterparts. However, they lack in individuality, creativity, and the capacity for intimacy (Bettleheim, 1969; Bronfenbrenner, 1970; Cagan, 1978; Kessen, 1975). While these studies call attention to the neglected collective-collaborative dimensions of childrearing in our society, they also point to the need for preserving the strengths of our American value traditions such as the valuing of individuality and creative, critical thinking, and point to the essential value dilemma of this book's field study.

An understanding of the power of familial childrearing relations allows us to begin to comprehend our society's ambivalence toward day care as supplementary childrearing. Psychoanalytic theory unveils this power, namely, that the primary attachment and daily childrearing relations between parents and young children are the essential foundation of children's self identity and conscience, both ego ideal and super ego. As significant others in their childrearing relations, parents ensure social continuity, that is, the continuity of society's ideals, practices, and prohibitions: Poster and Chodorow also, however, unveil limitations of familial childrearing. A recognition of these limitations and an awareness of alternative strategies for childrearing suggest day care's potential to ameliorate some of the shortcomings of familial childrearing. The following section examines current changes in our society's family structure and functioning that are resulting in an increase in the social childrearing context of day care for many of our young children.

Changing Fabric of Family Structure and Functioning

An overview of demographic characteristics of the modern family in the past two decades gives evidence of gradual changes in family structure that involve changes in family functioning and its relation to the social structure. Two factors are involved in these recent changes: an increase in divorce and an increase in married mothers in the workforce. Between 1960 and 1984, the proportion of children living in female-headed families more than doubled (CDF Reports, 1985). An equally striking aspect of the changing family structure is the increase in married mothers in the workforce. In 1983, 57 per cent of women with children between 3 and 5 years and 46 per cent of women with children younger than age 3 were in the labor force (Blank, 1983).

Recent changes raise a double-pronged question: first, what changes could occur in the internal functioning of the family, and second, what changes could occur in the family's relation to society? Within the family, patterns of experiences of women, men and children currently are either in the process of changing or have the potential for future change.

The increasing number of wives and mothers in the work force plus the women's movement of the 1960s and 1970s have been accompanied by a gradual loosening of the strict sex-role differentiation within the family. Traditionally most women's lives have been regulated by the family life cycles, and women's choices of work have been circumscribed by their familial roles. Van Dusen and Sheldon (1977) described current shifts in American women's 'life cycle': a larger proportion of women are seeking career education, are postponing marriage, and are rearing fewer children. As a result of these changes, women's lives are much less enmeshed in the family life cycle.

The changed status of women is not the only factor at work here. Changes involving the influence of television and school have altered childrearing in ways that are equally (if not more) significant. The school year has lengthened to an average of 180 days, which is more than double the time children spent in school in the late nineteenth century. And most children spend more time watching television than they spend either in school or with their parents. It is estimated that the average preschooler watches television one-third of her or his waking hours, and that the average sixth grader watches for thirty-one hours each week (Bane, 1976).

At the same time, many women have adopted the high value our society places on male activities and, in the process have depreciated the value of motherhood. With the professionalization of health, vocational, and educational services to the family, plus children's increased use of television, many mothers feel inadequate in their role. Already isolated and receiving little social support from society, now homemakers, in addition, experience deprecation from other women.[2]

As more mothers enter the work force, it also is becoming more common for fathers to be 'helping out' with housework and childcare (Ehrensaft, 1980). If fathers are sharing in the day-to-day maintenance of homemaking, their increasing accessibility allows for a lessening of rigid differentiation of psychological capacities between male and female. Further, many children are receiving surrogate parenting outside the home while mothers work. From their critical perspective, both Poster and Chodorow uncover shortcomings of the traditional family: (i) the sharply differentiated and unequal sex roles; (ii) the family's isolation from society; (iii) the accompanying restricted sources of identification for young children; and (iv) heightened dependency of the young child. If mothers are in the work force, fathers more accessible at home, and young children able to receive quality supplementary out-of-home care, then there exists the possibility of ameliorating some of those limitations. As increasing numbers of young children spend eight to ten hours, five days a week, in day care centers, day care teachers become significant others. Parents of day care children are no longer the exclusive source of identification; the social emotional context of childrearing has expanded. The day care child's identification process can be more diffuse and dependency can be less salient without traumatic loss of the child's crucial primary bonding with parents. Kagan (1978) has reviewed two studies of infants who spent a considerable amount of time with substitute caretakers outside of the home. Results of both of these studies support the assertion that the biological parent remains the preferred adult of attachment for these young children, in spite of their experiences with surrogate parenting. But the potential effects of day care depend heavily on the quality of the care and of the relationships that children develop in the day care setting. The next two sections examine the day care context, in terms of its historical development and current practices and social policy of day care.

Day Care

Historical Development of Day Care Policy and Practices

Day nurseries in America were initiated in the latter half of the nineteenth century as an attempt to strengthen and preserve the family. During the 1880s and 1890s there was massive European immigration and rapid urbanization resulting from increased industrialization. Installation of machinery in factories required unskilled labor; and immigrant mothers became a source of cheap labor. As an alternative to the previous pattern of institutionalizing neglected children in foundling homes, wealthy women began day nurseries.[3] Day nurseries multiplied rapidly after 1905, and by 1915 there were about 450 centers across the country (Joffe, 1977).

Wealthy women raised funds for these centers, served on the board that set policies, and supervised matrons who maintained these nurseries six days a week, twelve hours a day, for infants, toddlers, and preschoolers. These wealthy volunteers also regularly visited children's homes and taught night classes in 'homemaking' skills, child-care, and English. Socialization to the normative American values of middle class family life was the focal point of the day nursery, which represented benevolent propagation of normative domestic values. It was a new cultural intervention aimed at preserving the family. Steinfels (1973) notes that from its very inception, ' . . . like other forms of relief, the day nursery was thought of as a temporary expedient; ideally it would eventually go out of business, when mothers were restored to their proper places in their homes. Meantime, the nurseries should be operated as to hasten not delay, that day' (p. 50).

There are interesting underlying ironies within this day nursery movement. The upper class women, being apparently bored in their traditional role at home, liberated themselves through their charitable work, where they sought to promote middle class values. These reformers focused on the young child, yet they knew little about their own children, who for the most part were the responsibility of nurses and servants. Their focus was on the family; yet the industrial system which was controlled by their husbands and which weakened the family through non-living wages for men and maternal employment outside the home, was taken as a given and was not challenged.

In the early twentieth century, the first government social policy concerning children was enacted, a policy reinforcing the national family ideal of maternal childrearing. In 1909, the first White House children's conference, specifically a conference on the care of dependent children, was convened. Over 200 child welfare workers met and transmitted fifteen recommendations to the President. The first recommendation reads: 'Home life is the highest and finest product of civilization . . . children should not be deprived of it' (quoted in Steiner, 1976, p. 38). Conferees urged public pensions enabling widowed mothers to care for their children in their own homes. In 1911, Illinois enacted the first mothers' pension program, and within a decade, forty states had similar provisions.

After 1910, wealthy volunteers gradually were replaced by a middle class staff, whose 'friendly visiting' was the beginnings of social case work (Greenblatt, 1977, p. 84). Gradually the new social work profession gained control over day nurseries. Before the entry of social workers, day nurseries were seen as a service to families living in poverty, a poverty which was the result of conditions external to the family — immigration, urbanization, and industrialization. The day nurseries were a service to help families who were trying to better their lives by maternal employment. The professionalization of social work as a relief-oriented profession implanted the relief image onto day care. The ideal of mother at home remained, and day care was seen as an undesirable service, only for families that were not normal (the poor). Accompanying the social worker's relief image of day nurseries was the individualistic interpretation of poverty; that is, poverty was due to individual and family deficiencies.

Both psychoanalytic psychology and behavioral psychology were used to bolster this view of the deficient poor family. Though these two perspectives differ greatly, each stresses the significance of early childhood in human growth and learning. The primacy of the early years in the shaping of adult characteristics carried with it the notion of the family as the determining factor in how a child develops. From this point of view, the deficiencies of the poor child were traced *not* to social conditions in which poverty is embedded, but rather to the inadequacies of the child's family. In an early account of the day nursery, Beer (1938) stressed: 'Many of the difficulties the day nursery has with the child can be traced to the home environment' (p. 54). She summarized the four most common deficiencies in these homes as follows: the child is fed foreign food, the child is beaten frequently, the home is untidy, and the child is 'spoiled' since the parents have no time for discipline (pp. 54–7).

1920–1945

A parallel development beginning in the 1920s was a rapid growth in training schools for nursery school teachers, in laboratory nursery schools, and in child development research. With the popularization of the progressive educational theory of Dewey and the psychological theories of Freud, Gesell, and Watson, a vast number of middle-class families sought education for their young children. Reflecting Dewey's influence, the nursery schools devoted most of their time to play and direct experience with materials. From their inception, nursery schools were different in function and goals from day nurseries. Nursery schools served middle and upper middle-class children, and their primary purpose was the educational enrichment of the child. In contrast, day nurseries dealt exclusively with impoverished children in order to supplement home care given by their employed mothers.

Between 1924 and 1939 relatively few immigrants came to the United States due to restrictive legislation. However there was a large influx into the cities from rural areas, which felt the depression eight to ten years before the 1929 crash. During this period there was a decline in the charitable work of wealthy women. More generally, there was less social reform. As a result, the number of philanthropic day nurseries declined (Greenblatt, 1977).

Since the nursery schools could not absorb the growing number of trained teachers, the nursery school began to penetrate the day nursery field as a new coterie of trained teachers replaced the untrained matrons (Beer, 1938; Greenblatt, 1977). In 1930, the White House Conference on Child Health and Protection Committee published its survey of existing institutions for the education and care of young children (Anderson, 1930). This survey differentiated three main types of institutions: first, day nurseries with a relief purpose and wide age-range (one month through eight years), meeting for ten to twelve hours daily, six days a week; second, relief nursery schools meeting eight hours a day for five days each week, with both relief and educational purposes, for children between 2 and 6 years; and third, nursery schools with an education and training purpose and narrow age-range (2 through 6 years), meeting half-a-day for five days each week. Whereas the typical day nursery teacher had a high school degree and worked with approximately twenty-four children for forty-five hours each week; the typical relief nursery school teacher had special training beyond high school but was not a college graduate, worked thirty-five hours a week and was responsible for thirteen children; and the typical nursery school teacher had a college degree, worked twenty-eight hours a week and was responsible for approximately nineteen children (Anderson, 1930).

When trained teachers entered the day nurseries, they were not prepared to deal with infants and toddlers, nor did they want to work twelve hours daily. Hence programs for most centers were shortened to seven or eight hours, and toddlers and infants were eliminated (Steinfels, 1973). Working mothers continued to have the need for longer days and for infant-toddler care, but they had to look elsewhere. Initially day nursery care had been primarily custodial, with an emphasis on health and hygiene. In the 1920s, trained teachers instituted a play curriculum into relief day nurseries: activities like clay modeling, carpentry, painting and music were introduced (Beer, 1938). While the child's day was 'enriched' in relief nursery schools, many day nursery services to the family were curtailed (for example, lunch and afternoon recreation for older siblings and night classes for parents).

With the decrease in availability of day nurseries, the obvious question arises: How did working mothers obtain childcare? Greenblatt (1977) notes that 42 per cent of institutional child care in the 1920s was proprietary, that is, centers oriented toward earning a profit. Care was primarily custodial and child care workers rarely had early childhood training or experience. There is little mention of proprietary centers in early childhood literature, and there was no contribution to the literature by proprietors themselves until the 1970s. Professionals in the field ignored their existence. Since the 1920s, the day care market has expanded at a faster rate each decade; and the proprietary segment of child care has increased dramatically, in spite of its continued 'invisibility' in the early education professional literature. Auerbach (1979) reports: 'In 1978, proprietary centers comprised 70 per cent of child care services including family child care homes' (p. 68).

Public social policy regarding children in the 1930s and 1940s reflected our society's ambivalence toward social parenting. The national family ideal that even impoverished mothers should remain at home was supported by the Social Security Act of 1935 which provided Aid to Families of Dependent Children. Schorr (1968) describes the early years of the AFDC program:

> In the early years, the AFDC program fitted into the economy in such a way as to offer a genuine choice (of working) to a mother. The program was written when it seemed desirable to attract women out of the labor market, leaving more jobs for men. The effect however was that if a mother desired to work, she did. If she preferred staying at home, her right to do so was affirmed in accepting her for AFDC. (p. 27)

During the same decade that the government reinforced familial parenting through AFDC, the first federal support of day care was instituted through the WPA. Now social parenting was reinforced, justified in terms of the national interest — the economic crises of the thirties. The government subsidized WPA centers in public schools in order to provide employment for teachers, custodians, cooks, and nurses (Greenblatt, 1977; Steinfels, 1973, Steiner, 1976). Significantly, these WPA programs were educational, and clientele included both low and middle income children on a sliding fee scale. The differentiation between stigmatized day nursery for poor children and the more middle class nursery school was abandoned. With the onset of World War II, these WPA centers evolved into centers funded by the Lanham Act of 1941. Again federal policy was justified in terms of national interests, in this case, the wartime labor shortage. It is a significant feature of the WPA-Lanham centers that they were the only occasions where government policy ignored the distinction (relief versus education) between day care and nursery school. The government by-passed social welfare agencies and gave control of these centers to the public schools. Greenblatt (1977) observes that the social work profession and the Children's Bureau never did support the WPA-Lanham programs; they were ambivalent about the wisdom of providing institutional care for children under 3 and they were concerned that these programs weakened the national family ideal of maternal childrearing.

1946–1962

In February 1946, federal funds for day care centers were withdrawn. Except in Philadelphia, New York City, and the state of California, Lanham centers were closed. AFDC was continued however, so that impoverished mothers could choose to remain at home. Though the years 1946–62 involved no government support of day care and no significant increase in non-profit child care centers, there was a marked increase in working mothers. Steinfels (1973) notes that between 1948 and 1966, married women who worked and who had husbands present and children under 6 years old, increased from 10.8 per cent to 24.4 per cent of all adult women (p. 70). Steinfels further observes:

> In 1956 70 per cent of families with incomes in the middle class range of $7–15,000 had two wage earners. Two American dreams were at odds with one another — a mother at home, but in a middle class home; and for many, a middle class home required a mother to work. (p. 71)

During this period, proprietary day care continued to expand. Data is not available on the prevalence or quality of unlicensed child care centers. Greenblatt (1977) does report that of the 4426 licensed day care facilities in 1960, 64 per cent were proprietary (p. 279).

The contradiction between a growing need for childcare and a decline in public and philanthropic support of it can be understood by identifying prevailing American social patterns which reinforced the national family ideal of maternal childrearing. The mystique of the women's world of the post-war era was so widespread in popular culture that the reality of large numbers of mothers in the work force was invisible to many. This was an era of tremendous proliferation of mass media. Popular magazines and television shows, and the rapidly growing advertising industry, depicted a 'model' nuclear family with mother as director, supervising the children and creating a domestic haven from the workplace. The social sciences of psychology and child development that had guided social practices of the helping professions and affluent families before World War II were popularized in the 1950s. Patterns of appropriate maternal childrearing were now standardized for mass consumption, and increasingly became a taken-for-granted part of public consciousness.[4] Spock's widely circulated handbook abandoned notions of conditioning and rigid habit training, and softened the Freudian weight given to negative repressive characteristics of parent-child relations. Mother-child relations typical of the child-centered permissive tradition of the early nursery schools for the affluent were now promoted as a right of every child. Support for out-of-home care in this period would have negated these prevailing normative values.

Current Practices and Social Policy in Day Care

Social policy

The year 1962 marked the first federal involvement in out-of-home child care since 1946. An analysis of the social context of this period indicates that once again the federal assistance was justified in terms of national interests. In the early 1960s, the work of Piaget, Bloom, Hunt, and Bruner gave evidence that the first five years of life were the years of most rapid intellectual development, and had great consequences for later development. In particular, child development research on 'cultural deprivation' gained a large audience in politics. This cultural deprivation literature implied a critique of lower class culture and lower class parenting. It was thought that the poverty cycle might be broken by compensatory education, that is, education in the early years to compensate for deficient parenting. Compensatory education would allow poor children to be better prepared for success in schools. (Interestingly, the issue of inferior urban schools in impoverished areas was not discussed.) Fortuitously, dissemination of this social science research coincided with the Kennedy-Johnson anti-poverty political agenda, the civil rights movement, and the beginnings of a new women's movement. At the same time that scholarly research emerged on cultural deprivation and the significance of the early years, the soaring costs of public assistance programs were linked to the increased number of AFDC families. While researchers and policy makers were debating 'cultural deprivation', rioting erupted in many large cities beginning in 1964. Policy makers looked for ways to maintain order in the cities, lower welfare costs, and reverse the 'cycle of poverty'. In part, this concern was translated into child care legislation.

In 1962, Public Welfare Amendments authorized federal grants of funds to states for day care of impoverished children. This legislation was a dramatic departure from the ideal of maternal childrearing; however, it applied only to the lower class. This legislation was a means of getting AFDC mothers off the welfare rolls, for it removed from AFDC mothers the choice of whether or not they would work. Given the fact that these AFDC mothers had no advanced training, their earnings were very low, almost the same as their AFDC grants. The money earned was deducted from AFDC grants, so that they were no better off financially. Schorr (1968) comments on this 'catch-22' process: 'A conflict is inherent in the AFDC mother's situation. She is more or less officially pressed to work but work increases her load and does not add to her income' (p. 31). Now not only are children without fathers, but their mothers have left home to gain employment. Greenblatt (1977) observes:

> The relief cast given to day care in 1962 reinforced a pejorative image of day care and magnified it for some time to come. Furthermore, the scope of the program authorized, crumb-size in relation to the increasing number of employed mothers of pre-school children, added to the unfilled market demand for day care. The 1962 Day Care Amendment, therefore, gave added impetus to the proprietary sector in day care, at least for women who could afford commercial day care fees. (p. 154)

Through the summer of 1981, there were no significant departures from the day care legislation of the 1960s. Under that legislation, the federal government has been paying 75 per cent of day care costs, with the remaining costs paid by states and localities (Steinfels, 1973). With funding, the government defines who is eligible to use publicly-funded day care. Employed welfare mothers and welfare mothers in work training programs are given first priority, and any remaining slots are for other working mothers, who pay on a sliding scale. Beginning in 1968, all centers receiving federal funding were required to meet the Federal Interagency Day Care Requirements, the first federal standards for day care. FIDCR provides uniform standards such as staff-child ratio, size of group, suitability and safety of facilities, and staff training. Given these FIDCR standards, these publicly supported centers often have higher levels of staff training and lower staff-child ratios than other non-profit or proprietary centers.

Federally-funded centers must also be licensed, but this licensing is state controlled as is the enforcement of FIDCR standards. States also license other non-profit centers and proprietary centers. The licensing standards vary among the states; thus the quality of care is at different levels in different states. In addition, state standards are poorly enforced. For example, no state has ever withheld day care payments when FIDCR standards have not been met (Orton and Langham, 1980). The responsibility for state licensing is usually assigned to the state public welfare department; so again, the relief image rather than an educational or child development service image is projected onto day care.

The 1964 Economic Opportunity Act and the 1965 Elementary and Secondary Education Act authorized federal funding for preschool programs for impoverished children. Head Start became the widely publicized avenue to offer 'equal opportunity' to 'culturally deprived' young children. Once again, policy focused on education of the child as the avenue to resolve social class inequities. Interestingly, Head Start was not seen as weakening either the family or the maternal role, for parents have been an integral aspect of the program since its beginning. Head Start represented significant advances in the child care movement in that program content was linked to education and developmental needs. The traditional distinction between custodial care for the poor and educational care for the affluent was bypassed. The strategies of Head Start rested on the child development research and cultural deprivation theories of the 1960s. In turn, the establishment of Head Start gave a lot of publicity to this research and these theories. More generally, it lent heightened prestige to the field of early childhood education. Now day care providers became alerted to the educational needs of their clients, and educationally oriented programs became more common.

As the new decade began in 1970, circumstances for effective social policy for child care were more advantageous than ever before. Caldwell's (1964) widely publicized research demonstrated that high quality day care for infants, toddlers, and preschoolers can have positive developmental effects. Head Start had become a very popular program with considerable positive media coverage. The Nixon administration explicitly had made a commitment to child care as part of its welfare reform. The women's movement continued to gain momentum, and child care for all working mothers became a key issue of concern. In addition, the country was in a period of general economic prosperity. During this period, Mondale in the Senate and Brademas in the House were able to obtain bipartisan support for passage of the 1971 Child Development Bill. This Bill provided the framework for eventual universally available, community controlled child development programs for all families who needed and wanted them, on a sliding scale of fees. The Bill was the culmination of almost two years of carefully orchestrated congressional hearings. The Bill was vetoed by President Nixon on the grounds that day care would weaken the family and lead toward communal approaches to childrearing that would threaten our nation's values (Joffe, 1977). It is difficult to understand why the issue of social childrearing versus family childrearing on which this veto was based had never been discussed during the two-year congressional debate on this bill. Similar federal legislation was submitted in 1975 in the Child and Family Services Bill and was passed by Congress, but vetoed by President Ford (Fishhaut and Pastor, 1977, p. 39). The welfare rationale for day care was resurrected as the national norm, and the coalition of labor and public interest groups that had coalesced on behalf of day care dissolved.

With the new decade of the 1980s, circumstances for 'effective' day care policy seem bleak. The current administration has attempted to cut government social spending drastically. Federal money for day care, under Title XX, received a 19 per cent cut in funding in 1981, and the state matching requirement of 25 per cent was cut. States now may opt not to spend state money on Title XX day care services, making a total potential day care cut of 44 per cent (Voice of Children, 1981). The newsletter of the Children's Defense Fund (CDF) reported in January 1985:

> In 1984, despite increased need, higher costs, and an upsurge in interest in child care, 25 states are spending less overall for day care than in 1981, 27 states are serving fewer children, and 15 states are paying 1981 wages to child care workers. (p. 7)

Within this context, child care advocates currently are focusing their energies on protecting existing child care programs.

A constant obstacle to effective social policy is the lack of coordination of organizations of child advocacy, and the policy structure of government concerned with children's issues such as nutrition, education, and health. Though children are a part of each congressperson's constituency, children's issues are distributed to a variety of committees. This uncoordinated assortment of committees results in no focal point of either congressional leadership or attention to children's issues. In like manner, children's issues always have been dispersed through a conglomeration of different federal agencies, agencies that seldom work together and occasionally compete with each other. Auerbach (1979) observes:

> By 1971, more than forty programs in eight agencies in some way had an influence on the child and family; none of these programs and agencies cooperated with each other. The end result of these freewheeling programs is that services for the same population are harder to provide, cost more, and have little impact on those for whom they are intended. (p. 24)

There has been a similar lack of unity and coordination among child oriented professional and voluntary organizations. Lobbying for children's issues has been consistently inadequate. Steiner (1976) notes that many child oriented professional groups lack specific lobbying skills and instead of lobbying, '. . . behave more like educational institutions, reporting findings and conclusions and hoping that the product will trickle down to and affect legislative committees' (p. 153). Philanthropic associations occasionally have made efforts at lobbying; however, given different ideologies and priorities among the different groups, lobbying efforts have never been successful. Feminists have demonstrated effective lobbying skills, and have argued consistently that women's and children's issues are inseparable. Thus far, however, their lobbying has focused on women's issues like abortion and the Equal Rights Amendment, and not directly on children. Given our system of policy making, effective legislation probably will occur only if the self interests of a large proportion of our society can be invoked. Currently, the decreasing public school enrollment does give one potentially influential group, public school teachers, a stake in early childhood education. The American Federation of Teachers, in fact, has increasingly seen the need for child care coinciding with teachers' need for jobs. At the same time, however, many early childhood professionals see this public school movement as dysfunctional, for the traditional teacher-directed public school classroom is antithetical to much of early childhood theory and practice (Fishhaut and Pastor, 1977).

Day care practices

Given the government's guiding principle of non-intervention into childrearing, and the pluralistic yet highly stratified nature of our society, utilization of child care varies quite a bit while still reflecting our society's stratification. Woolsey (1978) summarized consistent patterns of working mothers' day care utilization. Relatives not living with the family babysit for 50 per cent of all families. Given the relevant role of the extended family among minorities, these families are the most common users of family child care. Middle income families are most likely to utilize nursery schools and housekeeping child care; whereas single parent families are the most common users of institutional day care. Almost all infants are cared for within homes, and the quality of family day care is largely undocumented.

There has been very little written about the quality of proprietary centers, which represented 70 per cent of institutional day care centers in 1978 (Auerbach, 1979). The most extensive available study is Keyserling's 1972 report on the National Council of Jewish Women's study of 127 proprietary and 304 non-profit centers in seventy-seven sections of the country. Keyserling reports that an eight to ten-fold expansion of existing day care would not meet the child care needs of the communities studied. Proprietary centers were unable to meet FIDCR standards and still make a profit. Half of the centers visited were considered of poor quality, 15 per cent good quality, and only a few of those considered good had an educational program.

Emerging from the last two decades is a large array of philosophically and programmatically diverse, sometimes opposing, approaches to early childhood education. Montessori, behavioristic Bereiter-Englemann programs, programs built on Piagetian theory, the open classroom of the British infant school, and the developmental approach of Bank Street College are all held up as models for day care. These programs generally are affiliated with universities, generously funded, and designed and evaluated by sophisticated child development researchers. Most available day care is not of this character, and the influence of these approaches on the typical day care center is largely undocumented.[5] We are left without a professional consensus on what constitutes appropriate day care.

Suransky (1982 and 1983) provides vivid depictions of the day by day relationships in these social childrearing settings.[6] She poignantly portrays children's lives within a profit-run franchise center, characterized by 'institutional coercion', differential treatment of children according to their race and income level, and fragmented, often hostile interactions among adults and children. Suransky describes how teachers utilize denial of conflict, containment, institutionalization of time, and acculturation to a work ethic to create '. . . the erosion of childhood' (1982, p. 98). Only two centers, a predominantly black low income, non-profit center and an alternative 'free' school, provide a social context where young children have the opportunity to play, to 'create their own landscape', and thus to master reality. Through these analyses Suransky puts into bold relief crucial issues concerning social childrearing; specifically the young child's need for consistent, nurturant, long term ties with significant others.

Conclusion

Our country never has had a unified national policy focused directly on child care. Day care in the sense of enhancing child development never has been an end in itself, but rather, a support for something else; jobs for the unemployed, workers for defense industries, combating poverty, maintaining order in the cities, or getting welfare mothers to work. Even among child care advocates, there is a divergence of interests: women concerned with 'liberation', teachers concerned with jobs, government bureaucracies concerned with welfare reform, and families concerned with rising costs of living. No one is focusing directly either on day care as a distinct social childrearing context or on the quality of child care within this context. Having examined the role of familial childrearing in our society, we can better understand this neglect of day care.

The field study reported in this book addresses the issue of the quality of social childrearing within day care. Specifically the study's concern is the value transmission within the childrearing interactions of day care teachers. As significant others, do these teachers' childrearing practices promote or threaten the continuity of America's tradition of individualism? Through observation of the actions and words of day care teachers and their children in their day to day activities over time, this study provides a conceptual model for an initial understanding of whether day care children experience values different from those within America's tradition of individualism.

Notes

1 Gilligan (1982) has documented male and female differences of morality and ways of structuring relationships that relate to this assymetry of parenting in males and females and consequent differences in experiencing attachment and separation. Gilligan gives evidence that women's moral judgment is essentially based on an ethic of care underlying a logic of relationships seen as complementary webs of connections. Whereas women define the self and moral responsibility from their awareness of interconnections, males define self and moral responsibility from their awareness of separation. Male

imagery of relationships are images of hierarchy and their moral logic is a formal logic of justice and respecting the rights of others.

2 Whereas feminist writers of the 1970s spoke of the loving nurturant mother and supportive wife as positions of weakness and mediocrity, some feminist writers of the 1980s are redressing this critique (Elshtain, 1982; Friedan, 1981). Friedan writes: 'To deny the part of one's being as woman that has through the ages been expressed in motherhood — nurturing, loving softness, and tiger strength — is to deny part of one's personhood as woman' (p. 86). These feminists restore the importance of the family, and view distinctive gender needs and strengths as valuable to preserve. Given this new position, the challenge then becomes one of creating political and economic equality within the family and society, for females and males — an equality that encompasses gender differences.

3 Before her marriage to Franklin, the young debutante Eleanor Roosevelt was an active member in this movement. She had been recruited into the movement by Mary Harrison and Nathalie Henderson, who had launched the Junior League. One of the Junior League's main purposes was assistance in settlement houses, where many day nurseries were established (Lash, 1973, pp. 136–48).

4 It is frequently noted that the affluent usually establish the patterns that become normative values. Young and Wilmott (1973) speak of the principle of 'stratified diffusion' to describe the pattern of social changes beginning with the most affluent classes and working their way downward. They observe, 'What the few have today the many demand tomorrow' (p. 19). Though implementation of the Feminine Mystique usually was confined to middle class and upper middle class women, the Mystique became the normative value for all women in the fifties. Currently, there is a large increase in the number of affluent women with young children who are choosing to work. And gradually, these women are beginning to utilize suburban child care centers. If this trend continues, the stigmatized image of day care might in fact be withdrawn, and the public may gradually accept the idea of out-of-home child care.

5 We do have the carefully documented longitudinal study of preschoolers through age 15 who were enrolled in the Perry Preschool Program. This study demonstrates significant differences between experimental and control groups of poor black preschool aged children with low recorded IQs in response to early intervention. Specifically, the experimental group who attended the cognitively oriented Perry Preschool Program did significantly better than their control group in later schooling, and expressed less anti-social behavior than did the control group. This Perry Preschool Project seems to justify the additional public cost invested in early schooling (Schweinhart and Weikart, 1980).

6 Social science has produced very little research that describes and analyzes what young children and teachers are doing in the day-to-day child care centers. Research such as Suransky's pungent descriptions and analyses of

children in five child care centers is long overdue. Her work provokes disturbing questions for all child advocates, and hopefully can serve as impetus for additional field studies. Field workers and students of field work could profit however, from a more explicit account of Suransky's methodology. Her chapter entitled 'The Question of Method' predominantly addresses questions of theoretical orientation. The reader learns why she rejects positivist, empiricist approaches and chooses to use an interpretative phenomenological stance (1982, pp. 29–40). In her 1983 essay, she labels her perspective critical phenomenology. Both accounts involve a discussion that is primarily at a metatheoretical level rather than a methodological level (Smith, 1979). That is, she does not deal directly with procedural techniques and issues that give credibility to field work, such as ways of compensating for researcher bias, temporal scheduling of observations, manner of recording data, flexibility of procedures (for example, direct observation vs. informal conversation vs. formal interview vs. documents — verbatim vs. interpretative notes) (Becker, 1970). Admittedly, upon careful reading, several concrete research approaches can be pulled from the narratives and analyses in chapters 4 through 8. For example, the reader learns that at the franchise center, initial visits were preplanned weeks in advance but later Suransky was able to '. . . float in and out of the structure' (1982, p. 128). Within her analysis of this center, Suransky provides over a dozen of the directors' or staff members' comments about center events and policy. Yet at Golda Meier Nursery School only one direct comment from a staff member is noted. Suransky claims that the teachers at Golda Meier '. . . conceive of themselves as a separate class . . .' '. . . the teachers believed in acknowledging the angry feelings of the children . . .' (1982, pp. 74–5); however, the reader has no information as to how Suransky knows this. Are these inferences from observation notes or information from direct conversations with teachers, or both? A brief 'methodological' essay would clarify many of these questions.

3 *Social Childrearing Within Day Care: Rosehill Day Care Center*

We have seen that as a society, America lacks a policy for and even a national commitment to — high-quality day care. Day care always has existed within the tensions between familial and social childrearing, for the American ideal always has been familial childrearing, even though this familial ideal cannot be put in practice by most families today. As recently as 1980, when the White House Conference of Education held hearings throughout the country, people continued to voice concern that day care weakens the family and America's tradition of individualism (Caldwell, 1983). Yet we have seen that families' need for day care is increasing at an accelerated rate and that day care centers are burgeoning.

It is within this broader cultural context that we now focus on the distinctive social childrearing of day care through an in depth study of the daily life of teachers and children in one day-care center, Rosehill. Once we have described the nature of the day-to-day life within this day care, we then can ask if this social childrearing promotes or threatens America's value tradition of individualism.

Rosehill Day Care Center as an Organization

Establishing Rosehill Day Care Center as an Organization

In a manner similar to the establishment of the first day nurseries in America, America's tradition of egalitarian social reform is exemplified in the founding of Rosehill Day Care. Rosehill was established by the Ecumenical Minister's Alliance in the suburb of Elton in response to the requests of parents to see if '. . . there is anything that the churches of Elton can do to provide a safe place for our children and others when we are at work. It's not only hard to find baby-sitters, but so often when we do, our children are pushed in front of the TV all day, or are left to roam the streets unattended' (Rosehill Board of Directors' Minutes, 1973).

Elton is a middle-class suburb of a large metropolitan city in the American mid-west. Near the old central business district are four large stone Protestant churches, and a new modern Catholic church. At an intersection near the next suburb is a large Catholic stone church, a large Presbyterian stone church, and a modern Disciples of Christ Church. All of those churches have prestigious social class memberships. Scattered throughout the residential areas of town are smaller 'mainline' Protestant churches. In the metropolitan area, Elton is known as a family and church-oriented community.

In January 1973, as an attempt to become more active in community affairs, the Elton Ministerial Alliance formed the Elton Ecumenical Ministry. In March 1973 this Ecumenical Ministry appointed a Task Force on Day Care, the group that established Rosehill Day Care Center. The task force membership included two representatives from eight churches. In early May, this task force submitted a detailed proposal to the Ecumenical Ministry which adopted the following statement on the policy on day care:

> Elton Day Care is designed to provide full day care for 3 through 5-year-old children of working mothers.
>
> The day care is interracial, interfaith and will operate according to standards and requirements prescribed by the state and the city of Elton. A professionally trained staff carries forward a program to meet the physical, social, educational and emotional needs of children.

In late May, the first meeting of the Board of Directors of Rosehill Day Care was held. This Board consisted of two representatives from each of the eight participating churches plus two community representatives. Once the center began, two parent representatives were added; and as the center expanded the number of parent representatives was increased to four. Initially the eight sponsoring churches contributed the 'seed money' to begin Rosehill's operations.

In early September 1973, Rosehill Day Care opened with one full-time Director, two full-time teachers and eighteen children in space within one of the eight sponsoring churches. The day care's opening was a culmination of four months of volunteer work and contributions by community and church members in Elton. Much of the original equipment was made by volunteers with donated materials (for example, child-sized tables made from doors set on legs, children's 'cubbies' made from prayer-kneeling racks, and a sand box made from a large tractor tire). Initially volunteers assisted in much of the day care's maintenance and management, such as helping in the kitchen, doing clerical work, and assisting the teachers.

Within four months, thirty-six children were enrolled at Rosehill, and by the following fall the number was increased to forty-four. By the end of the second year, the center was filled to capacity (fifty-four children) with a waiting list. Each year therafter, the center has maintained a waiting list of at least twenty children. In 1978, the Rosehill Board of Directors began a satellite center to serve children 5 through 7 years during hours when they were not in public schools. This second center is in another Protestant church one mile from the original one, and has had forty-five children enrolled.

Since this first year, 50 per cent of Rosehill children have received some scholarship money. Scholarship funds are paid through church and community donations. Each of the sponsoring churches has pledged a yearly contribution. In addition, the Director has been very skilled in receiving donations from community service organizations such as the Lions Club, Rotary Club, and the Jaycees. During the first few years, the day care Board of Directors, staff and parents also held periodic fund raising events such as bake sales and rummage sales. Each spring they sponsored a large 'gala' dinner and theatre performance to raise funds.

Raising funds has been a primary task of both the Director and Board of Directors. To save money, they sponsor a spring, summer and fall 'work-day' where parents, staff and board members complete needed maintenance at the center (for example, tiling the kitchen floor, washing and painting walls, landscaping the playground). In 1975, Rosehill was admitted into United Way, and received a substantial annual contribution from them. In 1976, the United States Department of Agriculture's 'Child Care Food Program' began subsidizing all food served at the day care. In addition, a major contribution to the day care's functioning was the design and building of their playground by an architectural design class at the School of Architecture at Metropolitan University. The day care furnished all materials to the students who designed and built a large innovative playground. Again, the day care received many donations, such as all telephone poles given by the local electric company and all lumber given by a local lumber yard.

Over the years the number of regular volunteers from churches and the community has decreased; however, the day care has had a regular pattern of student volunteer assistants. Students from Elton High School's community campus assist for two hours a day and students from several parochial high schools assist for a month each year. In addition, the day care has served as a practicum site for several local universities and community colleges.

In attempting to maintain a professional staff, the Rosehill Board of Directors supported the education of their Director and teachers through granting some monetary assistance and release time when necessary. During the day care's first year, the Director and two teachers enrolled in the Child Development Associate (CDA) training program at a local community college. This CDA training program followed a developmental approach to early childhood education, and was used as the philosophical framework for Rosehill Day Care. Rosehill's goal and philosophy is summarized in its brochure:

> The Center's goal is to serve families by enabling parents to work and yet feel secure in knowing that their children are cared for in a safe, stimulating, and loving environment.
>
> Each child is encouraged to realize his full potential individually and to develop confidence and a sense of self-worth. We include in our programs a wide range of experiences that will strengthen important skills as well as encourage and develop the more complex intellectual processes involving concepts, reasoning, judgment, mathematics concepts, and reading readiness.
>
> The philosophy of Rosehill Day Care is to provide more than custodial care for children, as important as that care is. More than that, we strive to be a place where children feel good — and a place where parents feel good about leaving their children. Our programs stress not only the educational development of children, but also skills in socialization and practical life. The centers' teachers or 'caregivers' provide a happy balance between a variety of daily activities ranging from group activities, free play time, quiet time, and structured activities in a safe and healthy environment.
>
> The centers' goals, in short, are to provide a warm, nurturing, home-like atmosphere and to foster a child's development as an individual by enhancing his or her physical, social, emotional, and intellectual well being. . . .

As the day care's enrollment increased and additional staff were hired, they were encouraged to gain further training. If a staff person began work with no early childhood education, s/he enrolled in the community college CDA program. Other staff members who had early childhood education training usually obtained their CDA Credential from the CDA National Credentialing Program.

The teaching staff began at minimum wage and gained yearly salary increments. Staff did receive health insurance and a one-month vacation, both of which were rare in the day care field in this metropolitan area. Initially staff turnover was quite frequent, but by the day care's third year, this turnover had diminished significantly. The Director explained that most often the resignations were due to a staff member's ability to gain a higher paying position outside the field of day care.

Data collection of this study was completed in the day care's seventh year. The four teachers who are the subjects in this study had been teaching at Rosehill for six years, five years, three years and four months respectively.

The Setting: Use of Time and Space at Rosehill

Several features of early educators' use of time and space offer challenges to an outsider interested in understanding the flow of people and activity during the course of a day. During free play periods, both children and teachers move about in several areas of one room, or several rooms. During some parts of the day, both children and teachers move from indoor play areas to the outdoor playground (for example, at the outset and end of the day). Some spatial areas are used for multiple purposes (for example, a table area used for free play, eating, and naps). In addition, the same space often is shared by several teachers and their groups of children (for example, the large meeting room is used by everyone during Early Care). And finally, day care centers usually are open from early morning until early evening and thus both children and staff's arrival and departure are staggered. All of these features are characteristics of Rosehill staff's use of time and space.

The center is open from 6.30 a.m. to 6.00 p.m. Arrival of the children is staggered between 6.30 a.m. and 9.00 a.m. as is their departure between 3.00 p.m. and 6.00 p.m. Children's arrival and departure is determined by parent need. The teaching staff's arrival and departure is spaced between these hours so that all teachers are present between 9.30 a.m. and 2.30 p.m, and enough are present for a minimum ratio of one teacher for every ten children at all other times. The following description of each teacher's activity schedule includes a description of use of time and space within the center. Figure 3 depicts an overview of the activity schedule of lead teachers and children within the given space and time at Rosehill.

The church's large meeting room with adjacent kitchen is used for early care from 6.30 to 9.45 a.m. In this study, this large room is termed

Figure 3: Activity Schedule and Use of Space for Each Teacher

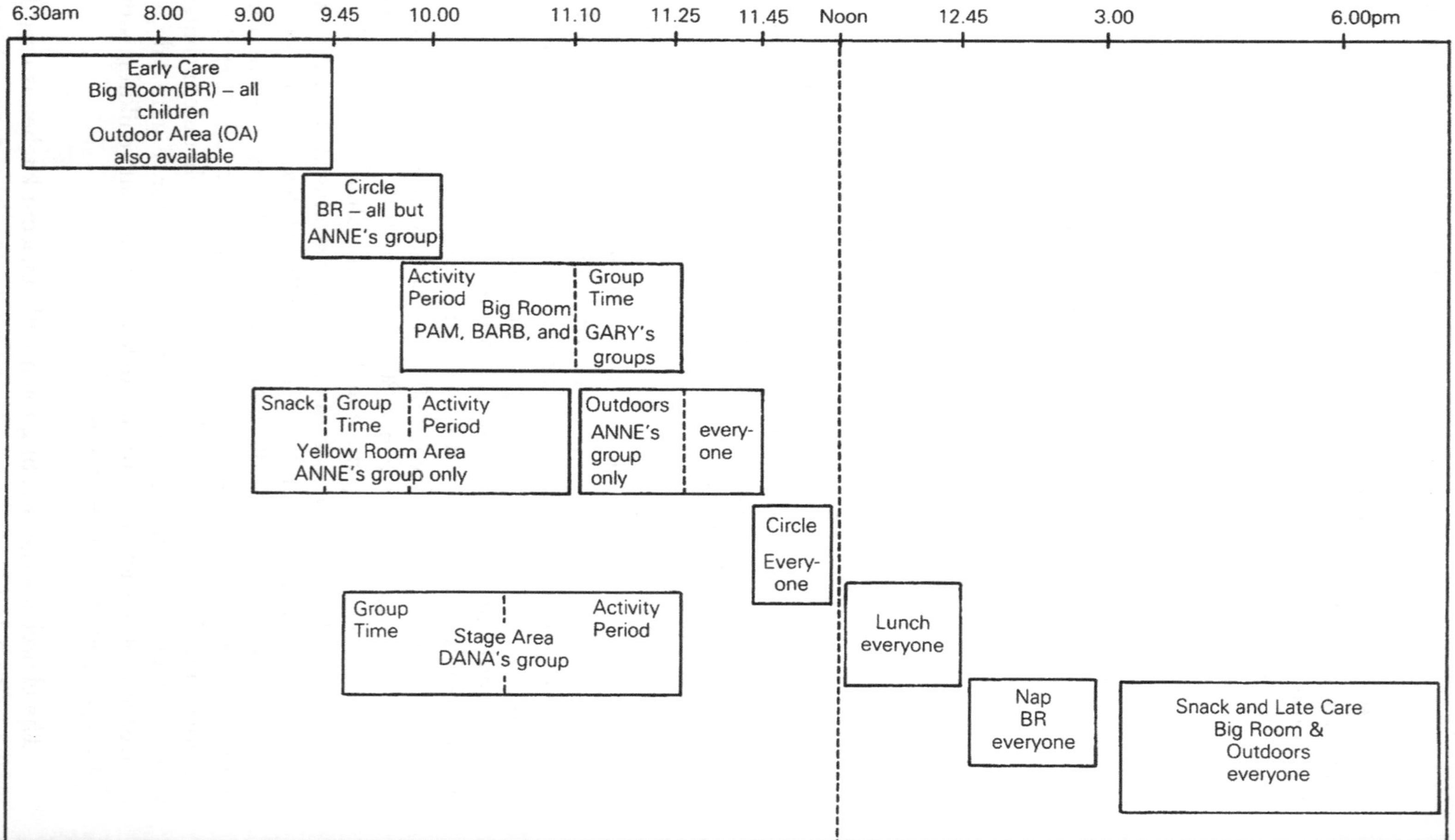

the Big Room. With brightly colored graphics painted on the long walls and children's free artwork hanging from the ceiling and displayed on the walls, the visitor senses that this cheerful looking space belongs to the children. The front third of the space has tables used for meals and choice activities. Two shelves containing a variety of manipulative toys to be used at the front tables are in this area. The remaining two-thirds of this room is divided by shelving and rugs into activity areas: a quiet book area, an art area, a housekeeping-dramatic play area, a unit block area, and a manipulative toy area. Throughout the room there is an abundance of high interest materials. A relaxed informal atmosphere is maintained during early care, even with the low steady hum of movement and voices of twenty to fifty young children and their teachers. Figure 4 is a map of the Big Room.

The fourteen youngest children comprise the entry class. *Anne*, one of the teachers in this study, is the lead teacher and *Tina* is her assistant. Between 6.30 a.m. and 9.00 a.m., these children join all other children in the Big Room, the church's large meeting room for early care. Weather permitting, children can choose to be either in the Big Room or on the outdoor playground between 8.00 and 9.00 a.m.. At 9.00 a.m., Anne, her assistant, and the children go to the Yellow Room area for snack, group time and activity period (free play). At 11.15 a.m., these children and their teachers go to the outdoor playground for twenty to thirty minutes.

The Yellow Room area comprises two small rooms next to one medium-sized room having yellow walls. As with the Big Room, this center room is cheerful with children's artwork displayed everywhere. The area's smaller size and careful placement of material communicate greater order than in the early care space. The small quiet room contains floor pillows, children's books on shelving, a circular table, and a shelf containing a toy barn, garage, vehicles and small wooden people. The small block room contains large hollow wooden blocks, small wooden unit blocks, and a three foot slide. In the Yellow Room is an art area, a housekeeping-dramatic play area, and a puzzle-manipulative toy area. All three rooms are used for activity period; the block room is used for group time; and the Yellow Room for snack and activity period. The Yellow Room area is depicted in figure 5.

Another headteacher, Dana, has the ten next oldest children for activity period and group time on the stage area. After Anne's children go to the Yellow Room, early care activities continue for all other children until 9.45 a.m. At this time Dana and her children go to the stage area in the back of the Big Room until 11.25 a.m., when they go outdoors. In Dana's carpeted room, there is a long shelf with a large

Figure 4: Big room area, kitchen, and stage area

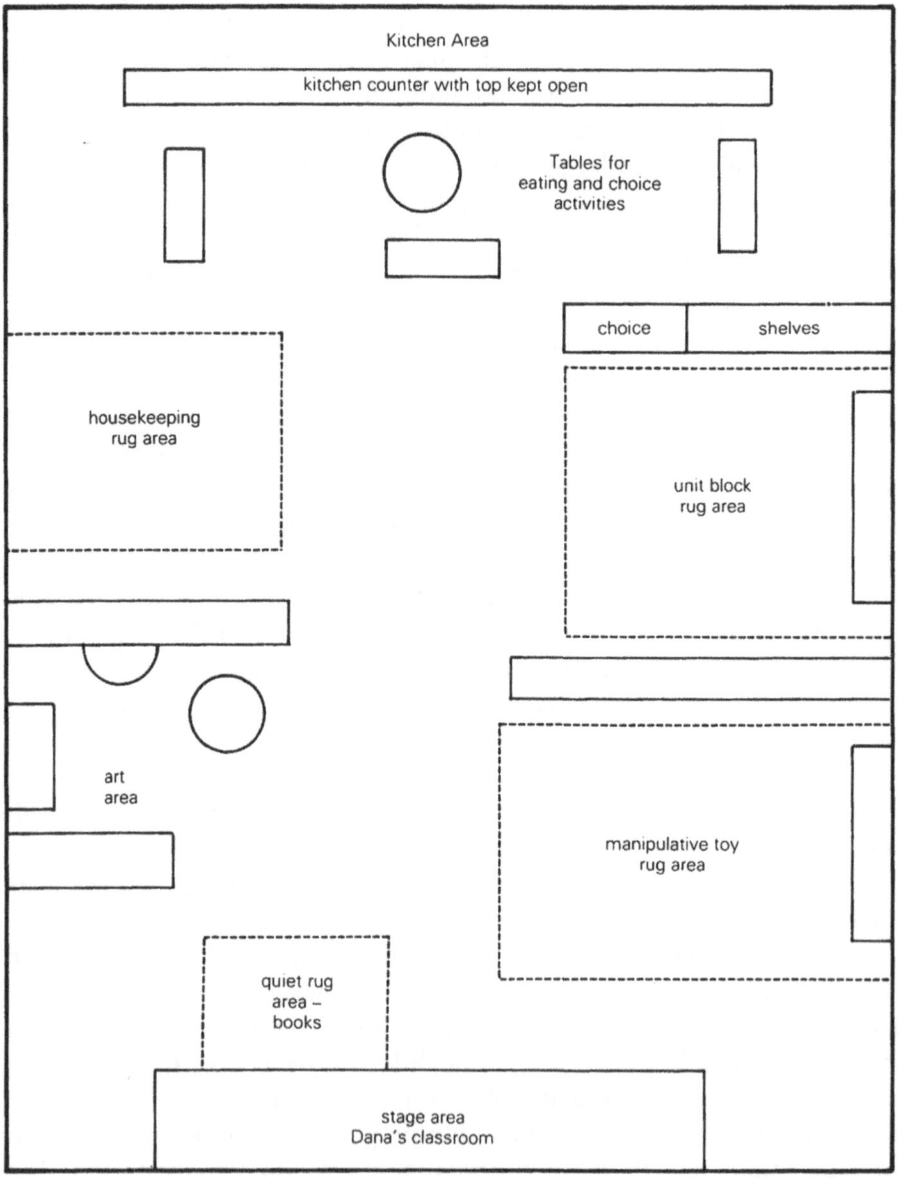

Figure 5: Yellow Room Area — Anne's Classrooms

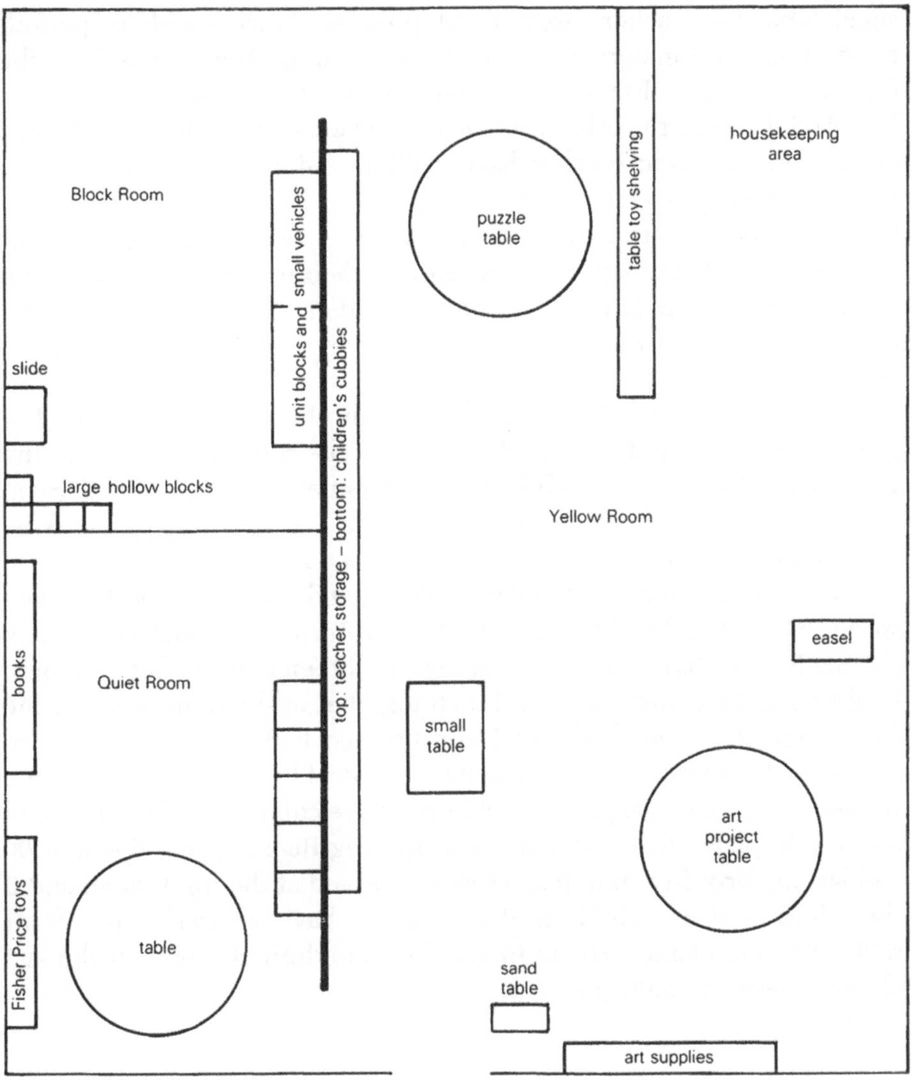

assortment of puzzles, other manipulative toys and children's books; a small shelf with paper, scissors, crayons and other art materials; and a small table for teacher directed art projects. During activity period, children can use materials either on the rug or on the long table in the front of the room. Figure 6 is a map of the stage area.

At 9.45 a.m., the other three lead teachers — *Pam, Barb*, and *Gary* — and one assistant teacher have a fifteen-minute circle period with their thirty children on the back manipulative toy rug area. Then these four teachers each are responsible for children's experiences in different activity areas. Each day the children can choose a cooking activity, an art activity, manipulative toys, blocks, and/or housekeeping-dramatic play. Upon completion of activities in one area, children may move to another area. At 11.10 a.m., group time is scheduled; however this activity is implemented in only 50 per cent of the days observed. For group time, Barb and Gary each use one of the activity rug areas in the Big Room. Pam and her children use Emmet's Room, a small room containing a rug and television. All children and adults go outdoors by 11.30 a.m.. Figure 7 maps the outdoor play area.

For the remainder of the day, children and teachers share the same space. By 11.45 all children and teachers return to the back rug area of the Big Room where they sing together for fifteen minutes before lunch. Children and teachers then eat lunch together at the front tables of the Big Room. After lunch the children use the bathrooms and listen to stories in Emmet's Room as teachers set up fifty-four cots in the Big Room for nap. By 3.00 p.m., all children have completed their naps and are free to play either outdoors or in the Big Room. Beginning at 3.00 and lasting forty-five minutes, a snack is served at the front table; and if they desire, twelve children at a time can have a snack at this front table. Parents begin arriving to get their children at 3.00 and the last children leave at 6.00 p.m..

The People: The Rosehill Community

The children enrolled in Rosehill live within five miles of the center. Of the fifty-four enrolled children, there is an equal number of 3 and 4-year-olds. Whereas 80 per cent of the children came from low and and/or single parent families when the center opened eight years ago, this year 50 per cent of the families are middle income and 45 per cent are from two parent homes. The Director shared with me that given the dramatic increase in applications from middle class families in the past four years, she no longer accepts children on a first-come first-serve

Figure 6: Stage area — Dana's classroom

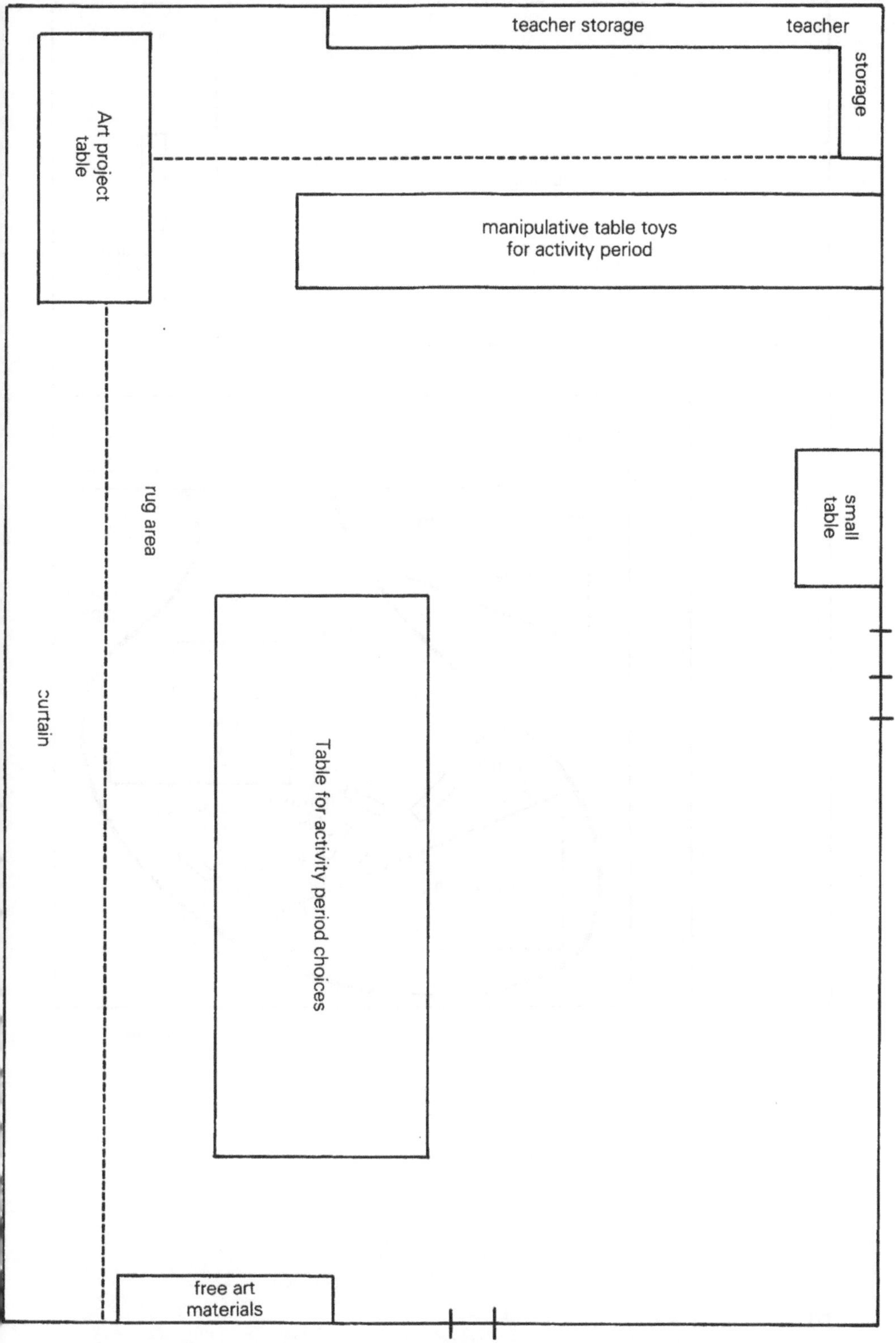

Figure 7: Outdoor Play Area

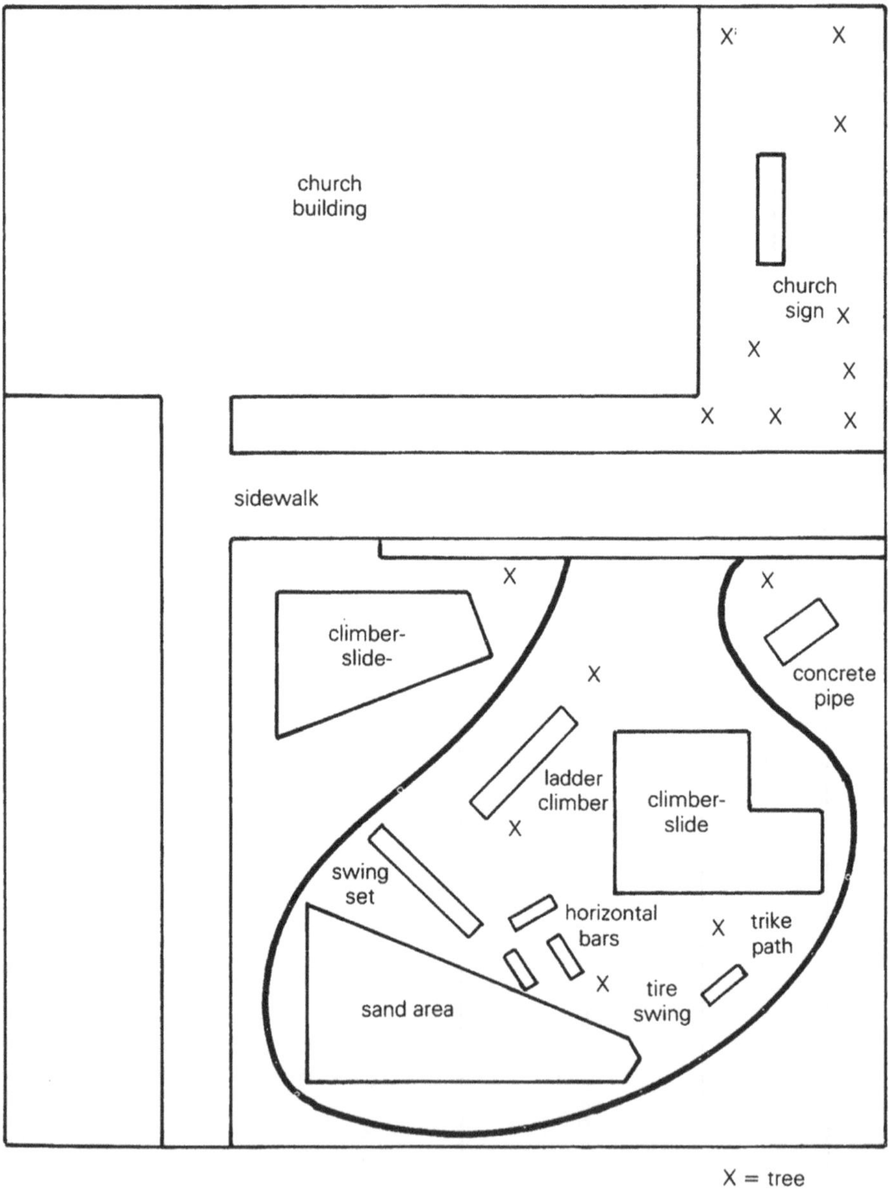

policy. Though this is the stated policy of Rosehill, low income children are always accepted first to maintain the center's commitment to heterogeneity. Twenty per cent of the children are black and the remainder Caucasian. The distribution of income and single parenting is proportionately the same for both races. One-quarter of the children spend ten hours each day at the center, half are present for nine hours, and one-quarter are present for eight hours.

Kate has been the center Director since Rosehill opened seven years before I began this study. She is an attractive 63-year-old woman who has lived in Elton for over thirty years. Prior to her work at Rosehill, Kate had many years of administrative business experience. She and her husband John had owned a shoe store in Elton. Kate has three grown children and six grandchildren, all of whom live in communities near Elton. Kate and John have retired from the shoe business, which has been continued and expanded by their two sons. Both Kate and John are very active at the local Presbyterian church. Kate was her church's representative to the Elton Ecumenical Ministry's board which sponsored the beginning of Rosehill Child Care Center.

Having administrative but no educational experience or training, Kate completed a two-year Child Development Associate (CDA) training program at a local college during her first two years as Director. The CDA program follows a developmental approach to early education similar to the Bank Street College of Education model. Rosehill teachers without formal early education training also enrolled in the CDA program, which became the framework for Rosehill's educational philsophy and goals.

Kate is exceptionally skilled in managing, fund-raising and community relations. She focuses primarily on administrative rather than educational aspects of center functioning. She meets with the staff during nap period once each week for about one hour. In these meetings, staff members share ongoing concerns and Kate gives updates on new enrollees, board decisions, forthcoming visitors, and news from the local day care association. Kate looks to Pam to decide and implement educational aspects of the day care's functioning. Several years ago, she had asked Pam to be Assistant Director. Pam refused this administrative title; however she unofficially functions as supervising teacher and educational decision maker, usually with consultation from Kate. Other teachers readily accept Pam's leadership.

Kate arrives each day by 7.30 a.m. and usually does not leave the center until after 5.00 p.m. Kate has an easy going relationship with each teacher, and often chats informally with them in the kitchen area where staff members congregate to take short breaks. She rarely is with the children and teachers unless she is guiding visitors through the center.

Kate supervises eleven staff members at Rosehill: a full-time bookkeeper/secretary, a full-time cook and part-time assistant cook, two full-time and one part-time assistant teachers, and five lead teachers. Pam, Anne, Barb, and Dana are lead teachers and are subjects in this study. The one male teacher, Gary, is omitted from the study for I did not want to focus on gender differences. Gary is a 38-year-old father of four young children, who received his associates degree in child care immediately after he returned from the Vietnam war. Gary has been working at Rosehill for five years, since he completed his associates degree. In his work with children and adults he maintains a very low 'profile'. Gary is the last adult to arrive at Rosehill and closes the center each evening. Though he is not observed taking any initiative, he consistently is dependable in completing his responsibilities at Rosehill.

The two young full-time assistant teachers, Tina and *Lisa* are new staff members. Tina started work three months before this study began and Lisa was hired six months later. The part-time assistant, *Ellen,* is somewhat limited with cerebral palsey, and works with small groups of two or three children. She has worked at the center three mornings a week for three years. On occasion one or two volunteers also work with the children. Several high schools have programs where students come to the center several hours a week for six weeks. In addition, several elderly women assist for a couple hours each week.

A Profile of Four Rosehill Teachers

As an early educator, I assume that 'teacher as person' is the most powerful instrument she contributes to the children she teaches. As a researcher at Rosehill, I have attempted to describe teachers' actions and to present an understanding of their aims and cognitions within the specific situational characteristics of Rosehill. Following Berlak and Berlak (1981) and Mills (1959), I strove to learn how each teacher's personal biography intersected with observed action. As Mead (1964) notes: 'Each person slices the world from a different time system' (p. 341). I engaged in frequent informal conversations and more structured interviews in which teachers spoke of their personal histories and of their views of the meaning of observed events. Given the constraints of both time and availability of just one researcher, these personal histories are somewhat thin; nevertheless, they can provide, on critical incidents, a significant lens in understanding the meaningfulness of particular teacher action.

Pam

This is Pam's sixth year at Rosehill. As mentioned, although she has refused the Director's offer to become a supervising teacher, nevertheless the Director and all teachers relate to Pam as if she were in that role. A 28-year-old woman, fine featured with a short pixie hair style, Pam's blithe spirit and graceful movements of her tall slender body communicate an understanding of 'being in charge.'

As a child, Pam lived in a middle-class suburb just west of Rosehill. Pam begins describing her childhood by saying: 'I had a boring childhood, for I remained at home most of the time. My father was in business and made enough money that my mother, my two older sisters and I never needed to work.' She continues, that as a child she had loved dancing; but when she entered high school her parents 'forced her' to quit dancing and begin piano lessions which she hated. When 15, Pam's father died. With her two older sisters away at college, Pam and her mother lived alone together until she left home to attend a state university. Pam explains: 'I never was a good student and went to college because it was expected of me. And I never thought of being a teacher. As a child, I didn't even baby-sit like many of my friends did.'

In college Pam majored in psychology. She was advised that she would need a graduate degree in psychology if she wanted a position in that field. Since she did not enjoy studying, she explored alternative career choices. A friend told her about the university laboratory preschool and their early childhood education program. Pam explains: 'I observed at the preschool, was excited about what I saw, and enrolled in the early childhood education program. During my last two years, I loved every minute at the preschool.' At the same time, Pam became involved in the university theatre where she assisted the stage crews.

After college Pam returned home and obtained a position teaching preschoolers in a half-day alternative high school program, and working with high schoolers for the remaining half-day. She explains that she felt clumsy working with the high schoolers and was relieved to get a half-day appointment as assistant teacher at Rosehill in January of that year, six years ago. Then in June she began work full-time as lead teacher. When asked what has influenced her teaching most, Pam explains that with six years of experience she has gained self confidence, and this self confidence has been her greatest resource.

Since college Pam has become active in theatre and dance. Her friend Sue, with whom she now lives, does freelance work full-time for local theatres. Sue, Pam, and several others began a local community theatre group, and each year this group performs several musicals. I asked Pam what work she would like to be doing in the distant future. Pam replied: 'I cannot see myself teaching forever. And you know, I have been asked if I would like to take Kate's position when she retires; but I have no interest in being a Director. I want to be with the kids. Sue and I have talked about someday beginning our own business creating greeting cards'.

Anne

Anne is a 35-year-old woman who is beginning her fourth year teaching at Rosehill. Short in stature, Anne's neatly groomed wavy hair and precise dress reflect her expressed valueing of order and structure. She has a 6-year-old son who attends a parochial school near their home in the southern section of the city, eight miles from Rosehill. Anne's husband is a baker whose evening work hours allow him to care for their son in the early morning when Anne works.

Anne lived with her parents on their farm in Poland until ten years ago, when she moved to America. That year she married Jim, an American whom Anne met when he had returned to Poland to visit his family. Fifteen years earlier, Jim had left Poland with several other teenagers to live in America. Anne explains: 'He hated the Russians you know, and they always heard on Radio Free America how wonderful everything is in America'.

For her first five years in America, Anne remained home and cared for her son until he was old enough to enter Rosehill where she began to teach. Anne, her husband and son are very active within the Polish Catholic Church. Their personal-social life involves experiences with Polish immigrants who also attend this church. Every three years the family returns to Poland for four weeks.

For five years in Poland, Anne taught twenty-five to thirty children in a state supported day care center that was controlled by the school system. The school system gave the teachers a set curriculum, which Anne describes as very structured. She explains that by structured she means that all the children do similar table projects as directed by the teacher. She showed me lessons that she has kept from her teacher training in Poland. A typical activity involves a teacher making an outline of the Polish flag for each child, and the 'art' project consists of the child coloring in the lines with the given color.

In Poland, Anne remained with the same children for three years. When they became six, Anne took them to their school teacher. 'We have meetings with the teachers and the physicians. They all really depend on us, to see if the children are ready for school.' Anne then stresses that unlike in America, the children respect the teachers. She explains: 'I mean, I never saw a child run away from me, hit me, or spit at me. But you know, the teachers got very much respect from the children's parents. And at home, the children always listen to the parents, who often say: "You need to listen to your teacher"'.

Anne frequently compares her Polish experience to America. She stresses that all day care teachers in Poland, unlike in America, must be qualified. 'We have two years of college and then get a diploma for teaching what in Poland is called kindergarten'. When asked what resources have helped her the most in her teaching, Anne replies:

> The teacher training in Poland. Over here, people work in day care just for a few months, and often they are not trained and are not good teachers. But all my life I wanted to be a teacher.

Anne then explains that once she began teaching at Rosehill, she enrolled in the Child Development Associate (CDA) program for early educators at a local community college. After one semester of CDA training, Anne arranged to complete her requirements independently. Then several months after my observation study, Anne obtained her CDA credential from the CDA National Credentialing Program. Prior to her CDA assessment, Anne asked me to read her portfolio, a notebook containing examples of her teaching and statements explaining the purposes of the given examples. After reading her portfolio, I shared with Anne that many of these statements seemed very different from those of our earlier discussions of teaching. Anne replied: 'Yes, that's right. But you know I did this portfolio by following the CDA guidelines.' I then asked her which theory and method, American or Polish, she thought was most effective and educational. She replied: 'Methods like in Poland, but you know, I am getting used to things here now. And it's okay'.

Barb

Barb's long wavy hair and casual dress reflect her youthful spontaneous manner in relating to both children and adults. At 24, Barb began work at Rosehill one month after I began my observations. Prior to that time she had worked at a half-day preschool for three years. Barb explained to me that she was eager to work full-time now that she and her husband had just purchased a home. Barb's home is in the southern section of the city, close to Anne's home. One year earlier Barb had married a young man who obtained a BS degree from the local state university. Though he has his degree, he continues to work in the warehouse of a large machinery company where he had worked in high school.

Barb grew up in a Catholic working class family in a small suburb south of the city. She is the middle of five children, and attended parochial elementary and public high school. Then she enrolled in a child care program at a local community college where she received her AA degree. Barb comments:

> I have never been much of a student. I am not a reader, and never have been. But in college I learned a lot even though I have never been a school person. From the first semester we worked in centers, and I learned a lot from teachers in these centers. My best semester was working at Rosehill. At the college, teachers shared their own experiences and always talked about how they would handle different situations. And when I left college I really felt prepared.

Barb shared with me that when her own children are infants, she does not plan on working. But she would like to remain in the field, and as soon as her infants are two or three years old, she would like to teach again. She comments: 'Of course I may not be able to afford to teach in day care; the pay is so terrible'. And in reality, she would earn twice as much money if she worked in a factory. I asked Barb how she became interested in early childhood education.

Barb: Since I was three I have taken dance lessons. And when I was ten, the teacher asked me if I would like to help her. And I began hanging around her studio. She was very helpful to me and I loved being around small children. It seems like small children really have always responded to me.

CSK: How did you become interested in day care?

Barb: I needed work. I love it here; and I think it's great for the kids.

CSK: Great in what way?

Barb: Day care expands the kids in all directions, and they become a lot more independent than if they were at home. And there is a lot of stability in coming to a place like this, a

> lot more security than being with a sitter and TV. And the children here get a lot of love from the adults and have many children to play with.

After her first few weeks at Rosehill, Barb became close friends with Pam. Pam encouraged Barb to become active in the local community theatre group, and the two women spent time together after work as they prepared for shows. One year after this field observation Barb gave birth to her first child and resigned at Rosehill.

Dana

Dana is a 29-year-old who is completing her fifth year at Rosehill. A short, slightly plump woman, with neatly arranged 'permed' curl and large glasses, Dana's demeanor suggests that of a nineteenth century schoolman, a characterization most vivid during naptime, when she sits next to the sleeping children and reads thick library books.

She also grew up in the southern section of the city. Her mother is a full time homemaker, her father manages a pharmacy at night, and Dana is their only child. After graduating from public schools, Dana enrolled in a local private college where she majored in English and art. After college, she returned to work in the large department store where she had been employed in high school. After three months in the department store, she resigned to look for more challenging work.

When asked how she chose to work in day care, Dana replied:

> I can't exactly explain it. Yet one day I said to myself: 'why not work with preschool children?' When in college I had visited a local private school where my friend was student teaching, and I loved what I saw. This same friend suggested that I visit Valley Preschool and I did. The Valley Preschool Director then suggested that I could volunteer at Rosehill to see if this is an area I would like to pursue. The next week I began volunteering three days a week at Rosehill. In two months I was hired as an assistant half-time, and began working full-time two more months later, five years ago.

Dana began working as a lead teacher three years ago. A consistent thread in her work is her solitary stance. She has a quiet almost bashful relationship with both newcomers and co-workers. She is very warm and friendly when approached by people but initiates few spontaneous exchanges with fellow workers. Other teachers seem to respect Dana though they occasionally describe her as 'different' (for example, '... more interested in academic skills like letters and numbers. ... wants to have Friday movement/motion sessions separate from us.').

Dana seemed to enjoy spontaneous conversations with me, and spoke very freely during our four formal interview sessions; however she asked that I not use a tape recorder. Given her seemingly separate stance, her description of what assists her most in her teaching gives evidence of her complexity.

> When the staff meets regularly and we discuss the children, and what things possibly have led to certain behavior, those sharing times are most helpful to me. And even when it is not a regular staff meeting, the informal conversations we have about the children are extremely helpful.

Dana lives alone in an apartment in a suburb west of the center. She loves to read and to travel, and last summer travelled alone in England. Shortly after I finished this field study Dana resigned from Rosehill to begin work in the city's art museum. Before leaving she shared with me that though she loves her work at Rosehill, this new position is a wonderful resumption of her college studies, and might offer exciting future possibilities.

A Day at Rosehill: The Schooling Acts of Four Day Care Teachers

Early Care — 6.30–9.45 a.m.

As Pam turns into the church parking lot at 6.30 a.m., she waves to Jill and Sally who are getting out of their cars with their mothers. After Pam opens the center, the children's mothers sign in at the entry. Jill and Sally follow Pam into the Big Room, and help her put the chairs under the front tables. Since it is Monday, Pam places on the two choice shelves the table toys that will be used for early care this week. Approximately twenty to thirty items are put on these shelves: a box of dominoes, a tray of six wooden puzzles, a can of small zoo animals and fencing, a bucket of snap-together plastic Bristle Blocks, a can of small plastic bears, a go-fish card game, pegs and pegboards, wooden beads and thread, a box of wooden pattern cubes, one inch cubes, and a tray of parquetry shape blocks.

Jill and Sally kiss their mothers goodbye and immediately get the bristle blocks and begin to snap them together as they sit next to each other at the table. By the time Pam has the room arranged, three more children have arrived, and another fifteen arrive during the second half-hour. The outsider is intrigued by the matter-of-fact routine manner in which these small children separate from their parents and begin their day at Rosehill. After saying goodbye to their parents, they put their coats in their individual cubbies, then get a toy from the choice shelf and take it to the front table area.

Once she has the Big Room arranged, Pam goes into the adjoining kitchen and begins cooking breakfast. As she is involved in these tasks, she enthusiastically greets children as they arrive. At 7.00 Anne arrives and either assists in breakfast preparation or sits with the children at the front table area. Anne frequently eats a light breakfast in the kitchen where she and Pam informally chat together. When the cook arrives at 7.30, both teachers leave the kitchen area and join the children in the Big Room. During this first hour, the relaxed even slow tempo of children and adult movement and interaction is reminiscent of an early morning homelike informality.

At 7.30 Pam 'opens' at least one and sometimes two other activity areas for the children to use in the Big Room. This process includes either placing bean bag chairs and rockers on the quiet library area, setting up an art table with paper and magic markers, or placing tubs of toys on the block area rug. Except for about twenty minutes when she supervises children on the playground, Pam works in the Big Room for the remainder of early care. During this time, Pam either is observing the children, conversing with children or with a teacher, participating in an activity with a child or children, or completing a maintenance task (for example, sorting materials in the art cabinet). Regardless of where she is located in the Big Room, children frequently come to Pam to share home happenings, to show her their work, to ask for assistance, or to ask her to play with them. Pam's response is uniformly cheerful and these spontaneous exchanges have an informal ease in tempo.

By 7.30, Kate has arrived. Before beginning work in her office, Kate usually chats informally with Pam and Anne. Between 7.30 and 8.00 another fifteen children arrive. As the number of people and movements increase, Pam and Anne's greeting of arriving children becomes less frequent. If an arriving child does walk by either teacher, they cheerfully welcome the child. Otherwise most children hang up their coats and then initiate their own activity without teacher greeting. A soft hum of voices and a calm atmosphere pervades throughout the Big Room. On a typical day, ten children are eating breakfast at the front table and are assisted by the cook. Six children are in the quiet area, each looking at a book. Four children play with tinkertoys and small rubber blocks on the block rug area. Another fifteen are using table toys at the front tables where Anne and Pam are seated.

With the exception of twenty minutes outdoors, Anne remains in the table area of the Big Room until 9.00, when she and her fourteen children go to the Yellow Room for snack, activity period, and group time. During this early care period, Anne sits with children as they work with table toys. As children in her group enter the center, she usually greets them with an enthusiastic hug, and frequently adds: 'I love you'. In addition, Anne occasionally has one of her children on her lap during early care. Often children initiate hugging and kissing with Anne, and she affectionately responds to these gestures. When children who often are non-compliant follow Anne's rules, she is quick to use physical affection to praise them; typically she hugs the child as she says: 'I like that' or 'I love you'. Pam also provides intimacy through affectionate touching, hugging or lap sitting during early care.

1/26 — Early care — Jim, typically sad during the outset of each morning and usually on the fringe of ongoing activities, stands next to the block area as he watches children play. As Pam walks by Jim, she cheerfully greets him and gives a quick tickling gesture on his stomach. Jim shyly smiles as he says hello.

12/15 — Early care — Pam has gathered five children who are roaming aimlessly about the room. She and the children sit on the back rug area and begin singing fingerplay songs together. Alicia is sitting on Pam's lap as Ronnie leans against her arm.

As Anne sits with the children at the front choice tables, she engages in many spontaneous conversations and is available to assist children upon their request. Children occasionally bring their picture or other completed project to Anne and she is quick to praise them. As her new enrollees enter the center, Anne helps them learn how to set and clear their utensils for breakfast, how to pour their own drinks, how to put on their own jackets, and how to choose their own table toy and return it to the shelf upon completion. Anne gives these directives in a simple, warm manner, often with demonstration. In turn the children quickly become independent in these tasks and seldom need adult help after their second week. All children are free to come and go outdoors after 8.15, and Anne spends a good proportion of her last hour in early care assisting the children in fastening their clothing. As she zips and buttons, she chats with individual children in a relaxed manner. Pam also is quick to assist children when asked. Whether the task is puzzle completion, coat fastening or shoe tying, Pam is very patient in her interactions with the children. Older children with the needed competency to assist another child occasionally are nearby Anne and Pam when they are helping a child. However, neither teacher is observed encouraging children to help each other, unless it is a child's first day.

When Barb comes to work at 8.00, she first looks for the children in her small group and enthusiastically greets each; in turn, her children often return her greeting with a spontaneous hug. If the weather is above thirty degrees, Barb then opens the outdoor play area, where she remains until Dana comes outdoors at 8.40.. Typically Barb is available outdoors but is not actively focused on the children. She does assist children upon their request; otherwise, she frequently is conversing informally with children and/or adults. On a few occasions Barb initiates a group activity outdoors — playing kickball with the children, chanting familiar rhymes as she structures turntaking on horizontal bars, or singing with the children as they slide together down into a gargantuan pile of leaves that they gleefully toss into the air around her.

All Rosehill teachers take turns in supervising the outdoor playground for a portion of early care. About one-third of the play area is grass and the children often race about this area. The remainder of the outdoor area contains a series of large permanent structures — swings, sand area, horizonal climbing bars, and two large wooden climbing structures that each have a four-foot wide slide, and several large platforms of varying heights. Thus teachers do not necessarily have to provide portable outdoor equipment such as balls or jump ropes; and in fact, these teachers usually choose not to add to the given outdoor environment.

Daily, children use the swings, ladder climber, and trikes, all of which are used individually. Other equipment can be used individually but also has the potential for varied social interaction — the large sand area, a large vertical tire swing hung from a tree, or the two wooden climbing structures. Sometimes several children are playing side by side on this equipment. At other times, children are playing together in the sand box, swinging together on the vertical tire swing, and engaging in some social role playing outdoors.

10/1 — Early care — Jill and Sally have just entered the playground and run to the church sign which they pretend is a restaurant. Jill: 'What do you want?'. Sally replies: 'An ice cream cone'. Jill then pretends to give one to Sally, who leaves as she pretends to be licking the cone. Annie comes to the area and Jill asks: 'What do you want?'. Annie: 'Cherry pie'. Jill: 'We only have chocolate pie. Do you want some?'. Annie nods yes and Jill pretends to give her some. As Annie leaves, Jill calls out: 'Anybody want food or drinks?. . .'.

10/20 — Early care — Corrie, Ronnie, and Lia play on the vertical tire swing. Lia and Corrie take turns sitting with Ronnie inside the swing. The other girl then twists the swing tightly and then lets go as the swing rapidly unravels and the children gleefully laugh together.

In these two sequences of spontaneous group activities, and in most other outdoor social play, no teacher is directly observing the children. Rather, they usually gather together and informally converse with each other. Only Dana supervises but she remains near the swing area where the children's play is individual.

When Dana comes to work at 8.30 she gets a cup of coffee and goes to the outdoor playground where she remains until 9.20, when she goes indoors to prepare materials for the next two activity periods. Dana is the only Rosehill teacher who uses a predictable period of time daily to leave the children and to prepare materials. Others do this preparation as they are with the children in early care.

During early care Dana engages in a limited range of interactions with children and adults. Whereas the other teachers use outdoors as a time to congregate and converse together, Dana is more likely to be separate and actively watching the children near the swing area. Her stance is so consistent and quiet that she almost seems invisible. Most of the children in her group are immersed in play when Dana arrives, and neither she nor the children usually greet each other. Rather, Dana is a presence, usually standing near the children. Children occasionally call to her to watch them (for example, sliding or swinging high), and she warmly responds to their initiatives. Expressing physical affection common on the part of the other teachers and children is not observed.

By 8.30 at least forty-five children have arrived, and all children are present by 9.00. Unless the temperature is below thirty degrees, children play in the Big Room and/or outdoors at their own choosing. Most of the children engage in individually focused activity. Areas in the Big Room that invite social interaction (for example, housekeeping and block area) are 'closed' on all but about 25 per cent of observed mornings. This individual focus is inherent in most of the table toys for use in the front table area. A few items could be used for joint construction (for example, Lego). However, it is the school policy that when children choose an item from the choice shelves they may decide whether or not they wish to share this item with other children. All children know this 'first choice' policy and conflicts over materials are infrequent. As they engage in these table activities, the children spontaneously chat with nearby children and adults. I asked each teacher the rationale for this first choice policy:

Pam: We always have enough materials for everyone. A child should have the chance to use materials in her own way.

CSK: And this morning, when Jesse was using Lego, he needn't share with Kay, even though there were enough for the two children?

Pam: Right. Jesse should have the chance to use them in his own way.

Anne: When I first started work here, they already had the rule. But I think it's good because the children know they have the right to play with what they choose.

Dana: It seems logical to me, for if it weren't the school policy, and the decision were up to me, I'd be inclined to do that.... It seems logical that a child would want to play alone. Children should have that prerogative....

Barb: I've never thought about it.... but I guess it protects the kids' rights.... And it's an easier way for us to handle a 'scuffle' between children.

Most Rosehill children are quick to learn to initiate their own tasks and upon completion, put away materials and begin another task with new materials. These children control how long to remain involved in a task and the manner of this involvement. Teachers speak of this time as time for '... children to do things in their own way', 'we don't have anything planned and the kids control'. An outside observer is impressed with the even tempo of movement and voices in a room with so many young 3 and 4-year-olds. But if the observer focuses on individual children for a lengthy period of time, five to fifteen minutes, s/he will see that many children have surface play patterns. That is, they move from one task to another and never maintain involvement in any one activity.

During the six month observation period, occasionally sequences were observed where children spontaneously play together either in pairs or small groups. In all of these observations, at least one of the children involved are those sixteen of the fifty-four children who have developed enduring friendships with another child at Rosehill. These sixteen children with best friends seem to have chosen their companions spontaneously; at least teacher initiation of friendship pairing is never observed.

Several types of social play occurred. First, some of the social play between children is activity that is structured either by the materials or by rules of the game. For example, children complete a puzzle together, rock in the rocking boat together, look at a book together, or play a commercial table game together.

> 1/26 — Early care — Eddie takes the bingo game from the choice shelf and says: 'Who wants to play with me?'. Alicia replies: 'I do!' and the children sit at the table together. As Eddie takes out the board, Alicia says: 'We take turns. I'll begin'. The two children then play bingo for about five minutes until Pam tells them it is time to clean up for circle.
>
> 2/8 — Early care — Four girls, each with a hula hoop are in a circle. Emy seems to be the leader, for she counts: '1, 2, 3, 4, 5, go!'. And then the girls begin twirling their hoops. In an authoritative manner, Emy gives the children directives as to their spatial location: 'Lea, you may go over there. No Corrie! over there'.

Second, other social play among children involves role playing, either spontaneous social role play without any dramatic play props or role play structured by materials either in the housekeeping area or block area. The housekeeping area is 'open' on about one-quarter of the mornings during the six-month observation. Most of the children's involvement in this area primarily involves mere manipulation of objects.

> 2/4 — Early care — In the housekeeping area, Eddie has stacked two pots and a teakettle as a tower on the small table. Evan, Alicia and Rita are hiding utensils in the large hollow blocks which are stored against the housekeeping wall.

Children frequently enter this area and dress and undress themselves in the adult clothing provided, or dress and undress the dolls without engaging in role play sequences. A few brief role play sequences were observed, and again the children able to engage in this type of extended play always include at least one of the sixteen who have enduring friendships with another child.

> 11/21 — Early care — Rachel, Nan, Jill and Mia have entered the housekeeping area. Rachel and Nan make two chairs from the large hollow blocks and sit on them. Mia gives each child a cup as she says: 'I'll go get the cake'. Mia then goes to the stove, pretends to crack a plastic egg into a bowl, mixes with a large spoon and then brings the bowl to the two girls. Mia: 'It's ready'. She pretends to 'dish out' the food. Jill crawls about the floor as she makes kitten sounds. Then Nan and Rachel pretend to sleep on the wedged hollow blocks. When they get up, Nan says: 'Let's go to the store now'. The four girls begin riding the wooden riding boat.

Teachers are neither directly involved or observing these play sequences in the housekeeping area. Similarly they are not observed participating or directly observing the children's spontaneous role play.

> 2/5 — Early care — Evan, Jimmie, Carl and Ricky are walking about the rug in the block area. Each boy has made a snap-together plastic block space ship, which he 'flies' as he walks about the rug area, with space ship held high.
>
> *Ricky:* 'Let's blast off!'
>
> *Carl:* 'Calling Batman, calling Superman!'
>
> *Evan:* 'Robin, we better go. Oh! Help me! I'm stuck in some molasses.' Evan stops walking as if to 'freeze'. Ricky touches Evan which seems to allow Evan to move again.
>
> *Carl:* 'When you heard that ding noise you saw the ship lost its motor and fell.'
>
> *Evan:* 'And then you found some bombs in it that Darth Vadar put in and you take them out.'
>
> *Carl:* 'You mean down here?' (He points to the back of his 'ship'.)
>
> *Evan:* 'Yes.'
>
> *Carl:* 'Let's pretend Darth Vadar drops some cryptamite on Superman.'
>
> *Evan:* 'And he dies.' Ricky (Superman) lies down for a moment and then sits up.

Ricky: 'I'm awake.'
Evan: 'Hi Superman. Now pretend Robin and Batman will get Darth Vader with a bat net.' David then comes to the rug area and makes a space ship.
David: 'Storm destroyer!'
Evan: 'No! we don't need a storm destroyer.' David moves about the rug area with his space ship in his hand held high.
Evan: 'My magnetic force, my lazar can do the trick!' All boys are walking about the rug area. If not talking they are making motor sounds as they hold their ships up.
Evan: 'Let's go to the art factory.' The boys then 'fly' their space ships to the art table. Barb tells the boys: 'The art area is closed. It's time to clean up for circle.' (This is the first exchange these children have had with a teacher. No teacher seems to be aware of these children's play.)

A third form of observed social play during early care consists of children's joint construction or creation within an extended sequence of interaction. This interaction is more complex than activities that are structured either by materials or by rules of the game. Here the children create something new as they work together on a common goal. As with the previously described social play, teachers are not observed either participating or directly observing most of these sequences.

12/30 — Early care, back of the room — Two girls and three boys are clapping their hands and stomping their feet to the rhythm that Alan is beating on the bottom of a cylindrical toy container. Ronnie seems to be the leader for occasionally he calls out 'stop' and all do in fact, stop. Then when he says 'o.k.' the children continue clapping and stomping.

Depending on their arrival time, most Rosehill children have from one to three hours of early care play. Observed social play sequences rarely lasted longer than ten minutes. Occasionally the playing children have a conflict and need adult intervention. However, on many occasions children end their disputes on their own. Three strategies to end disputes are observed. Children angrily shout at each other, which seems to give them needed release, for then they continue playing. Or, one child threatens 'I won't be your friend', which usually causes the other child to comply. Or most often, the offended child leaves the play area.

Recurrently during early care, there are brief periods of time when the children are on their own, either with no teacher present in the area, or with a teacher present but neither focused or aware of the children's activity. This is a pattern that occurs with all the teachers at one time or another. When the children are alone in the Big Room, a teacher usually is involved either in a maintenance task or teachers are conversing together in the kitchen area. Occasionally teachers are in the Big Room yet are preoccupied with one task and not aware or within view of happenings in other parts of the room. On these occasions when no teacher is with the children, the low hum of children's voices and movement usually is sustained. The observer is reminded of a homelike atmosphere, when parents do household chores in rooms nearby their young children.

In the early care period of the day, the teachers' most frequent type of interaction with the children occurs when they are responding to children's misbehavior. If children are roaming aimlessly about the room, misusing materials, being excessively loud indoors, doing something that is potentially dangerous, or engaged in a lengthy conflict, all four teachers redirect the children's action in a firm consistent manner. All the teachers give their redirections in repetitive phrases that become like slogans: children who are flitting are told to 'get a choice'; children who are excessively loud are told to 'use an inside voice'; if physical aggression is involved in a conflict, children are urged to 'use words', and the attacked child is urged to tell the offender to 'stop bothering you'; if children are grabbing materials from each other, the 'first choice policy' is implemented. Most frequently Anne, Pam, and Dana call to the misbehaving children from wherever they are situated. In contrast, Barb always goes directly to the misbehaving children rather than call from across the room. But unlike Pam and Anne, Barb rarely sits with children; rather she saunters about various areas as the children play. She remains within view of the children; yet she often does not seem focused or actively observing them. Observation notes contain recurrent interpretative questions as to whether Barb feels at ease during this time, for she often stares into space and seems either distracted or bored. I asked Barb to explain her rationale for always moving about:

> I hate to sit down, for when I do, I don't seem to be able to get to places fast enough. If I'm standing and see something happen, I can get there quickly. You know, sometimes, I just panic inside; the room is so open and big and I know I can't be everywhere.

Of the four teachers, Anne redirects the children most frequently. In all observed sequences Anne uses repetitive phrasing as do the other teachers; however Anne makes certain that she also tells the children 'I don't like that!'. Often when she hears a loud noise or children crying, Anne calls to the children and asks: 'What's going on?' However, this phrase seems to be more for getting the children's attention, for she doesn't wait for the children to reply; rather, she gives them a directive.

> 11/5 — Early care — Anne is in the kitchen and is conversing with Kate. Eighteen children play alone in the Big Room. From the block area which is not within view of the kitchen, two children begin to cry loudly. After the crying continues for about two minutes, Anne goes to the area and sternly says: 'What's going on in here? Get your coats and go outdoors!'. As they slowly stop crying, the two children do as directed without speaking to Anne.

Anne's management-rule orientation is seen in her comments to me during informal exchanges and in formal interviews. During formal interviews, I asked Anne to describe each of her children by giving what she considers to be the child's strengths, any areas needing improvement, and her teaching goals for the child. For seven of her fourteen children, Anne speaks in terms of the children's ability to learn the school rules and follow her directions:

> 10/1 — Sally is no problem. She learned the rules quickly and in group time, she's pretty good . . . A.J. is a nice boy, very smart, always willing to do what you ask . . . Jimmy is very stubborn, like today when I told him to change his wet pants, he just sat there and did nothing. Otherwise he's not a problem child — even in group he sits still . . . Kyle is very quiet and smart! . . . I wish we had more like him, you know, no problems . . . Eddie was a nice boy when he started last February . . . when I had my six week's vacation, he started having problems with the other teachers. But I never have that problem. But you know I'm strict.

Anne frequently describes herself as strict, and I asked her what she means when speaking of strictness:

> *Anne:* I expect all children to learn to follow the rules, or they won't when they grow up. Like I expect them to learn how many can play in the sandbox or block room, etc. You know, I expect the children to be responsible.

CSK: I'm not sure I know what you mean by responsible?
Anne: Following the rules — otherwise there'd be six in the sandbox or block room and there'd be fighting and too much noise.

Anne often shared her management concerns with me. On one occasion she came to me on the playground and described her experience at a parent's meeting the previous night.

> Last night, I went to a parent's meeting at my son's school. The principal is a nun, and she is like a soldier. And the parents respect her — the children and the parents; and I think that's good. In Poland everybody respected the teachers too. A child would ask a parent a question, and often the parent would say: 'Ask your teacher. She'll know!'

During early care, Pam expresses a wider range of interaction with the children beyond management. However, when children misbehave, her responses are similar to Anne's, with the omission of Anne's 'I messages.'

> 11/6 — Early care — Pam is in the art center and is preparing materials for activity period. Across the room in the block area three children walk about a table as they chant 'beep-beep'. Each child has hooked together plastic cars and trucks and they move the vehicles about the table as they walk one behind the other. Judy's car comes unattached and she stops abruptly. Jay accidentally but forcefully bumps into Judy, who cries out. When Judy cries out, Pam says: 'Jay use words if you are having problems'. Jay looks up as Pam speaks, then walks over to his cubbie where he puts on his coat and goes outdoors.

Indoors Pam frequently participates in activities with a child or children upon their request. Often children come to her and ask: 'Pammy, will you play with me?'. Usually these are the children from Pam's own small group. (They affectionately call her Pammy though Pam confides in me that she never is called this by anyone else.) Pam replies, 'sure', and enthusiastically enters into activities with the children. These tasks usually are 'open ended' and the child is the initiator of the approach. In these play sequences, Pam expresses spontaneity, and an ease in relating with the children.

> 12/28 — Early care block area — (This is the fourth day unit

> blocks are open during early care.) Ronnie and Kevin take a few blocks from the shelf and begin banging them against the shelf as if it were a drum. Pam enters and says: 'These blocks are for building boys'. Ronnie replies: 'Pammy will you play with us?'. Pam: 'Sure!'. and she begins making three fourths of a rectangle on the floor. Ronnie closes the rectangle and the boys begin making the walls higher. Ronnie: 'We're making the walls higher and higher'. Pam: 'A gigantic building!'. Pam begins a simple structure and together the boys make a third structure next to Pam's. This time they experiment with using triangles and half circles within the walls and the effect is very aesthetic.

When I asked Pam, 'What do you intend to happen when a child asks you to play with her/him?', she replies: 'Well, I don't want to be always just sitting and observing. Yet I do some of that too. When playing with the children, I don't see myself directing them but rather, helping their ability to focus'.

About once a week during the winter months, when outdoor play is eliminated due to cold weather, Pam initiates a teacher-directed small group activity. These sequences involve creative movement with record accompaniment, marching with musical instruments, reading stories to four to six children, or singing fingerplay games with five to ten children. I asked Pam what her goals were in these activities.

Pam: I think I started these spontaneous groups because it got to the point where the shelf had been used to its maximum and there weren't enough activities out for the children. And I knew I could probably get a group and it would take some of the strain off the other areas. And then the children would have another small group time during the day. Since it was so successful I continued to do this about once a week.

CSK: Did you explicitly plan to initiate these tasks about once each week?

Pam: No, I think I just judged it by how well the morning was flowing. If I felt that it could help the situation I would begin a group.

The other teachers neither initiated small group activities nor engaged in child initiated play with the children during early care. Frequently Barb's children would ask her to play with them, but Barb's reply consistently communicates the same message — that she will be near them, will watch them, and will help them if necessary. I asked

Barb how she views this recurrent request of the children.

> I hate when they say that. I feel that my attention needs to go too many places, and so I usually tell them: 'You get started and I'll see what you can do'. I always remember my training at college. The instructors always said that the central part of early childhood teaching is good observing.

Anne's children also request that she play with them, and though Anne makes one or two initial gestures of participation, she invariably becomes distracted and does not sustain involvement in the child's activity.

At 9.00 a.m., Anne, her assistant and the fourteen children in Anne's group leave the Big Room and go to the Yellow Room area where they remain for the rest of the morning. After Anne and her children leave the room, the cook places the morning snack at a front table. This snack becomes a choice for any child who desires to eat before the end of early care at 9.45 a.m..

Schooling in the Yellow Room Area — 9.00–11.10 a.m.

Snack

For Anne's children, morning snack is a total group activity that signifies the end of Early Care in the Big Room and the beginning of activities in the Yellow Room area with Anne and her assistant. Anne ensures that these young 3-year-olds participate in snack in a calm orderly routine manner. Before snack begins, Anne puts the children's name tags at places on the two circular tables. Once the children are seated, she asks one child to give everyone a napkin and another to give everyone a cup. Daily, children assume this responsibility, but no system exists to make certain that each child has a turn to pass items. Children are expected to sit with their hands on their laps while they wait for everyone to get napkins and cups. Then they pour their own juice, take their own crackers, and pass the basket. If children spill their juice, they independently clean up their spill. Children frequently initiate conversations with each other and with Anne, who warmly replies to their comments.

Group time

After snack, Anne and her children enter the small block room where they have a twenty-five minute teacher-directed group period. Before she sits down, Anne makes certain that she separates any close friends who may be sitting next to each other. Then she directs everyone to 'sit on your bottoms like me' (and everyone crosses their legs). As she gives directives, Anne speaks in a soft, whisper-tone voice to the children, who quickly comply. As soon as everyone is quietly seated, Anne begins to sing high interest songs and fingerplays. The children enthusiastically participate in this singing, and choose many of the songs. Even the new enrollees attempt the fingerplay motions and learn the songs very quickly. Anne leads this singing with animated expression and varied voice tone.

> 8/25 — Group time — Anne and twelve young 3-year-olds sit on the rug with their legs crossed. Anne: 'Okay now . . .' and she begins singing the fingerplay song: 'Open Shut Them'. The children, even Alan, who has only been at school four days, sing enthusiastically. Only AJ, this being his first day, does not sing; rather he sits, hands on knees with a serious face, and watches the others. Immediately after this first song Anne begins singing 'Twinkle, Twinkle Little Star'. When they finish the song, Anne says: 'I'm sure glad Sally and Alicia are singing today. But you need to sing softer'. (This is Alicia's third day at school.) Alicia replies emphatically: 'But that's all I have!'. Anne: 'Alicia, it hurts my ears when you sing loudly'. Again Alicia replies: 'My mommy likes it! That's all I have'. Anne: 'You need to get softer'. Anne then immediately begins singing the fingerplay song 'Gray Squirrel, Gray Squirrel' very softly, and the children begin the hand motions as they too sing softly.

During half of the thirty observations, Anne introduces a second group experience that is related to a weekly unit theme that the center staff has chosen (for example, 'family fun' — 'growing' — 'parent occupation' — 'our five senses' — 'our bodies'). After brief introductory comments, Anne invites each child around the circle to have a turn to either share home happenings or to individually explore the objects Anne has introduced.

> 8/28 — Anne holds a doll and asks five children individually to come to her and 'show us' a specific body part on the doll.
>
> 9/15 — Five cups are on a tray. In the cups are salt, sugar, mustard, honey and vinegar. Anne gives each child a

plastic spoon and then each has a turn to taste from a cup, and to tell if the taste is sweet, sour, or salty.

During each of these observed sequences, the children become increasingly restless as they wait for their turns. Anne responds to this restlessness in a firm repetitive manner: 'This is a time for listening and sitting quietly. You only talk when the teacher asks you a question. All you have to do is open your ears and listen'. Twice Anne has individual children who are restless, stand up, put their hands at their side, and remain in that position for about five minutes.

At the end of each group, Anne reviews the options for activity period. So too, she reviews the rules with the children (for example, two in the sand table, three at the play dough table, put away toys upon completion).

Activity period

During activity period, Anne's children spend slightly more than one hour playing in the Yellow Room and adjoining block and quiet room. Three children, usually boys, are always in the block room. Other high interest areas are the art project table, easel, and sand-water-rice table. Usually there is a flow of movement in and out of the quiet room, the housekeeping area, and the manipulative table area.

The children ordinarily use art materials, table toys and books independently; yet as they sit side-by-side and work in individual tasks they often engage in spontaneous conversations with each other or a teacher. The relaxed informal tempo of this activity segment is a shift from the earlier tightly structured group time.

Four of Anne's fourteen children are close friends and often choose to play together.

2/28 — Alicia and Sally together place pegs in all the holes of a pegboard. Alicia then says: 'I'm going to take them out now'. Sally helps her and when they finish she gleefully says: 'We did it!' Sally then gets a puzzle which they complete together.

9/22 — A.J. and Alan spend about ten minutes hooking together about two dozen three-inch plastic monkeys, which they hang on the back of a chair.

The sand-water-rice table and the blocks are two areas that invite material sharing and/or cooperative playing. Daily two children share the funnels, sifters and small cups in the sand box. As they play together, these children often hum or sing familiar songs. Children build simple structures together in the Block Room, where three children are allowed at one time.

> 10/6 — Brett and Eddie have placed a large pile of hollow blocks in the center of the room. Brett: 'This is a big house'. Then he stands back and says: 'I don't like this house,' and he knocks down the structure. Eddie suggests: 'Let's make a spaceship now, o.k.?'. Brett agrees and suggests 'Let's play Starwars; I'm Darth Vader and you be R.2.D.2.'. The boys then rearrange the large blocks. Anne then comes and tells the boys it's time to clean up.

Though the block room contains both unit blocks and large hollow blocks, the children invariably choose the large blocks. Builders are always boys and usually the structures are either houses, motorcycles or planes. Extended decision-making, planning, and/or language exchange typical of preschoolars do not occur; rather the short sequences of play seem more exploratory. Adults are not in the room unless there is a loud noise, crying, screaming, or when it is time to put the toys away.

During activity period, Anne's schooling acts are similar to those of early care. She usually is seated at a table and often engages in conversations with nearby children. She is not observed initiating activities with children or moving in and out of the children's play. As the children play, Anne spends part of each activity period sorting materials or completing other maintenance tasks. Frequent interpretative comments in observation notes question if these maintenance tasks are Anne's way of having the time pass as the children play, for she seems unable to know what to do as they play.

In the day to day, the ambience of the free play in the Yellow Room area does seem significantly different that that of early care. Whereas slightly over fifty people congregate in a large open space at the outset of the morning, no more than sixteen people are in Anne's three small rooms, rooms with clearly defined boundaries. Choices of activities are given at the end of group time and rules of appropriate behavior are reviewed. Within this context, children play with minimal misuse of materials or conflicts. Thus Anne's management focus is less dominant than in early care, a time when most of her interactions are management oriented.

When Anne does redirect inappropriate behavior during activity period, she continues to protect the rules and does not enter into the context of the children's activity; that is, she does not directly observe the sequence of events within which the children are involved. Her directives to the children involve the same repetitive phrasing typical of her early care interactions.

> 10/7 — Sam enters the housekeeping area which has been empty all morning. He opens the stove door and attempts to climb into it. From the puzzle table Anne says: 'Sam that's a stove to cook with. I don't like that'. Sam gets out of the stove and goes to the block room.

During a formal interview Anne shares her understanding of the value of the housekeeping area:

> It's very very good for social, for it's a place where the kids are talking and using their ideas ... and really playing their life, what they are seeing at home. Like, Mia with the doll — she's pretty rough. Often you can tell what kind of family life they have at home.

Though Anne speaks positively of the values of housekeeping, she remains uninvolved in the area except when redirecting misbehavior.

Schooling in the Big Room: 9.45–11.20 a.m.

Clean up and circle in the big room: 9.45–10.00 a.m.

Circle is a transition activity between early care and activity period. Teachers implement circle in order to help calm the children, to share options available during activity period, and to know that each child explicitly has chosen an area. Pam daily decides when to clean up materials from early care and to begin circle. Teachers neither decide together when to end early care nor does Pam assume leadership to direct them. As a result, children in different areas of the Big Room complete tasks at different times and 'dribble' to the circle for five or more minutes.

Pam begins each circle by singing familiar songs and fingerplays with the children, until everybody arrives. Then she either reads or tells a story, and often incorporates the children's participation in the story. Though over thirty children are gathered, their involvement is very high and misbehavior rarely occurs.

> 12/9 — Circle — Thirty children are seated on the pink rug with Pam and Gary. Pam teaches the children the first five verses of the song 'The Twelve Days of Christmas.'

> Then everyone sings 'Frosty the Snowman' with tremendous enthusiasm. With flannelboard figures in hand, Pam then tells the children: 'Today I'm going to tell you the story of "The Gingerbread Man" and you can help me'. (Gary goes to the kitchen area to prepare for activity period, and Barb continues preparing materials in the art area.) As she tells the story, Pam places the correct flannel figures on the board. She says: 'And the Gingerbread Man said — now you help me children'. And in unison the children chant: 'Run, run, run, catch me if you can. . .' . . .At the end of the story Pam says: 'Thank you all for helping. You were good storytellers'. And in fact, all the children had attended and had attempted to participate.

At the end of circle, Pam asks each teacher how many children s/he would like in her/his area for activity period. Then she asks the children to choose an area. Children choose without knowing what specific activity is planned for that day. Usually the areas available are art, manipulative, blocks and cooking.

Activity period in the big room

For approximately one hour, Pam Barb, Lisa, and Gary have Activity Period with thirty children. Each teacher is in charge of one of four areas for a month, and then they rotate. Each day children are free to choose from one or several of the four activity areas. When children complete activities in one area, they are free to go to another area. Daily observations of Pam's and Barb's schooling acts during this time segment were made when each teacher was in charge of the manipulative area and Barb in the art area.

During activity period, Pam has an explicit idea of the type of child involvement she wants to facilitate. When responsible for the manipulative area, she places about twelve items on the shelves. Though all these items are manipulative toys, many involve symbolic representational learning; that is, the tasks involve cognitive skills such as classification, ordering or matching and often use numerals. These tasks are more difficult to complete than items on early care choice shelves. A typical sampling includes: a fifty-piece interlocking US puzzle, a box of ten foam numerals and ten sets to match as puzzles, an alphabet puzzle, pegboard with cuphooks and a bag of keys to sort on the pegboard, box of complex cube design cards and cubes, box of cardboard strips to seriate, several interlocking puzzles of twenty or more pieces each, numeral cans and popsicle sticks for making appropriate sets.

When Pam is in the manipulative area five to ten children work on the rug with items they've chosen. Pam also sits on the rug and is either observing, assisting a child in understanding a specific task, or actively participating with a child in a task. Several children in Pam's group daily choose to work with her. Often she'll arrange that these children begin activity period in a different area; however, they inevitably navigate to her before the period ends. When participating in a task with a child, Pam's warmth, spontaneity and humor is evident in the same manner as when involved in indoor tasks during early care; however she more frequently demonstrates correct use of materials and requires children to complete their tasks. In other words, she takes on a more traditional classroom teaching role.

> 12/4 — Ned and Pam sit next to each other on the rug. Pam place four three inch wooden numerals on the floor and tells Ned: 'Close your eyes'. Ned does as directed and when he opens his eyes he tells Pam what numeral is missing. Then Pam closes her eyes as Ned takes a numeral away for Pam to identify.
>
> 12/17 — James has foam geometric squares and triangles of different sizes in front of him on the rug. Pam — assists him in beginning to seriate each of these shapes in order, according to size.

In December when Pam is in the manipulative area, a new assistant teacher, Lisa, is responsible for blocks. Lisa and the children daily construct elaborate structures. Before December no adult was observed working with children with blocks. Pam frequently praises Lisa and the children as she works in the adjoining manipulative area.

Both Pam and Barb are observed during the month they are responsible for cooking experiences. On three-quarters of these occasions, children either help fix part of the center's lunch (for example, making taco salad) or fix the afternoon snack (for example, cheese cubes wrapped with bologna for 'pigs in the blanket'). Both Pam and Barb utilize similar processes in these cooking activities. As children wash their hands, their teacher prepares the materials on the circle table. After all are seated, either Pam or Barb tells the children specifically what they will 'cook'. After a demonstration from their teacher, the children prepare the food. As they work, children and their teacher converse together and a relaxes tempo is maintained.

During the month of December Barb is responsible for art

activities. Of all the teachers, Barb seems to take the most initiative in art, in providing new open-ended materials for children to explore, construct, and express themselves. Daily easel painting is available. In addition a small side table is available for children to construct items with either scissors, varied paper, glue, markers, crayons and/or assorted collage items. Barb also has an open-ended daily art project at the center table (for example, fingerpainting, sculptures made from toothpicks and styrofoam packing 'squiggles', sponge printing). The children's involvement is very high in these projects and they use the materials in a variety of imaginative ways. The projects also demand quite a lot of teacher preparation of materials; and in fact, Barb often does this material preparation during early care and circle. When I asked Barb what she sees as the meaning and purpose of these art projects, she explained:

> *Barb:* I think a lot of art is experimenting with different things, and offering a place for independence — doing things on your own and being creative.
>
> *CSK:* What do you mean by creative?
>
> *Barb:* I think of free style, where I'm not looking for a specific product and where children can express themselves.

Focused observations of Barb's schooling patterns during activity period began on the third week of January, two weeks after she had taken responsibility for the manipulative area. On her first day in this area Barb asks Pam: 'What do I do in this area?'. Pam replied: 'You can change shelf items any time you want. You can either plan special activities or let the children merely choose from the shelf'. Barb's uncertainty concerning her role in this area is still apparent on the day I begin my focused observations.

Similar to Pam, Barb places in the area manipulative toys that are more symbolic and difficult to complete that those available in early care. However, unlike Pam, Barb does not participate in activities with the children. Usually six or seven children work on the rug for short periods of time. No conflicts are observed, and Barb redirects misuse of materials only once. If a child requests help, Barb assists; otherwise she sits on the rug, watches the children, and stares about the rest of the room. Usually the children use the materials in a random exploratory manner then go to another activity area.

> Manipulative area: Seven children are seated in varying areas of the rug with Barb and a high school volunteer. The high school boy hooks together a wooden train track with Ned and T.J. Eddie stacks the small cans as if they were blocks. Evan and Rita

put together a one inch cube pattern. They do not follow the paper patterns. Rather they place all the cubes in the wooden box, dump the cubes and begin again for three times. Then the two leave the area and go to the block area. Barb is seated next to Evan and seems to be staring into space. Timmy and Jay make happy faces with the felt circles on the apple trees rather that attempt to match the circles to the numerals on each tree. Barb calls to them and suggests that there is room for them in the art area. (She does not tell the boys the correct way to use the apple tree game.) The boys clean up the apple tree game and go to the art area. Twice Eddie stacks the cans, then leaves them on the floor and goes to the cooking area. Kevin says to Barb: 'Will you play with me?'. Barb replies: 'I'll watch you'. Kevin then gets a simple puzzle, empties and quickly completes it, then leaves the area. In five minutes only the high schooler, Barb and the two boys with the train tracks are left in the area.

In February, Pam is responsible for the block-housekeeping area during activity period. On all observed days only unit blocks are available and housekeeping is 'closed'. Within this period, Pam remains in the block area either observing the children, or moving in and out of the children's projects as facilitator and/or participant. Often she assists a child or children by giving simple suggestions which help them experience success and/or extend the project.

2/9 — Nan and Rachel are attempting to build a simple structure near Pam who is helping Ronnie build. (This is the first time I have observed either girl in the block area, and their structures are very immature, especially in contrast with their other play patterns.) Nan repetitively attempts to stack blocks on top of each other but they invariably fall down. She is using 1 × 12 inch blocks. She complains to Pam who replies: 'They have such skinny bottoms. Try supporting the bottom with other blocks'. Rachel and Nan do as Pam has suggested. Together they then make a tall bridge decorated with triangles on top. Nan: 'See Pammy!'. Pam replies: 'Neat!'. Then they build another bridge and call to Pam 'Look it's staying up!'.

During February children engage in extended joint construction as they had with Lisa in December. These joint projects are more complex and involve more collaboration than does most observed play at Rosehill.

Given the sharper spatial boundaries and more direct teacher involvement, children's misbehavior is rare during activity period. On the few observed occasions of needed teacher redirection, Barb utilizes similar reactive patterns of rule implementation that are observed during early care. In contrast, Pam attempts to enter into the children's experiences when she redirects in this activity segment.

> 2/10 — Five children each make her/his own structure with unit blocks. Pam and Kevin alternate putting blocks on top of his structure. One child, Sue, says to Janey as she gets up: 'You can use my building; I'm going to paint'. Janey then continues building on Sue's structure. Zack shouts: 'An earthquake! Let's get away from the earthquake!' and he knocks down his own building. Kevin knocks down Janey's building as Janey shouts: 'No!'. In response, Kevin grabs a block from Janey's hand. Pam: 'Kevin you have plenty of blocks over here.' Kevin begins to cry softly as Pam continues: 'Kevin, you have play people, cars, and blocks. What else do you need? I can't help you if you don't tell me.' Kevin says nothing, but slowly stops crying. Zack scoots to Kevin and diverts his attention by saying: 'Let's pretend this is a spook house'. Kevin replies: 'And this is a witch house'. Then in a screeching voice Janey says: 'Do you want to come visit me?' . . . Pam remains seated near the children as they continue to role play and build together.

The transition from activity period to the next scheduled group period has similar patterns as the ending of early case. Teachers begin cleaning their area without any coordinated scheduling decisions. Some expect the children to assist and others do not; no one gives the children a warning that activity period will soon end and clean up begin. Given this pattern, some area clean up is completed earlier than others and several children aimlessly roam about the room before group time begins.

Group time

In January Barb has group activities immediately after activity period in the Big Room. During discussions or games that involve turntaking Barb's children repeatedly are inattentive and disruptive, and Barb's redirection adds further disruptiveness to the activity flow. Then in February, Barb changes the time, the meeting place, and some of the content of these group experiences. After activity period, she and the children go outdoors for fifteen minutes and then use the Yellow Room area for group time. After vigorous outdoor play, Barb's children are able to sustain involvement in singing, listening to stories and story dramatization. Activities that require the children to take turns are completely eliminated.

Pam's group meets in Emmet's room, a small eight-foot square room named for the large clown figure painted on the wall. Each child sits in front of Pam on individual rug mats. After singing several high interest songs and fingerplays, Pam either reads or tells the children a story. And as in early circle, Pam often stimulates the children's participation. When directing group activities, Pam often initiates activities in which she and the children together create stories or discuss together stories as they are being read.

> 12/29 — Group time — Eight children sit in front of Pam who holds up a book as she says: 'This is a new book where we can tell the story while we look at the pictures. The book is about a snowman'. Each page has four pictures of action sequences portrayed. Pam alternates between telling the children a sequence of happenings and asking the children 'now what is he doing?'. Occasionally she also asks a question other than directed at the sequence of action such as: 'What do you think will happen if he sits near the fireplace?'. The children spontaneously respond and there seems to be no break in the flow if several respond simultaneously. At one point, Jay comments: 'I covered myself up with snow'. Pam replies: 'You made yourself into a snowman didn't you?' and continues the story. Though the story process takes fifteen minutes, the tempo remains 'upbeat' and all the children have participated.

At the completion of group time, Pam dismisses the children to get their jackets for twenty minutes of play outdoors.

Schooling in the Stage Area: 9.45–11.20 a.m.

As Pam, Barb, and Gary's children gather for circle, Dana directs her ten children in her group to the stage area where they have group time and activity period together.

Group time

As they arrive on the stage, Dana's children form a circle around Dana who initiates group time with a song. Group time entails a predictable sequence of three types of activities. First everyone sings one or two songs together; then there are either games or discussions that involve children's turn taking, and finally, Dana reads a story. Children's involvement in singing fingerplay songs is quite high. Though she does not have a strong singing voice, Dana chooses only those songs the children already know and love; thus the children 'carry' the singing. Similarly, Dana regularly gets books from the local library and uses only familiar action-oriented stories which the children love. Unlike Pam, Dana's reading does not involve teacher-child conversation.

The uneven tempo during games or discussions is a sharp contrast to children's involvement in song and story. Children are unable to maintain their attention as they wait for their own turn to talk or to take part in a game. When a child restlessly moves about, talks to another child or begins bothering another child, Dana's redirection becomes an additional distraction for the attending children and misbehavior escalates. Further disruptions involve the children's repetitive tattling and calling to Dana for their turn. Dana either ignores the pleading children or tells them: 'I will call on those who are sitting quietly'. Often she will comment: 'I like the way . . .' a specific child is attending. When a child calls her attention to another misbehaving child, she tells the tattler: 'You don't have to worry about other children'. Though many of Dana's group activities entail a great deal of teacher preparation, initiative, and creativity, children are unable to maintain involvement.

10/22–9.55 — Dana tells the children that on each of the ten trees that are on the wall, one of their names is written. She asks Ned: 'Will you show the children your name?'. Ned goes to the tree and identifies each letter of his first name. Then Dana asks him: 'What is on the tree trunk?'. Ned 'reads' his last name.

10.00 — Dana then asks the same of Kim and Corrie, and all other children watch.

10.05 — Jim and Eddie are lying on their backs and Dana tells them: 'Boys you must be very tired, but you'll have a chance to rest at nap time. Sit up now'. They ignore Dana and she physically sits both boys on their mats.

10.10 — As individuals have a turn, it becomes clear

that several do not understand the meaning of 'last name', for they are unable to know what to do when Dana asks: 'And where is your last name?'.

10.12 — As Cassie has a turn, Corrie begins to sing loudly. Dana: 'You had your turn Corrie and I can't hear Cassie'. Corrie stops singing as Dana gets up to remove Eddie to the opposite side of the room since he continues to refuse to sit up. Eddie immediately returns and Dana tells him: 'Then you must sit up; and you may not have a turn'. Eddie sulks, but remains seated.

10.15 — Dana then shows the children a bulletin board which has ten cards, each with a picture of a tool people use at work. Each child is asked: 'What kind of people use this?'. Eddie pleads for a turn but Dana replies: 'I'm sorry; next time you listen and then you can have a turn'.

10.17 — Four children have had turns and the restlessness increases. Ben pushes Rachel, Dana redirects Ben, yet continues to extend her discussion with Ned about fire officers, even as the restlessness increases.

At the end of group time, Dana directs the children to put away their rug mats and choose an activity, either from the shelves or on the art project table. In an interview, I asked Dana what her goals are for group time.

> My goals vary according to what we are doing. But I think it's always helpful for the children to have a quiet time within a small group to get to know a little about each other and to create a sense of belonging. Also, it is a good opportunity for me to discover how far along children are in basic skills and concepts.

Activity period

Activity period options include the table toys on a ten-foot long shelf, art materials on a three-foot long shelf, and teacher structured art projects on a small table. Materials on the art shelf remain constant and include assorted paper, crayons, markers, templates and scissors. The table toys are changed weekly. There are always a variety of puzzles, including very complex alphabet or map puzzles, small snap together toys, games for classifying, seriating, or matching, and a half dozen books. Many of these materials are very complex for young 3-year-olds, and Dana's children often need her assistance for task completion. A maximum of three children can work at the art project table. These projects typically involve time and creativity in teacher preparation, teacher assistance in construction, and result in lovely and products (for example, children use corn cob holders to punch out leaf patterns on construction paper, and then tape different colored tissue paper behind the leaf 'cut outs').

During the four-week observation period on the stage area, the same children initiate and sustain the same type of activity day after day. Of the ten children, three girls always begin at the art project table, and two boys choose to work with puzzles. With some of the art projects, the girls remain involved for the entire hour, and each of the boys is able to spend as long as thirty to forty minutes with a difficult puzzle. In contrast, Corrie, Eddie, Hal and Jim have short attention spans and their recurrent aimless flitting about the room invites continual teacher redirection. Jim seems to be somewhat of an isolate throughout the entire day. However, Corrie, Eddie and Hal are actively involved during early and late care; but their involvement always encompasses spontaneous social activities with other children rather than individually focused tasks like those on the stage area. The tenth child, Rachel, is very competent in both individual and social activities, and she usually engages in a wide variety of activities on the stage.

In contrast to her quiet distant posture during early care, Dana is actively involved in many exchanges with children during activity period. Given the difficulty of the available tasks children repeatedly seek her assistance. Dana helps children with undaunted patience in spite of frequent interruptions from other children who either are misbehaving or also need her assistance. Dana is not observed suggesting that one child help another, even though competent children are nearby when a child requests her help. Art projects invariably demand adult assistance. I asked Dana how she views the purpose of these projects.

> These activities encourage the children to use a variety of skills, such as following a line with scissors or using the hole puncher to gain strength in your hands. And the projects require the children to use their imagination — and the children are amazingly creative.

During the observation period, uniqueness of creative self expression among the children in these projects is not observed; rather differences in end products seem to reflect differences in children's eye-hand coordination.

A few individual children come to Dana and ask 'will you play with me'. Dana always agrees to play with them; so too, she occasionally sits on the floor with a child and begins reading a favorite story. Yet interruptions either to assist other children or to redirect misbehaving children prevent Dana from ever completing a story or other participation with children.

> 10/24 — Dana agrees to play with Rachel who brings a box of geometric blocks to the floor area. Dana takes out several diamond shapes and asks Rachel: 'Shall we make a design?'. Rachel nods as Dana begins to construct a flower with the diamonds. But when she sees that Eddie has left puzzle pieces on the floor, she gets up, reminds Eddie to pick up the puzzle pieces, and begins to help him. Dana assures Rachel: 'I'll be right back'. But in reality, other children ask for her assistance and Dana does not return for ten minutes. Meanwhile Rachel makes a large rectangular shape with the blocks.

Rachel is able to work at a task while she waits for Dana. However some of the less mature children either do nothing as they patiently wait, or aimlessly saunter about the room as they wait.

In addition to assisting individual children, Dana also recurrently redirects children's misbehavior. Children often engage in disputes over possession of materials. As during early care, Dana does not enter into the dispute until after the children's emotional outburst, when she first becomes aware of the problem. She redirects in a firm positive manner with repetitive phrases such as 'use words instead of your fists'. Often disputes involve children tattling on each other. Whereas in group time Dana tells the tattling child to 'take care of yourself', in activity period she redirects the misbehaving child and ignores the informer. In an interview Dana discussed this tattling with me.

> *Dana:* I just hate tattling.
> *CSK:* How do you respond to tattling?
> *Dana:* Well, if one child is talking about another child, I tell the child to look after her/himself. But if something is dangerous, I'll investigate.

Dana's conversation regarding children informing against one another is consistent with her behavior during group time, but not during activity period. It is possible that her attention is so fragmented during this second period that her responses are less thoughtful.

On Fridays Rosehill teachers initiate group movement/motion instead of activity period. Whereas the other four head teachers alternate directing movement/motion with each of the four groups, Dana chooses to implement this activity alone with her group. Dana's children always are eager for this weekly process, and actively participate.

> 11/7 — Dana and nine children are on the empty side of the asphalt parking lot. Dana tells the children they can run around the lot as she tapes fourteen balloons to the ground in a ten foot area. When the balloons are fastened, she calls the children to sit at the end of the area. Then each child has a turn, blindfolded, to pop a balloon with a stick. As one child takes a turn, others chant 'do me, do me, Dana!'. Dana: 'Ned, I'll choose you next for you are sitting quietly. Eddie, I'm not going to call on you if you don't sit down'. The children are fascinated with this game, and maintain full attention as their peers attempt to break a balloon. Several shout helpful suggestions — 'Step behind . . . go to the side'. Soon they are cheering as if at a football game.

Movement/motion seems to be the one activity segment in which Dana's children are able to maintain involvement with minimal need for teacher redirection.

At approximately 11.20 a.m., Dana dismisses the children to go outdoors, where they join the other children and teachers on the playground.

Outdoors and Lunch Circle: 11.20 a.m.–12.00 noon

Outdoors, the children choose to either run about the grassy area, play in the large sand area, play on one of the large climbers, swing, or ride tricycles. The teachers stand about in the yard as they chat together and are available to help children if needed. At 11.35 Anne, her assistant and their fourteen children go indoors and wash for lunch. Then they go to the rug area in the back of the Big Room and begin singing. By 11.45 all children and teachers come indoors. Two teachers monitor the bathrooms while all others join the singing, which Anne leads. Involvement is high, and the tempo is smooth and relaxing. Each adult has a child on her/his lap. At noon, bells from a neighboring church ring. All teachers and children silently pantomime the pulling of bell ropes until the twelfth ring. Then adults and children quietly sing 'The World is Round' as they do hand motions. They repeat the song with motions only. Everyone, even new enrollees participate, and though over fifty are gathered together, the room is very still. At the end of the song, Anne dismisses the children, who quietly go to the lunch tables in the front of the room.

Lunch and Nap: 12.00 noon–3.00 p.m.

Though teachers always eat at the same table, children choose to sit at any table for lunch. After everyone is seated a simple prayer in song is sung, and the food is served by teachers and children, family style. There is minimal conversing or playfulness typical of preschoolers when eating. The day has been lengthy and everyone seems eager to have a restful period. With such a large group of small children and adults eating together, the informal relaxed ambience is awesome to the outside observer.

In the twenty-minute transition period between lunch and nap, teachers share in maintenance tasks and management of the children: setting up cots, sweeping and washing lunch tables, monitoring children's use of the bathrooms, and leading activities in Emmet's room. The smoothness of this transition period when no child must wait idly, is a sharp contrast to transitions after early care and activity period. Pam posts the schedule for teacher rotation of responsibility for this transition period.

All fifty-four children rest in the Big Room on cots, and almost every child does go to sleep. Teachers sit by their children and rub backs to assist children in relaxing. Getting off one's cot or talking is not allowed. Even the most active child usually is able to rest for at least one hour. During this nap period, Pam's work day ends at 2.30 p.m. From 2.45 to 3.00, children half asleep, saunter down the hall to the Yellow Room, where Anne helps children put on their shoes and socks. Anne is firm in expecting each child to put on her/his own socks and shoes; then she ties the laces. Though some children know how to tie, Anne is not observed suggesting that these children assist others. At 3.00, Anne's work day ends.

Snack and Late Care: 3.00–6.00 p.m.

By 3.00 p.m., Pam and Anne's work day has ended. Before they go home at 4.00 and 4.30 p.m., Barb and Dana interact with the children minimally. Hence a description of the last portion of the day will be brief.

At approximately 2.30, Dana prepares snack, which is served at the front table at 3.00 p.m. If they desire, twelve children at a time eat afternoon snack at this front table. Children come and go at this table for about an hour. They then may play either outdoors or in the Big Room until their parent arrives to take them home.

Once she has prepared the snack, Dana goes outdoors to supervise the playground activity. Her outdoor involvement is similar to early care; she usually stands alone near the swing area and watches the playing children. By 3.45 each day she returns to the kitchen to clean up materials used at snack, and to wash counters and sinks in the kitchen. Often she remains here until it is time for her to leave work at 4.30 p.m.. During this time, Kate frequently comes to the kitchen and talks informally with Dana. The only occasions where Dana is observed with children during this last forty-five minutes is when there is a loud noise, crying or screaming in the Big Room. Then she immediately goes to the children to assist them.

Immediately after nap, Barb helps other teachers put away cots and set up tables for Late Care. Activity options are very similar to early care. The only exception is Gary's choice of many Fisher Price play people, vehicles and buildings that he invariably places on the back rug areas. Weather permitting, Barb remains outdoors for her last hour of work until she leaves at 4.00 p.m. If indoors, she saunters about the Big Room in a manner similar to her early care stance. Two high school students also supervise the children's play.

Parents begin to arrive to get their children at 3.00 p.m., and by 4.00, the fifty-four children have decreased in number to about thirty-five. Gary is the headteacher who closes the center at 6.00. By 5.30, he closes outdoors and all areas of the room except the front choice tables. Approximately twelve children are present during this last half-hour.

Having portrayed the experiences, actions and words of Rosehill children and teachers, we now can analyze the meaning of these events in terms of the teachers' emphasis of individual and social experiences. This analysis is the task of the following chapter.

4 *Individual and Social: Analyzing the Tilt at Rosehill*

Resetting the Problem in Context

In America the family always has been the primary vehicle for young children's internalization of society's values and practices. In their everyday childrearing interactions, parents are significant others in their children's internalizations of society's prohibitions and ideals. Thus, familial childrearing interactions ensure continuity of America's values. At the same time, however, literature on the family raise concern regarding the possible limitations of modern familial childrearing. The young child's sources of identification are severely restricted now that the child's own parents are the main available adult models. Further, when mothers are the sole source of primary bonding and fathers work and masculine activities are removed from the home, this familial childrearing reproduces sex-role differentiation of males and females, an asymmetry that can inhibit full development of children's capacities.

Given America's ideal of family childrearing, and its power in young children's development of self and internalization of society's values and practices, it should not be surprising that critics see day care as a threat to the social continuity of America's value traditions. We have seen that day care critics, most notably President Nixon in his 1971 veto of the Child Development Act, claim that this social childrearing within day care will promote collectivist rather than individualistic values, and thereby threaten the social continuity of the dominant value tradition of individualism.

America's ambivalence toward day care as a social childrearing context is depicted in the absence of a unified national policy focused directly on day care. The history of day care practices and policies in America give evidence that day care has not been supported as an end in itself to enhance child development, but rather, as a means to support some national interest such as jobs for the unemployed during the depression, workers for defense industries during World War II, or alleviating poverty and combating welfare costs in the 1960s and 1970s. Yet in spite of ambivalence in policy toward day care, dramatic increases in divorce and maternal employment have led to tremendous increases in the American family's need for out-of-home child care, and the concomitant burgeoning of day cares throughout the nation.

It is within this context that this field study's problem has been formulated. The focus of this study has been on individual and social value orientations. By focusing on the daily childrearing actions and interactions of four day care teachers over time, this field study can provide an initial understanding of whether day care does in fact threaten the continuity of America's values.

The narrative description in chapter 3 describes the daily activities of children and teachers, and their relationship with each other. In this chapter, I will examine these data in terms of the four teachers' emphasis on children's individual and social experiences. In this examination I will argue that these day care teachers, in their daily actions and interactions, emphasize individual more than social experiences; and these teachers' actions have significant consequences for young children's individual and social learning.

Although as we shall see, in Rosehill teachers' perspective, there seems to be a difference between 'school time' and 'free play' in early and late care, I assume that young children are learning in every experience they have at Rosehill; that is, learning and experience occur simultaneously. In other words, every experience children have at Rosehill involves learning. The specific aspect of children's learning and experience that is the focus of this study involves individual and social knowledge, skills and values. As defined in chapter 1, teachers' emphasis of individual experiences is characterized by independent action, individual accomplishment, individual rights and self-esteem; whereas teachers' emphasis of social experiences is characterized by conversation, helping and sharing action, combined efforts and empathy.

From my observational data, I have uncovered four domains involved in these teachers' emphasis of individual and social experiences: first, teachers' arrangement of environment; second, teacher-child interaction patterns; third, the children's actions that teachers either allow or encourage; and fourth, teachers' interactions with each other. A structural model of these four domains is portrayed in figure 8.

Though these four features are reciprocally intertwined, for clarity each will be discussed separately. Further, the complexity of adult and

Figure 8: Domains of Teachers' Emphasis of Children's Individual and Social Experiences

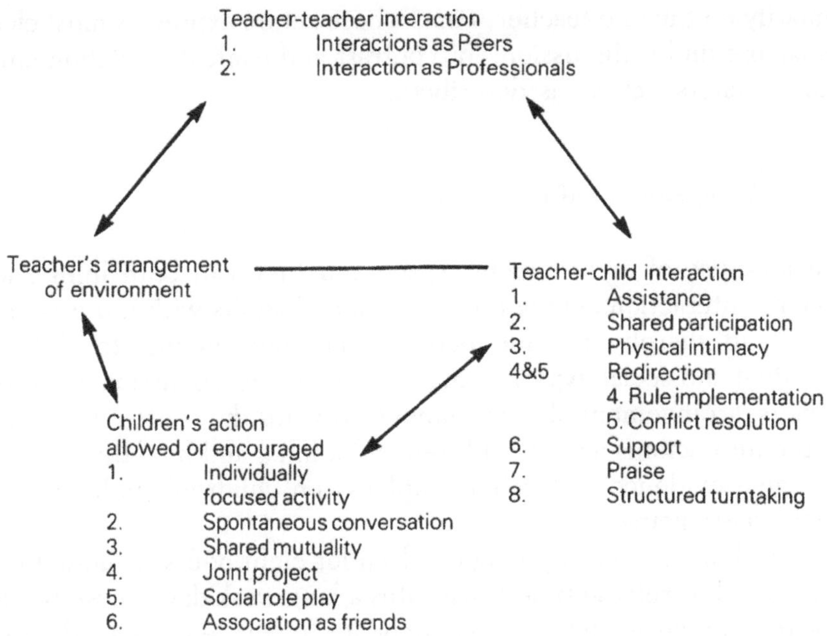

child action at Rosehill is reduced by using only key time segments: early care, activity period, and group periods. Discussion focuses primarily on the one teacher, *Pam*, whose action expresses most clearly the factors under discussion; for contrast and context, variation among other teachers' actions is described.

Arrangement of Environment

Teachers' use of environment, space and time can both limit and/or promote interaction among the children and adults within the environment, and thereby provide barriers and inducements to children's individual and social experiencing. The following discussion of Rosehill teachers' arrangement of environment provides the context for examining the interactions among children and adults, and how these interactions give evidence of teacher emphasis on children's individual and social experiencing.

Teaching groups of young children for eight hours without a lunch break or other release time constitutes a long work day. These teachers appear to organize time to accommodate to this lengthy work day by having a three-hour morning and three-hour afternoon activity segment — early and late care — in which they are available but need not be actively focused on the children. As Barb comments: 'We just hang loose during early and late care . . . it seems like we just kind of go with the wind'. Pam's comments add clarification:

> In early care children can do things their own way, and I don't interfere except when someone is hurting someone else or it is not safe for the children. In contrast, in activity time, I expect every child to use materials correctly; but in early care the children have more freedom.

Once early care clean up is complete, teachers become directly involved with the children. When Pam initiates singing in the total group circle at 9.45 a.m., it is as if the bell rang for 'school' to begin. In the teachers' mind there seems to be a difference between time segments, as if there were 'day care' and 'school' time, or free time and educational time.

In the following section, I will discuss two time segments, early care and activity period. Discussion of late care is omitted because it involves patterns similar to early care, only two of the four teachers are present, and neither teacher is involved with children beyond the outdoor area.

Arrangement of Environment During Early Care

Indoors

During early care all teachers and children use the same space, the Big Room and the outdoor playground. In this time period, teachers emphasize individual and social experiencing in terms of their choice of materials and use of indoor space in a similar manner. For though each teacher acknowledges that she has the right to change or add materials during early care, Pam takes primary responsibility for use of indoor space. Pam chooses the materials to put on the front shelves and decides if and when other activity areas are to be opened.

A vast array of materials and enough activity centers to invite both individual and social experiencing are in the Big Room. Yet only a limited portion of this Big Room space is 'open' for use during early care. The open areas are the front choice shelves, the quiet area and an art table — most of which involve primarily individually focused activity. A small proportion of shelf items such as Lego or dominoes could be used for joint construction, and occasionally two children do work together with the same material.

> 1/26 — Early care — Ronnie gets small foam blocks from the choice shelf, Kevin gets a can of small plastic bears, and they sit next to each other at a front table. The boys then build a four room structure together and place a few bears in each room.

The most common use of choice shelf materials is individual. Individual use is reinforced by the center's first choice policy — that when a child chooses a toy, s/he may decide whether or not s/he wishes to share this toy with another child.

Pam opens the housekeeping area on about one-quarter of early care mornings; and when this area is open several children do play either together or side-by-side. But the mere availability of material for thirty to fifty young children in an area does not ensure sustained social interaction. In housekeeping, the children either initiate brief disconnected role play sequences or manipulate materials in an exploratory manner, a manner typical of much younger children and which developmentally precedes social role playing (Hutt, 1971; Sutton-Smith, 1971). Sustained conversations and joint construction of role play sequences typical of threes and fours are rare occurrences, and typically are initiated by two children, Nan and Rachel, who are friends.

11/26 — Early care — Nan, and Mary are seated at the small table in the housekeeping area. Rachel puts dishes on the table while Sally passes out plastic utensils. Nan and Mary pretend to be eating. Rachel then goes to the stove and begins to pretend to mix in a pot.... Nan then makes a bed by arranging three chairs side-by-side. As she lies down she says to Rachel: 'I'm the baby'. Rachel lies down in the rocking boat and replies: 'No, I'm the baby and you're going to cover me up'. Nan replies: 'okay' as she covers Rachel with a doll quilt. Nan: 'I'll be the mommy'. Evan enters the area and Nan says to him: 'You can be the 6-year-old brother'. Evan repeats: 'I'm the 6-year-old brother', and he gets a sports jacket out of the clothes cupboard and puts it on.... Evan then sits at the table and Nan asks him: 'What do you want to drink?'. Evan: 'Nothing, I'm just watching T.V.....'.

The three mornings that Pam opens unit blocks during early care give further evidence that materials alone are not sufficient to stimulate children's social interaction; but sustained social collaboration can be enhanced by the presence of an enabling adult. During their first two mornings with blocks, children construct simple towers and piles of blocks, which they gleefully knock down. Two weeks later Pam remains in the block area and intermittently builds with the children. Then the children build complex structures together for forty minutes. Teacher involvement in the area enhances the level of social interaction.

In summary, most of these teachers' use of indoor space encourages individual involvement. Only Pam provides socially oriented material; and when she does, children's play with these materials tends to be surface in quality except on those few occasions when an adult is present. In their arrangement of the indoor environment during early care, all four teachers lean toward an emphasis on individual experiencing.

Outdoors

Outdoors, teachers need to take minimal responsibility for environmental arrangement since there are both ample space and permanent equipment outdoors. The playground furnishings offer equal opportunity for individual and social activity, independent of teacher involvement. And outdoors, these teachers remain available but are neither focused nor involved in activities with the children. Frequently Pam,

Anne, and Barb cluster together and converse with each other. These adult-adult interactions are important and will be considered in a later section. As a result of their alternative focus, these teachers usually are not aware of any spontaneous social interaction among children that occurs.

> 10/30 — Early care — Four boys pretend that the large horizontal concrete pipe is a haunted house. Dave sits on top of the west opening and Tim sits on the opposite side. Ray is a 'bat' and continually makes bat movements with his arm. Carl is a ghost and makes 'whooooo' sounds, as he moves his arms about. Dave and Tim act as gatekeepers, and when a child wants to enter the pipe, he whispers a magic word to Dave who gives permission to enter the pipe. . . .

No teacher is in the vicinity to observe this social role play sequence which lasts about fifteen minutes.

The one exception to this lack of teacher focus outdoors occurs when Barb occasionally takes initiative to utilize or extend the given outdoor materials. On these occasions Barb successfully uses outdoor facilities to foster children's social interaction.

> 10/22 — Early care — A.J. climbs on a tree stump, reaches to an horizontal bar, swings on it, then jumps down. Mia watches and repetitively tells A.J. to get down but A.J. ignores her. Barb comes and suggests that the children take turns. Soon five children are in line, each has a turn climbing onto the stump, swinging and jumping. Barb begins chanting 'one little monkey' and the children join in the chant as they wait their turn to swing and jump.

In summary, only Barb actively uses the outdoor area for children's social learning, and only occasionally when she is outdoors with the children. The rest of the time she and the other teachers depend on the center's permanent equipment to structure children's outdoor activities.

Arrangement of Environment During Activity Period

In activity period, each teacher works within her own spatial boundaries. Anne and Dana have their own classrooms. Barb and Pam remain in one of the four Big Room activity areas for a month, and then rotate to another area. Within the limits of available space, the teachers have considerable freedom in determining which materials will be available to the children. The following discussion focuses on how these teachers' choice of materials limits and/or promotes children's individual and social experiencing.

Pam, Barb, and Anne's material choices provide equal opportunities for children's individual and social activity. In contrast, almost all of Dana's material choices encourage individually focused activity. The predominance of individual experiencing of Dana's children is evident in my daily activity scans:

10/26 — nine children present

10:30 a.m. — Cammy, Jim and Jessie join Dana at the art project table. Dana tells the children: 'I want you to hammer on the line' (leaf pattern drawn on wooden block). Jim hammers without difficulty but the two girls need Dana's assistance.
— Brett completes an alphabet puzzle on the floor. (He completes this puzzle at least once each day for the past five days.)
— Rachel draws with markers at the table.
— Corrie looks at the book Dana had read during group time.
— Kay unsuccessfully attempts to match face blocks and calls for Dana's help.
— Eddie works on complex world puzzle.
— Howie roams about the room.

11:00 a.m. — Dana continues to assist the same two girls at the art project table.
— Eddie continues to work with world puzzle (45 minutes).
— Corrie has dumped attribute blocks on the floor and is waiting for Dana to play with her.
— Rachel continues to draw pictures at the table.
— Kay sits next to Rachel and begins cutting paper.
— Jim and Howie wrestle together on the floor.
— Brett completes an animal puzzle.

Many of Dana's shelf items and art projects are difficult for young threes and require teacher assistance. As a result, children repeatedly call for Dana's assistance. Since Dana works alone with ten children, these children daily spend much time waiting for her help and compete against each other for her attention.

In contrast to Dana's predominantly individual emphasis in her arrangement of her classroom environment, Pam and Barb provide approximately equal amounts of social and individually oriented materials. During activity period, Pam and Barb are responsible for one activity area for a month. Pam and Barb make similar material choices in both cooking and manipulative areas. They structure joint projects for several children and themselves, to prepare food used for either lunch or snack at least three days each week. These projects are the one time within this center when teachers direct a project that entails collaboration among the children. Both teachers speak of these experiences as being significant because the children '. . . are being responsible for what happens in their center . . . are being contributing members'.

Whereas in cooking these teachers' dominant emphasis is social learning experiences, in contrast, their material choices in the manipulative area point toward an emphasis on individual learning activities. This difference in emphasis of individual versus social learning experience is dependent partially on the nature of the activity setting, independent of teacher action; that is, an activity setting can affect the amount and kind of social interaction independent of teacher action. A group of six children and one teacher cooking is more likely to involve social interaction than manipulative activities with six children, for manipulative materials most often invite individual activity. Choice of activity per se can affect the degree and kind of social interaction between children (Gump and Sutton-Smith, 1971). At the same time, however, we will see in the following section that the quality of interaction among children and among children and adults also is influenced by the quality of pedagogical skill.

When responsible for the art area, Barb primarily offers individual tasks. When describing the value of these art projects, Barb speaks of '. . . a place for independence, doing things on your own, in your own way, expressing yourself'. Yet she also structures two days of children's joint construction of a large mural made with sponge painting, and on days when holiday paper chains are constructed, she helps several children join their chains together to make a twenty foot long chain to hang from the ceiling. Further, the open ended type of material in Barb's art projects sets an informal relaxed atmosphere, where children freely converse with each other as they construct. Within her dominant orientation toward individual experiencing in art, Barb's material provisioning gives evidence of an alternative pull toward social experiencing.

In February, Pam is responsible for activities in the block-housekeeping area. On all observed days she chooses to use only the unit blocks, and to participate with the children who daily share materials and cooperate in building structures. These children's social interaction is qualitatively different than when Barb or Gary are responsible for the block area. Since these differences are based on differences in teacher involvement with the children, they will be discussed in the next section on teacher interaction. With housekeeping closed in February, Pam in effect 'structures out' any possibility for much sociodramatic play to emerge during Activity Period. And Pam honestly comments to me: '. . . housekeeping is closed so often because it is a headache to all the teachers here, for it involves so much clean up hassle'.

In contrast to Dana's confinement to the small stage and Barb and Pam's confinement to one activity area in activity period, Anne has three rooms with a large number and variety of materials. And similar to the Big Room, there is a balance of materials stimulating children's social interaction (for example, block room, housekeeping area, and sand table) and areas stimulating individual activities (for example, puzzle/table toy area, art area, and quiet book area). Materials are developmentally appropriate, mostly open ended, and two teachers are available; thus there is no need for children to compete against each other for their teacher's assistance such as in Dana's room.

> 10/14 — Activity period: Yellow Room — 10.25 a.m.: Tina is seated next to three children who are forming shapes with play dough clay at the art table. Two children are filling assorted containers with sand in the small sand table. In the block room, three boys use the large wooden hollow blocks to build a 'clump', which they refer to as their space ship. Anne sits at the puzzle table where four children individually work with puzzles.

With a greater number of open ended material choices, such as the daily availability of the block room, housekeeping area, and sand table, there is more opportunity for the emergence of children's own extended play construction than the Activity Period boundaries of the Big Room allow. Yet Anne is not focused on the children's involvement in these areas; and as in early care, materials alone do not seem sufficient to enable these young children to engage in extended sequences of social interaction. Neither housekeeping nor the block room has an adult available as a supporting stabilizing presence, or facilitator of social interaction. Daily Mary and Mia play in the housekeeping area but the play has a surface quality; that is, sequences are repetitive and disconnected. Often the same boys do work together with blocks and build motorcycles or planes, but week after week, the buildings remain the same 'clump' like structures, and often the game is as much 'knock it down' as the actual construction. To understand Anne's lack of involvement in these areas requires understanding her interaction patterns which are the topic of the next section.

In summary, each teacher takes responsibility for arrangement of her own assigned space during activity period. Pam, Anne, and Barb provide approximately equal amounts of social and individually oriented materials. In contrast, most of Dana's materials stimulate individual involvement.

Teacher Interaction Patterns with Children

By definition any teacher interaction with a child is a social situation. Within this social context, however, the teacher's way of relating to the child can communicate valuing and behavioral expectations that primarily emphasize individual learning, primarily emphasize social learning or simultaneously emphasize individual and social learning. The following examples depict these two emphases. Within a small group period, a teacher gives each child a turn to identify her/his name card and letters within the name. In this social context, the teacher expresses an individual emphasis — each child's successful learning of name and letter recognition. Within a free play period, a boy asks the teacher to help him with a puzzle. The teacher suggests that the child sitting nearby knows how to complete that puzzle and will be able to help him. Here the teacher facilitates both individual and social learning as she encourages children to assist one another in mastering tasks, for both individual achievement and the social skill and valuing of assisting one another takes place. In the following analysis I will argue that while the teachers in this study inevitably are involved in individual and social interactions, they recurrently choose an emphasis on individual experiencing and concomitant learning of individual values and behaviors (for example, independence, task mastery).

In this study of the day-to-day lived experiences of Rosehill teachers and young children, distinct patterns of teacher child interaction emerge. These nine categories of interaction were developed from my daily observation records of these teachers' action.[1] The nine interaction patterns depict recurrent teacher action that is salient to the teachers' individual and social emphasis and that cuts across different situations and different teachers. In developing these patterns from my data, I followed the Glaser and Strauss (1967) guideline for theoretical sampling: 'The categories should not be so abstract as to lose their sensitizing aspect, but yet must be abstract enough to make his theory a general guide to multi-conditional, ever changing daily situations' (p. 242). These nine interaction patterns are portrayed in figure 9.

These interaction patterns are viewed as central to the young child's learning both in terms of development of self and internalization of society's values and practices. Although not developed here, the teachers' interactions may be conscious or unconscious — intentional or unwitting, and may be very important for subsequent analysis and interpretation. However, the issue is what is the result in terms of the meaning young children receive through these daily interactions; For the child's social-emotional context of childrearing has expanded to include day care teachers as well as parents as significant others. Day care children are forming secondary attachments within this social childrearing accompaniment to familial childrearing. And as noted in chapter 1, social-psychological theory gives clear evidence that it is the very early years, and within the young child's relation to significant adults that self identity and the internalization of society's values and practices develop.

In my claim that day care teacher and children's interactions, recurring day after day, month after month, are significant in the child's developing self and internalization of societal values and practices, I am not inferring a necessary cause effect relationship between teachers' schooling acts and child behavior. Following Mead (1962), I assume each child is a creator as well as a social product. Further, what teachers do is only one aspect of the child's personal experience with others, most important being the family influences on the child. At the same time however, I assume that daily recurrent patterns of young children's interactions potentially can influence the internalization of organized sets of attitudes, conceptions and expectations of 'the group' — what Mead terms the generalized other and psychoanalytic theory terms conscience.

In the day-to-day, there are variations within each teacher's interaction pattern as related to different children, different activity segments, and different spatial locations in which she is working. So too there are differences among these four teachers' interaction patterns. Yet to completely portray the complexity of these variations within and among the four teachers' behavior would obscure the dominant individual-social focus of this study.

In order to demonstrate the argument that these teachers lean

Figure 9: Teachers' Patterns of Interaction With Children

			Emphasizing Individual and Social	**Emphasizing the Individual**
	1.	Assistance	Teacher encourages children to help one another	Teacher helps children
	2.	Shared Participation	Teacher shares as participant in activities with child/ children	Teacher does not participate in activities with children
	3.	Intimacy	Teacher provides intimacy with body contact	Teacher maintains social distance of respective teacher/child roles
Redirection	4.	Rule Implementation	Teacher implements rules within the context of child activity	Teacher protects norms and rules, and ignores/ interrupts child activity
Redirection	5.	Conflict Resolution	Teacher enters into conflict to foster empathy and promote joint problem solving	Teacher responds to conflict to uphold ground rules that end the conflict
	6.	Support	Teacher supports children's interaction: — by being a stabilizing presence — by extending/expanding an activity	Children are on their own: — with no teacher present — with teacher present, but unaware of children's behavior
	7.	Spontaneous conversations	Teacher engages in spontaneous small talk with children	Teachers' conversations with children focus on individual task mastery
	8.	Praise	Teacher affirms children's group performance	Teacher affirms children's individual performance
	9.	Structured Turntaking	Teacher structures turntaking to foster simultaneously individual and social learning	Teacher structures turntaking to foster individual skill development

toward an emphasis on individual experiencing and concomitant learning of individual values and behaviors, I first will examine the interaction pattern of one teacher, Pam. Pam's action is similar to that of the other teachers and most clearly expresses the patterns being discussed. She is the lead teacher who is more skilled pedagogically and more open in talking about center happenings than are the other three teachers. Once the dynamics central to a specific interaction pattern are analyzed, relevant variations within and among teachers will be noted. In concluding this section a summary profile of all eight interaction patterns will be discussed.

Assistance

Preschool aged children often need three types of assistance: first, help in mastering self-care skills such as pouring a glass of milk or fastening clothes; second, in learning to successfully complete activities such as puzzles; and third, in learning the school rules and routines such as putting away materials after use. When children need assistance in a task, a teacher has the opportunity either to assist the children herself, and thereby foster individual skill development, or to encourage children to assist one another, and thereby simultaneously foster individual and social development.

Recurrently Pam is quick to assist a child who needs help, and does not encourage children to help one another, even when competent children are nearby. And with some teacher assistance, the children in this center readily become independent in routine self care habits, learn to choose their own activities, put away materials upon task completion, and master many of the provided tasks. If the children do experience difficulty in tasks, they do not hesitate in asking for Pam's help; however, children are rarely observed seeking help from one another. Anne, Barb, and Dana's assistance patterns are very similar to Pam's. The only variation for all these teachers occurs on a new child's first day attending Rosehill, when a child is asked to assist the new child to the playground, to the lunch table, etc.

Shared Participation

In this study, when teachers become involved as active participants in children's experiences this involvement is termed shared participation. Teachers' shared participation with children can occur either in teacher directed group activities such as singing together or jointly telling stories, or within child initiated activity segments. Rosehill children initiate their own activity during early care, activity period, and late care — activity segments which consume a very large proportion of the children's eight to ten hours at Rosehill. Lunch, nap, and the two or three brief teacher-directed group activities are the only exceptions to child-initiated activity segments. When children are playing in self-initiated activities, teachers have the choice of remaining separate from the children's activities or becoming involved in them. When they share as participants in children's activities, teachers can be significant role models and facilitators of children's individual and social learning. For example, as a teacher and children role play going on a family vacation, a teacher can suggest new role playing sequences and thereby extend the sociodramatic play and at the same time, clarify each child's understanding of travel.

Pam skillfully participates in activities with children in several different contexts, when children ask her to play with them during early care and activity period, and when Pam initiates singing and story telling or reading during group periods. When involved in shared participation with children, Pam enhances the children's level of individual and social learning.

> 1/9 — Corrie sits next to Pam and puts a coffee can full of colored small plastic bears on the table. Corrie makes a small circle of blue bears with a circle of red bears surrounding the blue ones. Then Pam makes a circle of green bears about ten inches from Corrie's circles. Pam: 'Let's see. One of these green bears is going to take a walk around the circle to pick up a friend'. Pam 'walks' one green bear around her circle, gets a yellow bear from the can, and puts it in back of the green bear in the circle. Then she says to Corrie: 'Now you do that Corrie'. Corrie puts a blue bear behind Pam's yellow one. Jim then comes to the table and asks Pam: 'What are you doing?'. Pam: 'Taking our bears for a walk'.
>
> Then Ned comes to the table and sits on the other side of Pam. Ned places a tub of six inch wooden figures on the table. As he begins to make a sculpture with these figures, Pam assists him in balancing the structure. As soon as Corrie sees Pam assist Ned, she says: 'Pammy will you play with me?'.
>
> Pam says with a questioning look on her face: 'What

am I doing? Sitting here cutting my hair?'. Corrie then walks behind Pam and pretends to cut Pam's hair. She holds a bear in her hand as she says: 'I'm giving you a bear cut'.

Pam laughs as she says: 'You're giving me a bear cut!'. Ella comes to the area and joins Corrie in pretending to cut Pam's hair. Then the two girls sit together and continue role playing with the bears as Pam assists Ned in making different structures. Lia arrives and sits on Pam's lap as Lia watches the wooden figure construction. Pam participates with Corrie, Ned and the other children at the table for about twenty minutes.

In this observed sequence, Pam and Corrie experience enjoyment together as they engage in cooperative role play with the small bears. Even as Pam begins building with Ned, she provides a stabilizing presence for Corrie, who is able to extend her role playing with Ella. On most days Corrie is unable to remain focused on tasks or play cooperatively in the manner observed in this sequence.

When directing group activities, Pam often initiates activities in which she reads or tells the children stories. And as in early circle, Pam is very skilled in stimulating children's participation. Without losing either the tempo or the children's focus, she asks questions which invite the children to hypothesize, to make judgments, to relate sequences of events, or to comment on their own personal life. Similarly, children spontaneously share personal experiences or feelings as Pam reads, and she is able to utilize this individual participation to extend and move along the group process.

1/7 — Nine children have just returned to their individual mats after 'standing and getting the wiggles out' as directed by Pam. Pam holds up a book as she says: 'This is a book about grownups crying. What are the things that make you cry?'. The children spontaneously share examples, such as 'fall down — get spanked — stub your toe?'. Pam then asks: 'What is the same about all these things?'. Children: 'It makes you cry?'. Pam: 'But why?'. Children: 'Because it hurts'. Pam then says: 'Yes, all that is hurting, but on the outside of your body. What about the inside of your body?'. One child replies: 'It gets sick'. Pam: 'Yes, but people's feelings also get hurt don't they?'. The children nod and Pam begins to read. Robbie then asks: 'But how do people talk inside their bodies?'. Pam: 'You

> can think inside your body can't you?'. Robbie looks puzzled but nods yes. Occasionally as she reads, a child shares something personal. Pam nods affirmatively and continues reading. Children remain attentive throughout the story. . . .

During this six-month participant observation study, the children's most collaborative, sustained experiences occur when Pam is actively involved as a participant, either in teacher-directed or child-initiated experiences. Admittedly, this interaction process occurs only during a small proportion of these fifty-four children's day. During most of the three hour early care period Pam is available but not directly involved with the children. Further, only six to ten children interact with Pam during activity period or group period.

Pam is the only teacher studied who has sustained shared participation with the children in a variety of contexts. Barb, Anne, and Dana do participate in activities with children during teacher-directed group periods, but rarely participate in child-initiated activities during early or late care or activity period. When children ask Barb to play with them she refuses. Barb explains to me that she is concerned about fostering dependency in the children were she to play with them. Though Anne agrees to play with children when they ask her, her initial gesturing and subsequent distraction in participation suggests her lack of valuing the learning potential of these play experiences. And though Dana eagerly accepts the children's play requests in activity period, repetitive interruptions either to assist or to redirect other children prevent Dana from completing a single sequence with a child.

Physical Intimacy

In receiving physical comfort when upset, in spontaneous giving and receiving of physical affection, and/or in the informal snuggling in an adult's lap, young children experience bodily contact with caring adults. These intimate contacts are basic forms of relationship for young children and contribute to their sense of trust in others and in themselves (Erikson, 1950). On the other hand, when young day care children experience consistent social distance of respective teacher and child roles, they very likely are encountering experiences in separateness, as literally and figuratively they 'stand alone'.

In her relationships with the children at Rosehill, Pam spontaneously expresses affection through physical contact with the children, a teasing tickle, a soothing arm, or an enthusiastic enveloping hug. She is exceptionally affectionate with the children in her group who have special needs, such as Ronnie who lacks self control or James who resists adult directives.

12/18–7.30 a.m. — early care — James is seated on Pam's lap as the two make a complex cube pattern design together. As they complete the pattern design, they sing together the song 'High Hopes'.

10/26–8.00 a.m. — early care — Pam is seated with several children at a front choice table. Ronnie comes to speak with her and as he speaks, he frowns angrily. (I cannot hear the conversation.) As she speaks softly to Ronnie, Pam has her arm around him, and he in turn leans against her.

In a similar manner, Barb and Anne provide intimacy in their relationship with the children. They too are affectionate most frequently with the children in their small group. In these interactions of physical intimacy, young children are experiencing self-in-relation as well as being affirmed as individuals. These three teachers' gestures of physical intimacy point to their alternative pull toward social and individual experience, in contrast to their dominant individual emphasis in most other interaction patterns.

Pam, Anne, and Barb freely speak of their rationale for providing intimacy with the children. Barb and Pam observe that their nurturance is one of their most important roles. Barb comments on the children's need for belonging, and Pam notes the emotional support children receive through hugging and lap sitting. On the other hand, Anne speaks of telling the children 'I love you' and thereby reinforcing obedience: '. . . the children know that if they follow the rules they get a hug'. For Anne intimacy is a form of control.

In contrast, Dana shows minimal affection by physical contact with the children. Admittedly she shows her affection and caring through her unswerving patience in assisting children, her diligence in supervision, and her calming presence during nap period. So too, the listener is aware of her concern for each child as she sensitively describes each of her children. But the only observed gesture of physical intimacy is child-initiated during one activity segment; children daily come to sit on her lap at circle before lunch, and she readily accepts them.

Rule Implementation

Rules contribute to individuals functioning together smoothly and productively, and are the foundation of group management. For children to be cared for in a group setting such as Rosehill, group management is essential, the alternative being recurrent incidents of chaos. The even tempo and smooth flow of the functioning of several dozen children and their teachers at Rosehill gives evidence of these teachers' skill in rule implementation. In this section I will analyze these teachers' patterns of rule implementation in terms of teacher emphasis on individual and social.

The processes of rule implementation depicted in figure 9 involve two methods of rule implementation, both of which effectively manage groups, but involve different emphases of individual and social. When a teacher implements rules within the context of children's ongoing activity, she has the opportunity to help the children understand the need for rule adherence in order for the children to function together productively. By implementing rules within the context of children's activity, teachers assist children's understanding of the interdependence of each person's functioning within the day care context. When a child shouts loudly across the room and Pam explains to the child that her shouting disturbs the other children who are listening to a story, Pam is assisting the child's ability to take the perspective of others.

Another method of rule implementation consists of teacher directive to follow a given rule for the purpose of children learning to comply with authority. As the teacher redirects the child she ignores or interrupts the child's ongoing activity. When Joy, Alicia, and Jill are role playing in the housekeeping area, and Pam calls to Joy to return to the front table and put away her puzzle, Pam has interrupted Joy's ongoing project with Alicia and Jill. Here the teacher communicates clearly the need for Joy to adhere to the given rules at Rosehill — namely, put away your materials when you are finished with them. In complying, Joy gives evidence that she has learned to follow teacher directives. This type of rule implementation can facilitate individual children's internalization of rules and adherence to authority. And in fact, these children's behavior at Rosehill indicates that they have learned to abide by the rules and to comply to adult directives. During the day they move from area to area or one activity to another in an independent manner with little need for adult redirection. This second method of rule implementation results in each child's learning to function independently through internalization of adult directives for the sake of rule adherence and adult compliance in and of themselves.

Pam's rule implementation patterns are consistent from day to day. She redirects children's misbehavior by positively stating the center's rules 'use inside voices', 'go outdoors to run', 'get a choice'. These rules are used in repetitive phrasing as slogans. During the lengthy early care period, Pam is available to the children but often is not directly observing or interacting with them. Given this lack of focused observation she does not act to prevent misbehavior; rather her stance is reactive. Pam 'catches' the child's violation and in her repetitive slogans, she protects the school rules. She does not enter into the children's experiences to understand the project they are working on or to give children an explanation of the need for rule adherence. Some of the children's misbehavior involves social experiencing; but in her ignoring or interrupting these children's ongoing projects, Pam expresses minimal valuing of these social activities.

> 11/11 — Early care — Ricky, Jill, Evan and Alicia are crawling about the housekeeping floor. As Alicia puts necklaces on Jill and Evan she says: 'Okay, I'll put your flea collar on. I'm the momma'. Alicia then goes to the stove and puts pots on the burners. Barking like dogs, Ricky and Evan crawl across the floor, and then climb into the 'dress up' cupboard. Evan: 'This is our dog house'. Pam is seated with children at the nearby front table. She calls to the boys and says: 'Evan and Ricky the clothes closet isn't a good place to climb in'. The boys climb out of the cupboard.

During activity period and group time, children's misbehavior is much less frequent than in early care, for these activity segments involve clearer spatial boundaries, more teacher focus and structure and less people are present. In contrast to her early care redirection patterns Pam simultaneously emphasizes social learning as well as compliance to rules during activity period and group time.

> 9/24 — Group time: Eight children sit in front of Pam who holds a baby picture of each of the children. Pam moves each picture from child to child so that each can see it. For each picture she asks a question. For example, 'Can you tell what James is eating? — Does Mia have a lot of hair?' Without raising their hands children respond enthusiastically. Often Pam elaborates on their response; for example, 'Not all babies have no hair. Some

> have a lot'. Though the children are not raising their hands to be called on, amazingly, each seems to wait until the other is finished before spontaneously talking. Near the end, when Joanna is speaking Patrick begins talking. Pam: 'Patrick, the rest of us can't hear Joanna when you speak at the same time. I know you have something to share too, but let's let Joanna finish her turn first'. When Joanna is finished, Patrick asks a question.

In these interactions Pam has entered into the context of children's experiencing and provides explanations for the expected rule adherence, explanations that help young children recognize and understand their own and other children's feelings and intentions.

In their interactions with children throughout the day, Anne, Barb, and Dana's rule implementation is reactive, and either ignores or interrupts the ongoing child activity, in the same manner as Pam's early care patterns. These teachers also are consistent in their use of similar slogans such as 'Use an inside voice'. In her redirections, Anne has a distinctive pattern of using 'I messages' such as 'I don't like that,' or 'That makes me angry'. These 'I messages' are not to be confused with the modern techniques promoted by human potential movements such as parent effectiveness training, where adult and child are urged to jointly solve problems (Gordon, 1970). Rather, Anne's 'I messages' communicate that the children are to behave in order to please their teacher.

In summary, during early care all four teachers implement rules through positively stated slogans as they ignore or interrupt the children's ongoing activity. This interaction pattern effectively facilitates the individual children's internalization of rules and compliance to authority, such that they quickly learn to autonomously play in the various areas. Only Pam enters into the children's experiences and implements rules with explanation; and she redirects in this way only during 'school time', that is, activity period and group time.

Conflict Resolution

Two methods of teacher redirection of children's conflicts have been observed in this study and are portrayed in figure 9. The first method — 'Teacher enters into children's conflict to foster empathy and promote joint problem solving' — involves the teacher entering into the children's experiencing. When a teacher enters into children's disputes, she has the opportunity to reconstruct the situation with each child's feelings and intentions made explicit. Often young children in conflict are acting impulsively with little or no awareness of their own feelings. When they hear a teacher recognize and care about their own feelings, they are more able to hear the teacher's report of other children's feelings. Then with teacher assistance they can help in reaching a joint solution to the dispute. In this manner conflict can be basic curriculum for learning in early education. In this type of teacher redirection, the conflict becomes a social learning context for perspective taking and joint problem solving. In addition children learn to respect each other's feelings and rights.

The second observed method of teacher redirection in conflict is 'Teacher responds to children's conflict by upholding ground rules that end the conflict'. Here the teacher resolves the conflict by implementing rules that are familiar to the children and that end the dispute. For example, when a child at Rosehill grabs the toy of another child, the teachers remind the child that grabbing is against the center's 'first choice policy', that the first child need not share her/his toy. When teachers consistently implement ground rules to resolve conflicts, young children learn these rules and often are able to settle disputes on their own. As in the previous rule implementation pattern, this type of teacher behavior results in children learning to function independently through internalization of adult directives. This teacher resolution pattern has a more distinctly individual emphasis than does the first.

In early care, Pam's redirection strategies in children's conflict situations involve the second interaction pattern, and are a consistent analogue to her early care rule implementation pattern. Ordinarily she is not focused actively enough on the children to grasp anything other than the emotional outburst of the conflict. Then she provides a quick resolution by implementing a rule that is external to the ongoing events within the conflict.

> 10/10 — 9.15 a.m. — Early care: Pam is preparing materials in the art area in the Big Room. Across from her on the checkered rug area four boys each make structures with Tinker Toys. Rachel, wearing a floor length formal, enters the area and with Tinker Toys she makes a structure that looks like ten lollipops on a stand. She then begins chanting: 'A dollar ninety-five for one of these lollipops'. Billy takes two and pretends to give her money, then walks away as he pretends to lick the lollipops. Rachel calls to Billy: 'Give one to

> your kid!'. (No adult is observing these sequences.)
>
> Chuck walks about the rug area with his Tinker Toy space ship as he chants motor sounds. When he comes to Rachel he takes her lollipops from her and Rachel yells: 'I had it. No! I had it'. Pam looks up, comes to the children and says: 'Rachel, with your formal on you need to be in the housekeeping area'. Rachel immediately goes to housekeeping, removes the dress, and then goes outdoors. Pam returns to the art area.

Pam's responses to children's conflict always are stated positively and she has similar solutions to most disputes. Children are told to work in their own area, to leave the scene of the dispute, to use words rather than to hit, and to adhere to the 'first choice policy'. In early care, Anne, Dana, and Barb respond to conflicts with similar slogans stated positively. Similar to Pam, they consistently maintain a reactive stance as they focus on protecting rules without entering into the children's experiencing. Given these teachers' consistency in positively stating slogans to end children's disputes, children quickly adapt to these directives and in fact, learn to end many of their own disputes, by leaving the scene or shouting at each other rather than hitting. The disputes are not solved but are aborted. Within this social context, these teachers' resolution to conflict and resulting children's learning is tilted toward an individual emphasis in the sense that children learn what is allowed (for example, using words) and what is not allowed (for example, physical aggression) and can learn to independently end disputes through internalization of adult directives.

With more defined spatial boundaries, more structured activity choices, and closer teacher supervision, Anne, Pam, and Barb's children rarely engage in conflicts during activity period. If a conflict should occur, Barb and Anne's behavior is the same as their reactive stance during early care. In contrast, Pam enters into the children's relationships, talks together with the children and attempts to reconstruct the episode to help the children understand what happened. Here Pam's interaction has a more social emphasis as she helps children understand each other's feelings and jointly solve the dispute. Unlike Anne, Barb, and Pam, Dana's children repetitively engage in conflict during activity period. These disputes seem to stem from contextual features of Dana's environment. That is, the complexity of tasks and small amount of highly desirable toys provoke tattling and competition among the children, competition to gain help and competition to gain access to materials.

Support of Children's Interaction

Teachers have the opportunity to support children's interaction through being a stabilizing presence and through facilitative intervention. As young children are playing, a teacher's presence provides an affirming and stabilizing effect on the children's action (Bronfenbrenner, 1979; Isaacs, 1966 and 1972; Snyder, Snyder and Snyder Jr., 1980; Weber, 1971). The teacher who sits at a table where children are building together with lego influences the involvement of these children. Her presence supports these children's experience in several ways. They know their teacher is interested in their activity, that she is available to help if needed, and that she can share in their delight. Beyond being a presence, a teacher offers support when she enters into children's experience, interacts with them, and then departs from the area. This moving in and out of children's involvement, termed facilitative intervention in this study, is a basic strategy in early education and offers support beyond being a presence only. For in her involvement, the teacher has the opportunity to extend, expand, and/or clarify the children's experience. For example, three children put on adult clothing, assume family roles, and stand about the mirror in the housekeeping area. A teacher enters, sits at the 'kitchen' table, and suggests that the children cook breakfast before they go to work. Here the teacher has helped the children organize a sequence of role playing events and extends their involvement. Her interaction simultaneously strengthens the children's individual and social experiencing. Whereas teacher redirection is reactive action, teachers take a pro-active stance in facilitative intervention.

When children are playing together, a teacher can choose to be separate, either in terms of being in a separate geographical area or in terms of being physically present but psychologically unaware of the children's activity. Without teacher supervision young children learn strategies of independent behavior. For example, when two children argue over the possession of a toy and no adult is present, the children may learn to solve the dispute themselves or merely leave the scene with the dispute unsettled. In contrast to teacher presence, the teacher separation reflects an individual orientation.

Pam is present and supports children's experiences during all activity periods except the three-hour early care period. Her early care 'teaching' consists of primarily providing many materials and managing inappropriate behavior. Her interactions with children are primarily reactive; that is, she relates to children in response, either to their request to help them, their request for her to play with them, or in response to their misbehavior. In contrast, in activity period, Pam is present and observing the children, often actively participates with them, or moves in and out of children's activity to extend or expand their involvement.

> 2/13 — Activity period — block area: Pam has been on the floor with four boys who each build a simple structure. Eddie says: 'This will be a zoo!'. Jay then comments 'And mine is too'. Pam suggests: 'Let's get some zoo animals and then you all have cages for the same zoo'. Pam and the children then go to the puzzle room and return with small plastic zoo animals. The children continue building, but now are making walkways, ice cream stands and other structures together as they imaginatively talk about zoo happenings within their structure.

Pam's strength as a presence for the children's growth and development is strongest in her one-to-one interactions, a strength that is portrayed most vividly in her relation to Ronnie. In early November, all eight Rosehill teachers list Ronnie as the child who causes them the greatest difficulty in management. In mid-February no teacher lists Ronnie as being a problem. And within that time span, Ronnie not only gains in self-control, but gains a special friend, Kevin, with whom he participates in many pro-social activities, that is, activities characterized by mutuality of positive relationship. During the fall and winter, Pam allows Ronnie to remain near her. Daily she enters into his play as an active participant, or moves in and out of his play to affirm and extend his involvement. As the weeks progress, this child seems to gain in his trust of a significant adult, Pam, and in this relationship he gains self trust and accompanying self control.

Anne, Dana, and Barb provide a presence during activity segments other than early and late care however, they do not have Pam's skill in entering into children's spontaneous activity. Similar to Pam, they rarely are focused on the children during early or late care. These teachers do provide an informal atmosphere where children feel free to enter into many spontaneous conversations together throughout the day. And occasionally, the children engage in pro-social behavior — structured mutuality, social role playing, and construction of joint projects. A consistent thread in most of these pro-social interactions is the lack of teacher awareness of their occurrence. These teachers' insensitivity to ongoing pro-social child behavior suggests that they are more oriented to children's individual rather than social development. As Bettleheim (1969) notes: 'Often what the educators of a system are insensitive about can tell more about the system than anything claimed for it on the positive side' (p. 119).

Periodically children at Rosehill are on their own in early and late care for brief periods of time with either no teacher present or a teacher in the room, but unaware of the children's behavior. Even when aware of this lack of supervision, these teachers do not view this pattern as problematic. The teachers speak of early care as being homelike in atmosphere, and preschoolers are left alone as parents do household chores. And admittedly, these children are able to maintain activity 'as usual' when teachers are not focused on their activity. In fact, many children seem to develop strategies of 'coping' with each other when no adult is present. When frustrated by another child, often the frustrated child merely leaves the area. Or when in a dispute, children learn to use acceptable means of expressing their frustration, such as shouting at each other rather than hitting. These strategies do not solve the initial dispute, but they do end the conflict. On one occasion I shared with Pam a ten minute conflict with Ronnie and Kevin that I had observed in which each boy hurled blasphemous curses of each other and mimed kicking and hitting. Pam commented: 'I think it's good . . . I mean, they are using words as we've been trying to teach them. The words may be ugly but it's better than hitting. And we do want the children to be able to solve their own problems'. These children's response to a conflict and their teacher's evaluation of their response is one resolution of a social situation, a resolution that seems to represent an individualistic understanding of social relationships.

Spontaneous Conversation

In early education settings such as Rosehill Day Care Center, children spend a large proportion of their day in play activities. As children move about the classroom and engage in play activities, teachers have the opportunity to have many spontaneous conversations with the children, or they can maintain distance from the children and only intervene to redirect children's misbehavior. Teachers can limit their conversations with children to the tasks at hand and thereby maintain focus on children's learning of task mastery. In addition teachers can engage in many informal conversations that are not goal directed, but rather, can be characterized as friendly 'small talk' — in which adults and children share personal experiences, thoughts, feelings and/or desires. When there is abundant spontaneous shared information between children and teachers, a relaxed informal ambience is created in the school environment. Further, the children develop a sense of companionship and belonging as they spontaneously engage in small talk with one another and with their teachers.

Throughout early and late care and during activity period, Anne, Barb and Pam initiate and respond to a great deal of spontaneous conversation with the children. Though she does not initiate such conversation, Dana enthusiastically listens and responds to children when they begin chatting with her. Given this informal ambience, the outsider senses that this is a cheerful child-centered environment in which children enjoy being with each other and with adults. As with physical intimacy, these teachers' involvement in and condoning of spontaneous conversation point to their alternative pull toward social and individual experience, in contrast to their dominant individual emphasis within other interaction patterns.

Praise

Teachers have the opportunity to interact with children to affirm children's action and thereby influence children's understanding of self and others. Teachers can praise individual accomplishments and thereby enhance the child's self-esteem. A child is swinging and a teacher comments: 'You've learned to pump your legs so you can swing high. What fun!'. A teacher also can praise children's group accomplishments and thereby let children know she values their social interaction with their peers. Several children build a city with unit blocks and their teacher comments: 'Your apartment building is very tall!'. Here the teacher is letting the children know that she values their joint project.

Throughout the day Pam calls attention to the children's accomplishments enthusiastically. In these interactions, she describes the children's ongoing project and in this manner, affirms the children's accomplishment for its own sake and helps children recognize their own success. For example she tells Ronnie: 'Your skyscraper is terrific! It's balanced very well'; or she tells Suzy: 'The colors in your painting are so happy'. Anne, Barb, and Dana also frequently praise children's individual performance, but in different ways. Rather than call attention to what the child did, Anne usually lets the child know how much s/he is pleasing her, for example: 'I like the way you put away your toys', or 'That makes me happy'. Barb and Dana frequently praise children through use of general evaluative comments such as 'good', 'neat', 'nice' — comments that also communicate that the child is pleasing the adult. Though their approach may vary, all four teachers compliment individual accomplishment. This teacher affirmation is in contrast to their lack of awareness or involvement in children's spontaneous projects. They seem to enter group situations only when redirection of children's misbehavior is needed.

Teacher Structured Turntaking

The nature of turntaking is an individual act within a social context. When a teacher utilizes turntaking with a group of children, she can place different emphases on the individual and the social. Within a group process the teacher may primarily emphasize the individual such as when in a group, children wait to have individual turns to practice reciting their address and phone number. On the other hand, a teacher can structure turntaking in a way that each individual's participation adds to the flow of the group process and the individual and social are simultaneously emphasized. For example, within a small group movement activity, all children and teacher rhythmically chant each child's name and move their hands and arms in the manner initiated by the named child. As each child has a turn to initiate a hand-arm movement to accompany her/his name, all members together chant and move in unison. Here the individual act transforms the group process into a new social experience.

Distinct contours of turntaking that emphasize the individual are a central component of Dana's daily group time. Each day Dana initiates a learning game in which each of her ten children have a turn to participate individually. As Dana directs her attention to teaching individuals, the waiting children become restless. In her zeal to foster this individual learning Dana loses effective group management. Children begin misbehaving, and as Dana calls on misbehaving individuals, her own redirection deepens the ruptured flow of the children's attention. This fragmentation of the group process is a pungent example of what Kounin (1977), in his research on classroom discipline, terms the 'ripple effect' of a teacher's handling of one child's misbehavior influencing the behavior of children who are the 'audience'. In addition, Dana's group process is fragmented by the children's competing for a turn. The frantic pleading for turns of these young 3 year-olds is a reminder of what Jules Henry (1963) describes as the 'forest waving' of hands so typical of public school children.

This daily turntaking during Dana's group time contrasts sharply with the simultaneous individual and social emphasis of her one outdoor balloon popping game. In the balloon game, the children who are not having a turn are active participants as observers; their gleeful cheering of the blindfolded child resembles spectators at a football game. This cheering creates a momentum filled with suspense. Yet Dana doesn't seem able to understand the change in her children's involvement, for she continues her indoor group strategies, for example, 'I'll only call on those children who are sitting quietly'. Differences between the structuring of this balloon activity and indoor group time games give insight into the fragmentation of indoor games. First, this outdoor game allows plenty of space for the children's diversity of participation. And second, the task is understood clearly by all, for it is on target with the children's developmental levels. Indoors, the task is always the same for all, but these children of varying ability do not always understand the task. For example, Eric easily recognizes his first and last name written on the wall; yet other children don't even understand the meaning of 'last name'.

In contrast to Dana, Pam and Barb omit any turntaking structure from their group process. They explain to me that the omission is because they had been having frequent management problems with individual turntaking. Anne occasionally structures turntaking into her group time activities, and like Dana she is unable to maintain total group involvement in these activities. But unlike Dana, Anne is secure in her role as authority, speaks firmly and disapprovingly to the misbehaving children and communicates that they are making her angry. Having been sternly scolded, the misbehaving children comply.

This turntaking structure is not a dominant teacher-child interaction pattern that cuts across all teachers and all situations at Rosehill. Yet a brief examination is warranted for at least two reasons: first, turntaking clearly outlines how a social structure can have an individual emphasis. And second, the prevalence of the turntaking structure within the early education field warrants a discussion of its meaning. For like Dana, in their zeal to ensure their children's readiness for kindergarten, many early educators see taking turns in a group as a skill needing to be mastered.

Observed Children's Action

The parameters of children's action at Rosehill are defined by three contexts: (i) the activities, materials, space and time provided by the teachers: (ii) the teacher-child interactions or lack thereof; and (iii) the teacher-teacher interactions or lack thereof. The reciprocal intertwining of these three contexts and children's action are considered to be the basic dynamics influencing children's individual and social learning at Rosehill.

Six distinct patterns of children's action have been developed from my daily observation records during this six-month field study. The first pattern, termed *individually focused activity*, refers to children's action that involves no social exchange. The five other patterns involve pro-social action, that is, action characterized by mutuality of positive relationship between two or more people. The five pro-social patterns are: (i) *spontaneous conversation*; (ii) *structured mutuality*,; (iii) *joint projects*; (iv) *social role play*; and (v) *association as friends*. In chapter 1, social experiences that teachers might emphasize initially were identified as involving conversation, helping action, sharing action, combined efforts and empathy. All five observed patterns of children's pro-social action included observations of combined efforts, sharing action and conversation. In contrast, throughout the six months of observation, children initiated helping action only twice. Empathetic action was observed infrequently, and only in social role play and friendship patterns. Figure 10 depicts a profile of children's pro-social action at Rosehill, and the role of their teachers within these actions.

These patterns are not meant to depict all possible child action, but rather to depict that observed child action which teachers allow or encourage and which is recurrent, that is, cuts across different activity

Figure 10: Children's Pro-social Action and Teacher's Mode of Emphasis

		Children's pro-social action				
	Modes of teacher emphasis	Spontaneous conversation	Structured mutuality	Joint projects	Social role play	Association as friends
Modes of Teacher Emphasis	Punishing					
	Discouraging					Sometimes: Anne
	Ignoring	All four teachers	All four teachers	All four teachers	All four teachers	All four teachers
	Allowing	All four teachers	All four teachers	All four teachers	All four teachers	All four teachers
	Supporting	All four teachers		Pam: activity period		
	Stimulating	Everyone except Dana		Pam and Barb: occasionally		

periods, different spatial areas and different teachers. The focal point of this field study is teacher emphasis of children's individual and social experiences. However, as we will see in the following section, a consistent pattern in the observed pro-social action of children is that this action most often is *independent* of the teachers; in fact, teachers usually do not seem to be in the vicinity or observing these children's action.

Three forms of children's action considered to be anti-social were observed: conflicts, competition and tattling. Conflicts among children occasionally do occur in different activity periods and with different teachers. However, since these conflicts are not condoned by the teachers, and have been discussed extensively in the previous section, discussion is omitted here. Competition and tattling occur very infrequently, and only on the stage area with Dana. The same children who compete and tattle on the stage with Dana neither compete nor tattle when observed in other spatial areas or when enrolled in other teachers' groups. Since competition and tattling were not salient children's action at Rosehill they are omitted in the following discussion.

Individually Focused Activity

The fact that most Rosehill children are involved in individually focused activity during early care, activity period, and late care is one of the clearest indications of these four teachers' dominant pull toward individual learning. In these time periods most of the children participate in individual activities as opposed to activities involving social groupings (see activity scans in appendix A). During early and late care when teachers are available but not directly focused on the children, the children are free to initiate their own activities in their own way, with materials which contain no explicit requirement for interaction with other children or adults. Children control not only the choice of activity, but onset, duration, and even manner of involvement during the six hours of early and late care.

> 11/14 — Early care — At a front choice table, James builds different objects with eight three inch shape puzzle inserts. Brett completes an alphabet puzzle across from James. James rearranges the puzzle shapes into different objects as he talks to himself, identifying the objects he has made. James first makes a train engine, then a wagon, and several rocket ships which he

> wrecks after counting backward from ten to one and calling 'blast off'. Then after he completes another design he says to Brett: 'I made a clown mask for you'. Brett does not reply but watches as James wrecks the mask and makes another object which he labels an 'erp . . . this erp makes cars. . . . This is a car machine'. Brett then leaves the table and James continues making new designs with the eight puzzle shape inserts. James to self: 'Now this will be a cookie machine. The fan turns around here, (he swivels a rectangle as he speaks) and the cookies come out here'.

James is able to play alone with full concentration at different table activities for over an hour at a time, day after day, throughout the six-month observation period. He and at least another dozen Rosehill children are able to initiate their own activities, sustain focused involvement, and learn to master most tasks available. And almost all these 3 and 4-year-olds at Rosehill can initiate tasks on their own, clean up materials upon task completion, and seldom need to ask help from other children or teachers. Yet most Rosehill children do not have James' ability to remain focused on one task; rather they tend to frequently change materials and their play has a surface quality. They do learn to be self reliant and follow the routine rules at Rosehill; however with minimal adult facilitation during early and late care, their growth in task involvement or mastery of increasingly complex tasks is minimal.

In the following discussion of children's pro-social action, we will see that their teachers most often are not in the vicinity or aware of these actions. In contrast, we have seen that frequently Rosehill teachers *praise* individually focused activity and give children *assistance* to master individual tasks, and thereby support and stimulate this form of learning.

Spontaneous Conversation

As Rosehill children engage in individual tasks during early and late care and activity period, they frequently engage in spontaneous conversations with other children or teachers. Many of the children spend a large amount of time during each day in small talk, listening and conversing with other children and/or adults.

> 9/5 — Early care outdoors — A.J. and Alan are filling coffee

cans with sand. A.J.: 'I got a sore here (points to his index finger)'. Alan: 'What happened? Where you fell at?'. A.J.: 'Nowhere, I just got a sore here'.

1/26 — Early care — Alicia is eating breakfast and Zachary enters. He comes to Alicia and say: 'I have a new shirt'. (He points to the Superman picture on it.) 'Do you like the sparkly part?'. Alicia nods yes, clears her place at the table, and the two special friends go outdoors together.

10/8 — Early care outdoors — Anne is seated on a railroad tie across from the sandbox. Jill has just arrived and is greeted by Anne. Jill: 'I went to the movies with Daddy'. Anne: 'That was special! What did you see?'. Jill: '*Star Wars*, and I ate so much popcorn I was sick'.

Within these teachers' dominant orientation toward individual learning they sanction and in fact, often are involved in conversations. The ease with which children spontaneously converse together and with teachers suggests that within their dominant orientation toward individual learning, these teachers concomitantly value social interaction.

Structured Mutuality

In this study, when two or more children are involved in an activity together, and their involvement is organized by the structure of the materials or by the rules of the game, this involvement is termed structured mutuality. The materials or the rules of the game define boundaries of the children's (for example, using a puzzle together or playing 'capture the flag').

In structured mutuality, the play is pro-social, for it often involves the children sharing materials and always involves combined efforts toward the same goal. Unlike social role play and joint projects, creative self-expression and use of imagination are minimally present if at all. Children's structured mutuality is observed in early care, activity period and late care. All observed sequences are child initiated and are experiences characterized by the children's shared enjoyment, combining of efforts, and on some occasions, one child's positive leadership with other children.

10/20 — outdoors — Five girls sit in a circle in the dust behind the large climber. The children are playing the game — 'doggie, doggie, where is your bone'. Jamie seems to be the leader for she tells individuals 'Now lay in the middle and lie down like a doggie'. After about five minutes, Sally suggests that they play 'duck, duck, goose', and the children do so. Again Jamie is the leader as she tells individual children when it is their turn. As the children play, Barb, Tina, and Anne converse together at the other end of the playground.

Though the Rosehill teachers arrange the environment in a manner in which children's structured mutuality is possible and it does occur occasionally, the teachers rarely initiate such interaction, and do not seem aware of its occurrence when children engage in this type of involvement. Once again, these teachers lack of involvement point to their dominant pull toward individual learning experiences.

Joint Projects

In this study, children implementing a plan together to create something new is termed joint project. This type of collaboration is observed in Pam and Barb's cooking projects, on a few occasions during early care, especially when children build with varied blocks, and in activity period block building in the Yellow Room area and Big Room.

1/28 — Early care — block area — Ronnie and Kevin are seated next to each other at a front choice table. Each boy is snapping together plastic Bristle Blocks. Together they are making a tower-like structure.

During early and late care, teachers most often are not observed in the vicinity of children creating joint projects. Rosehill teachers' lack of awareness of these children's pro-social actions indicates these teachers' orientation toward individual learning experiences. With no adult present, Anne's children engage in very simple repetitive block constructions during activity period. In contrast, during activity period in the Big Room, children work together for thirty to sixty minutes as they build increasingly elaborate block structures. In these sequences Pam is present, and at the very least, provides a stabilizing presence for the children. Occasionally Pam also participates in building with the children, or she extends the construction with a suggestion or with new materials.

Social Role Play

Role play is a common mode of play for all young children. Imitative and imaginative elements are basic to role play. The child takes on a role; and in utilizing her his own past and present experience, the child imitates other persons in action and speech with the aid of real or imagined objects. Often the child's verbalizations serve as a substitute for objects, actions or situations.

> 1/30 — Early care — Rachel and Nan have just climbed into the wooden rocking boat in the housekeeping area. Each child lies down on one of the seats. Rachel says to Nan: 'Sister, pretend I'm the mother and I sleep next to you so you won't have a bad dream'.

When there are at least two players interacting within the play episode, and verbal communication is an element the play becomes cooperative and is termed sociodramatic or social role play.

At Rosehill children initiate social role playing indoors and outdoors, role playing that is structured by materials such as in the block or housekeeping area, and role playing that occurs through the use of imagination and imitation. Central to almost all observed social role playing at Rosehill is its surface quality. That is, children begin role playing sequences that dissipate into manipulation of materials (for example, dressing and undressing), entail *non sequitur* sequencing (for example, setting the table, then combing one's own hair, then talking on the phone), and/or repetitive action (for example, continual dressing and undressing of a doll). Though children do share materials and space, the low level of verbalization, imagination, and cooperation indicates a surface quality in the play. The two special friends, Rachel and Nan, are the only children able to engage in extended role play sequences that involve a lot of verbalization, imagination and cooperation.

In almost all of the observed social role play sequences at Rosehill, there is no teacher in the vicinity of the playing children. No teacher is observed guiding social role play in the housekeeping area; their involvement in this area is confined to maintenance and management. In formal interviews, Pam, Barb and Anne do state that positive social learning occurs through social role play; however they seem unskilled in guiding this form of play.

Association as Friends

During the six-month observation period, sixteen of the fifty-four Rosehill children develop special friends with whom they play. All of these companionship relations seem to develop spontaneously without teacher facilitation. Often these sixteen children are in different small groups; yet they have several hours together in early and late care. I spoke to eight of these children about their special friends. All but one child told me that a child was her/his special friend '. . . because s/he plays with me'. This primitive understanding conforms with Damon's (1977) extensive research on young children's social development.[2] Damon reports that children under six years understand friends as '. . . associates with whom one plays or comes into frequent contact . . . there is no sense of liking or disliking the stable traits of another' (p. 153). With increasing age there is movement in children's understanding from an understanding of a material basis for friendship to an understanding of a psychological basis, and an increasing appreciation of the mutuality of friendship.

Though these children have primitive understandings of the meaning of friendship, significantly, at least one of these sixteen children always is involved in all of the observed pro-social interactions at Rosehill. Further, when these friends are playing together, their social role play and joint projects entail more complexity and greater duration of involvement than in other children's observed play sequences. It seems as if the children who have close friends also are the children with more mature social skills than their peers.

All four teachers speak of friendships as a positive aspect of a child's experience at Rosehill. So too all are aware that these friendships develop spontaneously.

Barb: Children seem to develop friends on their own. I think they're wonderful for they allow the children to be more happy when they're here.

Pam: Some of the children just seem to pair off.

CSK: Once friendships are formed, do you or other teachers nurture the friendship?

Pam: It depends on the children. Like Jim and Dave. They don't behave well together, so that one is discouraged by all the teachers. It just doesn't work out when they play together, for they get loud, and play pieces end up all over the floor. But then when I see A.J. and Alan play together I'll sometimes go by them and tell them how nicely I think they are playing together and that I'm glad that they are friends.

In conversations with me, Anne also speaks positively about any newly-formed friendships in her group. Yet she frequently separates close friends, seemingly, to ease her group management process. Daily she separates close friends before she sits down for group time. So too, she seems to promote children to the next, older class in order to separate close friendships and simplify her management.

> 9/3 — Sally (3 years 2 months) and Alicia (3 years 8 months) have been inseparable friends since they've entered school ten days ago. Though Alicia is very verbal and completes tasks with ease, she cries each morning when her mother leaves. On Alicia's sixth day, Anne whispers to me: 'Alicia is smart, but she gets on my nerves. And she and Sally never stop talking in group time'. When Anne obtains three new children in her class on 9/2, she promotes Alicia to another class in the Big Room.

Anne's concern with management leads to recurrent inconsistencies in her espoused 'theory' about friendships and her observed actions.

Both observations and teachers' explanations suggest that the children who have more mature social skills and who have developed close friendships have developed these friendships and skills relatively independent of their teachers.

Teacher Interaction With Other Teachers

The most significant aspect of an early education environment is the climate created by the teachers' relations with the children and with each other (Isaacs, 1974; Snyder, Snyder and Snyder Jr., 1980; Weber, 1971). As significant adults in the development of the young day care child, day care teachers' relations with each other create the climate for children's acting, valuing, knowing and understanding. Teachers' relations with each other have further influence beyond affecting the climate or ambience of the center. For in their interactions with each other, teachers have the opportunity to affirm or ignore, assist or inhibit, facilitate or threaten each other's teaching, and thereby influence the nature of the children's experiences within the center. Since Rosehill teachers spend a large proportion of their workday with other teachers and children beyond their own small group, their relations with each other are a significant dynamic within the center. In the following discussion, these teachers' interactions with each other are examined in order to give further insight into their influencing of children's individual and social experience.

Interaction as Peers

Throughout the child's day at Rosehill, these teachers engage in a great deal of spontaneous informal conversation with each other. These spontaneous relations are primarily peer relations, relations with a social basis, the sheer enjoyment of being with one another. Teachers' informal conversations are most numerous during times when they share child care responsibilities in the same space, namely, early and late care, outdoors, and during the children's nap. As these teachers share in responsibilities and enjoy the companionship of each other, they model companionship and mutual respect, and as role models, influence the children's social learning. Further, these amiable relations provide an informal pleasant ambience which allows the children to feel comfortable and secure enough to initiate interactions with other children and adults.

Interaction as Professionals

Rosehill teachers have more skill in relating as peers than as professional colleagues. More specifically, these teachers rarely make decisions together or coordinate their work with children during times when they are in the same space. Further, they lack skill in assisting and facilitating each others' teaching. Just as teachers are the fulcrum for much of children's action, so too, the director's role is pivotal to teachers' actions. Rosehill's Director, Kate, is a skilled administrator but is not an educator. As Director, Kate remains separate from the day to day flow of activity and interaction of children and teachers. She neither observes nor participates and thus has limited data to interpret or understand either ongoing happenings or the total context at Rosehill. Kate maintains an individualistic manner of relating in her many spontaneous conversations with teachers. In the early morning, she has long conversations with Pam, and delegates responsibility to Pam to 'pass on' to the other teachers (for example, rearrangement of the Big Room, cleaning and decorating in preparation for visitors, scheduling vacations). Since Anne also is at Rosehill in the early morning, Kate also converses with her, but with less frequency and intimacy than with

Pam. In the afternoon as Dana washes snack items in the kitchen, Kate often visits with her. Kate's conversations with Barb, Gary and assistant teachers are cordial but not frequent. Given the lengthy administrative agenda of most weekly staff meetings, Kate and the teachers rarely discuss the daily teaching learning'process during these meetings. As Director, Kate neither provides a structure nor does she expect the teachers to develop a time where they could regularly meet to plan together, to review ongoing events together, or to brainstorm together about possible teaching strategies. And without explicit expectations or structure for this type of collaboration, Rosehill teachers tend to function independently. And joint decision making (for example, choosing to walk to a park for the morning or outlining unit theme topics for a month) occurs ad hoc during their conversations in early care or the children's nap period. With Kate's separation from the daily lived experience of teachers and children, her dependence on Pam's skill as unofficial supervising teacher becomes central to these teachers' relations with each other.

Though Pam has refused Kate's offer to assume the roles of Assistant Director and supervising teacher, Kate and all staff members relate to Pam as if she were in those roles. No one, including herself, questions Pam's authority. Yet in the day to day flow of events, Pam organizes her activities as an individual and not as a team member. Though she does take responsibility for the physical maintenance of the center and scheduling of the teachers' work, she does not take responsibility to guide the functioning of the other teachers. And though Kate delegates authority to Pam, Pam does not delegate responsibility to other teachers. When asked about her role at Rosehill, Pam expresses ambivalence:

CSK: I've noticed that it is usually you that changes materials or opens new areas. Why?

Pam: Otherwise things wouldn't be set up for the children.

CSK: It seems as if you and the other teachers function as if you are supervising teacher. Is this role explicit?

Pam: Not really; we've never talked about it together. But nothing would happen if I didn't do things. Like circle time. On some days I wait around to see if any teacher will begin circle; and I end up doing it each day.

CSK: Do you think maybe Kate considers you to be supervising teacher. I notice she shares more information with you and requests that you do more jobs.

Pam: Right; but when she asked me to be her assistant I said

> no . . . yet she does give me extra responsibilities. You know, sometimes I wonder . . . maybe everyone talks about me behind my back. For Kate does give me more responsibility. . . .

Pam's ambivalence regarding her leadership role is evident during transition periods at Rosehill. The two morning transition periods that involve several teachers and large numbers of children occur between early care and circle and between activity period and group time. Daily Pam decides when to clean up early care materials and to begin circle. Teachers neither decide together when to end early care nor does Pam assume leadership to direct them. Rather she quietly tells children in one or two areas to begin cleaning up and come to the circle rug; then she begins circle with these few children. As Pam leads circle activities, other teachers either assist in cleaning up materials or continue to prepare their own materials for activity period. As Pam begins circle activities, several children aimlessly roam about the room and others begin putting away materials. The transition between activity period and group time has similar patterns as each teacher begins to clean her/his area without any coordinated scheduling.

In summary, these teachers' amiable relations with each other provide an informal pleasant environment in which the children feel secure enough to initiate many activities. Further, the teachers' peer relations with each other model mutual respect and companionship. But these same teachers miss opportunities for many additional social learning experiences when they do not coordinate their teaching and ignore rather than assist or guide each other's teaching.

Understanding Teachers' Emphasis of Children's Individual and Social Experiences

Very young children need both individual and social learning experiences, and at Rosehill, both individual and social experiences take place. However, the findings from this field study give evidence that Rosehill teachers' actions predominantly lean toward an individual learning emphasis, even within many social situations. We have seen this individualistic orientation in four areas: first, teachers' arrangement of environment; second, teachers' interactions with the children; third, the observed children's actions that are allowed and/or encouraged; and fourth, teachers' interactions with other teachers.

Several possible reasons can be suggested tentatively to understand these observed teachers' actions. My understanding of the dynamics involved in their use of environment is based on four sources: (i) my extended observation; (ii) teacher explanations of events; (iii) teachers' personal histories; and (iv) my own personal and professional history as it intersects with the above. Some of the observed teacher action is intentional, such as Anne's strictness originating from her stated goal that children need to learn to be obedient and to respect adult authority. Other teacher action is unintentional. For example, Dana conscientiously makes certain that her children have a variety of new materials to use on the stage each week. However, given her lack of understanding of children's developmental levels, many of her choices are too difficult for the children, who become frustrated and either compete against each other for her assistance or roam aimlessly about the room. Dana unwittingly chooses materials that result in recurrent management problems.

In the following I will discuss possible reasons for these teachers' emphasis of children's individual and social experiences: four characteristics of the Rosehill teachers — (i) teachers' personal history; (ii) teachers' personal needs; (iii) teachers' educational assumptions; and (iv) teachers' level of pedagogical skill and knowledge; three characteristics of the Rosehill schooling process — (i) maintenance and lesson preparation needs; (ii) group management needs; (iii) the given environment at Rosehill, and finally, the children's actions.

Characteristics of Rosehill Teachers

Teachers' personal history

Anne's *rule implementation* pattern delineates most clearly this intersection of personal history and teacher child interaction. Anne's most frequent interactions with children involve rule implementation, and she sees her main goal as making certain that her children are ready for school. Anne defines readiness in terms of compliance to authority and rule adherence. Frequently Anne speaks to me about her five years of teaching in Poland where authoritarian teaching was a given. Her ethnic community within her son's parochial school appears to be congruent with her educational experiences in Poland. Anne frequently confides in me that she sees most of her day as mere babysitting while the children play. And to the outside observer, Anne seems distracted during most of the day; her relationships with the children primarily are reactive. The one time she is totally involved with the children is when she enthusiastically sings with the children in group periods. Knowing that

Anne loved to perform in song and dance as a youth and young teacher in Poland, one wonders if Anne's singing at Rosehill is one aspect of her American teaching that she finds congruent with her past history.

Similarly, Dana's personal history no doubt is interwoven with her schooling actions, which clearly are tilted toward individual experiences. Dana maintains social distance in her relations with adults and children. Unlike the other teachers, she does not initiate *physical intimacy* with the children. Whereas other teachers use the playground to relate spontaneously to one another as peers, Dana usually maintains a solitary stance. In her environmental arrangement, Dana structures group activities for individual performance and chooses activity period materials that involve individually focused activities. Dana's personal life seems a consistent analogue to the individual emphasis of her schooling actions. She is an only child, who as an adult chooses to live alone and to travel abroad alone.

Similar personal histories no doubt assisted Rosehill teachers in feeling comfortable with each other and in providing topics for their many informal conversations. For example, Barb, Tina and Gary occasionally share memories of their experiences in Catholic high schools. And since her first days at Rosehill, Barb is able to have many spontaneous exchanges with teachers. Barb's ease in relating seems at least partially related to the intersection of her personal-social life and that of other teachers. Barb and Gary were in the same community college classes six years earlier. She and Tina are both recently married. Like Anne, Gary and Tina, she lives in the southern part of the city and is from a large Catholic family. In contrast, two teachers that had been hired the previous summer were never accepted by Rosehill teachers and chose not to remain at the center more than two months. One of these teachers was a woman in her early fifties with grown children. The other teacher was young, but she was shy, from a northern suburb, and dressed more formally than did the Rosehill teachers.

Teachers' personal needs

Rosehill teachers frequently gather together and informally converse with each other during Early Care and outdoor play periods. As mentioned, they are available but not focused on the children. With no official time off periods during their long work day, these teachers seem to use these times to relax and relate to each other as peers. This personal need for release time is similar to these teachers' management decisions based on personal preferences to do what is easiest.

With minimal involvement during early and late care, these

teachers have a reactive stance in their redirection of children's misbehavior. This reactive stance, whether for *rule implementation* or *conflict resolution*, seems to be at least partially explained in terms of the ease in management when using this method. That is, when all teachers react to children's misbehavior with the same rules given in slogan manner, children quickly learn adult expectations and both conflict resolution and rule adherence are 'quick and easy' to implement. (Whether what 'works in the short run' is the best method a teacher can use for young children 'in the long run' is a separate question.)

Teachers' educational assumptions

During frequent informal and formal conversations with me, teachers shared their rationale for use of the environment and their understanding of the meaning and purpose of observed events at Rosehill.

Different educational assumptions among Pam, Anne, and Barb partially explain their differences in *shared participation* in children's play. Pam speaks of her active involvement with children as being her way of helping the children's ability to focus. In contrast, Barb always refuses children's request for her to play with them. Barb explains to me: 'When the children ask me to play with them, I feel as if they're clinging to me, and by my agreeing, I'd be supporting their dependency. . .' Though Anne agrees to play with children when they ask her, her initial gesturing and subsequent distraction in participating suggests her lack of valuing the learning potential of these play experiences.

> *Anne:* During early care I just baby-sit. For in early care it's free and not a learning time. But in the Yellow Room it is a work period, where children learn to be responsible. . . .

Pam, Barb, and Anne are quick to give their rationale for providing *physical intimacy* with the children. Both Pam and Barb observe that they see nurturance as one of their most important roles. Barb comments on the children's need for belonging and Pam notes the emotional support children receive through lap sitting and hugging. On the other hand, Anne speaks of showing the children that she loves them through physical intimacy, and in this way, reinforcing their obedience.

> *Anne:* I think it is important for me to say 'I love you', to hug and to kiss, because I am strict. And the children need to

> know that 'she can love too' — that 'I'm being good and I get a hug for it'.

Anne speaks of physical intimacy as one of her ways of achieving control.

During interviews each teacher described each child in their group, in terms of child's strengths, weaknesses, and the teacher's goal for the child's continuing growth and development. Repeatedly all four teachers emphasize their desire for their children to develop independence and successful achievement of task mastery.

> *Pam:* Denise needs help in beginning her own task and then staying with it. . . . Jimmy enjoys being a baby and needs to be more self sufficient. . . . Ronnie has made dramatic progress in following directions. Now he needs to sharpen his letter recognition skills for kindergarten next fall. . . . Jill needs to be less dependent on Rachel. . . .

These teachers' dominant patterns of *assistance* of individual children's task mastery and their *praising* individual accomplishments reflects these educational goals of fostering independence and individual achievement.

Teachers also were asked to explain how they viewed the meaning and purpose of early care and activity period, and each activity area within their classroom. All four teachers speak of striving to create an early care environment similar to a home environment in which children are free to '. . . do what they want in their own way'. The large amount of materials and the individually focused nature of the materials used in early care reflect this educational perspective. It contrast to their view of early care, Pam, Barb and Anne view materials provided in activity period in terms of fostering both children's individual and social development. They speak of blocks and housekeeping as areas that are '. . . good for social . . . where children work together to make something . . . are sharing materials'. Art materials and table toys are depicted as providing opportunities for '. . . fostering independence, creativity, and fine motor development'. In contrast to Pam, Barb, and Anne, Dana has primarily an individual perspective. She speaks of housekeeping as stimulating imagination, blocks as fostering an understanding of mathematical relations and shelf items on the stage as encouraging math skills or letter recognition.

Looking at these teachers' view of early and late care helps in understanding the dynamics involved in their reactive redirection patterns. All four teacher speak of early and late care as a time in which 'kids control', separate from 'school time'. Pam comments: 'I don't interfere unless someone is hurting someone else or it is not safe'.

Dana: 'I wouldn't step in if the children are involved', and Barb: 'We just go with the wind — I mean we just really hang loose'. No one sees early and late care as a time for guiding children's activity. Children are on their own in a manner similar to these teachers' view of a 'homelike atmosphere'. Teacher *support of children's interactions* occurs primarily during activity period; then teachers are focused on the children, for they view this as 'school time'.

> *Pam:* In activity period, I expect every child to use materials correctly. And I have a specific plan as to what I want the children to be learning.

Teachers' level of pedagogical skill and/or knowledge

Repeated observations demonstrate that to facilitate social learning experiences demands a high level of pedagogical skill and knowledge which Rosehill teachers often lack.

These teachers' lack of pedagogical skill is involved in their actions during early and late care. Pam, Anne, Barb, and Dana provide few materials that invite spontaneous social interaction among children during the six hours of early and late care. Similarly, they often are not aware of the frequent spontaneous social interaction among the children. Though in interviews they espouse 'educational theory' to indicate an understanding of social needs of the children, in practice their provisioning and involvement are minimal.

Pam is the only teacher skilled in varied *shared participation* experiences with the children. Pam skillfully participates in spontaneous play activities with children. Further she skillfully guides individual children's participation in group stories and discussions, such that individual contributions add to the flow of the group process. In this *shared participation*, children learn to collaborate together and experience perspective taking. Though Pam is exceptionally skillful in these activities with children, she is unable to facilitate the other teachers' growth in these areas. Barb, who is a new teacher at Rosehill, occasionally asks Pam for advice. Pam invariably reassures Barb, 'You're doing fine', but does not suggest teaching strategies or invite Barb to observe her own approach. Kate the Director, as we have seen is similarly not involved.

These teachers primarily are bystanders and not participants in the children's experiences. When in fact children engage in pro-social interaction, teachers usually are neither involved nor observing. Were teachers to be more actively involved in children's experiences, they could facilitate greater social learning — through modeling, clarifying, suggesting, questioning, adding materials, or merely providing a stabilizing presence for the children's involvement.

A teacher need not be always totally immersed as a full participant to be an effective facilitator; rather they can move in and out of the children's involvement to extend, clarify, expand or reinforce the children's play. In this study, this moving in and out of children's play is termed facilitative intervention, and Pam is the only teacher observed in facilitative intervention. Both early education theory and research emphasize this need for teachers to circulate from individual to individual and from group to group — to enter into the middle of children's action in order to provide continuity and extension of children's learning (Hymes, 1968; Isaacs, 1972 and 1974; Schweinhart and Weikart, 1980; Snyder, Snyder and Snyder Jr., 1980; Weber, 1971).

This need for Rosehill teachers' facilitative intervention is most obvious in the housekeeping area. Though they speak of this area as being valuable for giving children opportunities to 'take on familiar roles', Rosehill teachers usually have the area closed, and when it is available, teachers remain distant from the area.

There is consensus among child development and early education theorists, that social role playing is a central avenue for young children's mastery of their everyday experiences and relations (Erikson, 1950; Isaacs, 1966; Krown, 1974; Piaget, 1972; Smilansky, 1968; Weber, 1971). Loevinger (1977) notes that in Erikson's theory of play, he makes explicit two of Freud's basic principles: the principle of mastery through active repetition of what one has experienced more passively, and the principle that schemas can be transposed from one realm to another. Interpersonal schemas can serve as a model and impetus for intrapersonal schemas.

> The three realms of the child's life are those of play and toys, of real relations with others, and of his own body. A problem in any one of the realms can be reenacted in the others via a transposition of the scheme. Optimally this is the child's means of planning, experimenting and growing. (p. 375)

Piaget (1972) argues that it is through repeated interactions with peers that young children learn to take another's perspective, and dramatic play with peers provides an excellent vehicle for this decentering process. As they daily ignore children's spontaneous social role play, and provide minimal role play props, Rosehill teachers give evidence of their lack of understanding and valuing of the social learning that emerges from social role play.

Child care in collectivist settings as in Russia, China, or the kibbutz in Israel demonstrates that young children's social skill development is dependent upon clear *adult expectations* (Bettleheim, 1969; Bronfenbrenner, 1970; Kessen, 1975; Sidel, 1972). Teachers in these child care centers explicitly encourage children to help each other, and it is common to see very young children spontaneously assisting and comforting one another. In contrast, Rosehill teachers are skilled in assisting the children in self care skills and task completion; yet seem unaware of their option to encourage nearby children, competent in the needed skill, to assist their peers. In turn, Rosehill children rarely assist each other.

Similarly, Rosehill teachers seem unaware of their many opportunities to incorporate children into routine maintenance operations in order that children experience social responsibility. Routine maintenance operations such as preparing for meals and naps are basic components in early education. In these tasks teachers can structure social learning experiences in which young children can have a contributing role in the maintenance of their classroom process. At Rosehill, Barb and Pam do initiate cooking experiences for lunch or snack, and Anne asks children to set the table for snack. However none of these teachers structures these experiences with an overall plan in which each child regularly participates. Were Rosehill teachers to focus on fostering children's social responsibility, additional routine operations could be incorporated into the children's daily schooling (for example, folding cot covers, watering plants, washing tables after projects). Again, reports from early education in collectivist settings indicate that productive work such as tending the garden or folding bed quilts can be an integral part of school so that even the youngest child has a contributing role in society (Bronfenbrenner, 1970; Chan, 1975; Sidel, 1972).

A final area in which Rosehill teachers demonstrate a lack of pedagogical skill and knowledge is in their patterns of *conflict resolution*. These teachers frequently use a developmental frame of reference in explaining the meaning and purposes of observed events. For example, when Pam and Barb discuss their rationale for giving and receiving affection, it is evident that they view themselves as significant others with regard to children's emotional development. However, none of these teachers seem to be aware that the years from three to five are crucial years for conscience formation — that young children's conscience is very accessible to influence — and in their relations with children, teachers are significant others in children's internalization of prohibitions and ideals (Damon, 1983; Erikson, 1950; Freud, 1960; Honig, 1985a and 1985b; Katz, 1984; Snyder, Snyder, and Snyder, Jr.,

1980). Accompanying a discussion of conflicts, children can learn to put themselves in another's place, to have empathy for another, or in Piagetian terms, to 'decenter'. This decentering is the basis of Piaget's (1965) claim that social conflict facilitates cognitive growth. Once desires and intentions are made explicit, conflicts also can function to assist children in learning to jointly find solutions to problems. To value this use of conflict as curriculum for social learning, teachers first need to understand the importance of focused observation accompanied by interpretation of the language of children's actions. Then they can understand the projects children are working on, can predict potential disputes, and/or can intervene to assist children's comprehension and skill in dealing with disputes.

Characteristics of the Rosehill Schooling Process

Teachers' maintenance and lesson preparation needs

Pam and Anne speak of using early care to complete maintenance tasks and all four teachers explain that they use part of early care to prepare materials for activity period and group time, the two activity segments they think of as 'school time'. And in the day to day, these teachers involvement in either maintenance tasks or material preparation often results both in children being completely on their own without any *teacher support*, and in teachers maintaining a reactive stance in their *conflict resolution* and *rule implementation*. Pam comments that '... early care is partially for convenience, for the children come in staggered hours and we need to help with breakfast and do other jobs'. And occasionally Pam uses this part of the day for tasks such as putting new name tags on children's cubbies or cleaning an art cabinet. Anne comments that in early care '... we do lots more than just sit with the children ... like clearing the breakfast tables and fastening the kids' jackets'.

Teachers' management needs

Teacher comments, my inferences from observations, and my own professional experiences suggest that these teachers' choice of predominantly individually focused materials during early care is based partially on ease in teacher management of a large number of very small children.

When materials offer multiple ways of use by more than one young child, the likelihood of disputes among children increases. The unit block and housekeeping area of the Big Room are these types of areas that invite spontaneous groupings of children; these areas most often are closed and teachers' ease in management seems to be partially the reason. Pam also comments that when the entire Big Room is open during early care, children race about and '. . . it is more difficult for us to see what the children are doing'. When Barb explains her understanding of the center's first choice policy, she states that this material use '. . . avoids or easily manages the children's fights with each other.'

The given environment at Rosehill

Some aspects of Rosehill's physical space are fixed components of the center, and thus limit teachers' choices. Rosehill operates within a church that does not have enough space for individual classrooms. Thus the Big Room serves multiple uses for several teachers and a large number of young children — for eating, napping, early and late care, and activity period and group time. This fact, that each teacher must share a large space with other teachers and many children, sets limits on teachers' choices of environmental arrangement. Similarly, the large amount of permanent outdoor playground equipment is a given. Teachers could choose to add balls, jump ropes, sand box toys or other portable equipment to this given, but this teacher initiative is not required.

The given environment at Rosehill facilitates frequent teacher relations with each other. That is, use of a church building requires these teachers to spend a large part of each day in the same space together. As they share the same space, these teachers frequent conversations offer an opportunity for them to relax during their work day which has no official time off periods.

As mentioned, these teachers neither coordinate their schooling actions nor give each other feedback. This lack of effective team teaching partially stems from there being no structured time in this center for teachers to gather together to make decisions or review happenings together. In addition, there is no effective leadership to guide this needed team teaching.

Children's action

Just as teachers' actions influence children's activity, so too children's actions affect teachers' activity. This dialectic is seen most clearly in Pam's evolving use of unit blocks. For the first four observation months, children rarely were able to use unit blocks, and when they did, their structures were simple clumps or towers typical of much younger children. Then during the fourth observation month, a new assistant, Lisa, was responsible for the block area during activity period. Daily Lisa participated with the children until they gradually were able to build elaborate structures on their own. Pam frequently praised Lisa and the children's block constructions, and Pam seemed to learn new possibilities of block use from her observations. When she was responsible for the housekeeping-block area two months later, each day, Pam only had unit blocks available, and she increasingly shared in the children's involvement. During a spontaneous conversation with me Pam commented:

> At Rosehill all the teachers always have hated blocks and housekeeping, for they always demanded so much clean up. But now that the children have experience with blocks, their buildings are fantastic! And since Lisa put labels on the block shelving, putting blocks away has become a sorting game.

Earlier in the year, in formal interviews, all four teachers had given many educational purposes for block play; yet none became involved in this area in their day to day practice. Once Pam was able to view the children's growth in their involvement with Lisa, she seemed to put into practice her formerly stated theory.

When teachers are focused on young children's involvement, they often can extend or enrich this involvement by adding or changing materials, rearranging furniture, or changing the schedule of activity segments. Because these teachers often are not directly focused on the children's activity, they frequently miss opportunities to enrich or extend the children's involvement. Of the four observed teachers, Pam seems able to alter her action based on her observations of the children. When children developed an elaborate zoo and began to role play in the block area, Pam extended the length of activity period so that the children could continue playing. Similarly, if the children seemed exceedingly restless during early care, Pam occasionally shortened early care and began the next activity earlier than usual. A further example was observed when Pam had moved a circular table but left the circle of chairs in the front area of the Big Room one morning before the children arrived. When the circle of chairs remained on the third day I asked Pam to explain her rationale for this new arrangement:

> When I left the chairs there on Monday, I noticed that several children gathered together and chatted there, and then they

> even began singing fingerplays as if it were group time. I felt it was interesting and so I decided to keep it like this for the remainder of the week.

To achieve clarity, I have discussed these eight factors involved in these teachers' arrangement of environment separately. Yet as is evident in the discussion, more than one of these dynamics may occur at the same time and often they are reflexively inter-intertwined. For example, the arrangement of the Big Room in early care meets teachers' needs for maintenance, their personal needs for release time, their need for ease in management, and it reflects their view of the meaning of early care. The reflexivity of the dynamics involved in these teachers' environmental arrangement is represented in the structural model in figure 11.

Conclusion

Within their daily experiences at Rosehill, children are developing knowledge, expectations, practices and values. Regardless of whether their teachers' actions are intentional or unwitting, the result may well be the same in terms of the meanings children take from their teachers' actions. Day care teachers provide both individual and social learning experiences in which day care children gain knowledge, practices and values. For example, in individual learning experiences, children learn to identify their own name and learn to autonomously choose their own materials and activities. In social learning experiences, children develop a sense of self in relation to others, learn skills in working with other children, and learn values of assisting and caring for others. Just as individual and social self are complementary, so too, childrens' individual and social learning are interdependent. For example, a child cannot assist another child in tying her/his shoe unless the helping child previously has mastered this skill, and unless the child being helped is accepting of the assistance.

Very young children need both individual and social learning experiences, and at Rosehill, both individual and social experiences take place. However, the findings from this field study presented in this chapter give evidence that Rosehill teachers' actions predominantly lean toward an individual learning emphasis, even within many social situations. We have seen this individualistic orientation in four areas: first, teachers' arrangement of environment; second, teachers' interactions with the children; third, their interactions with each other; and

Figure 11: Understanding Teachers' Emphasis of Children's Individual and Social experiences

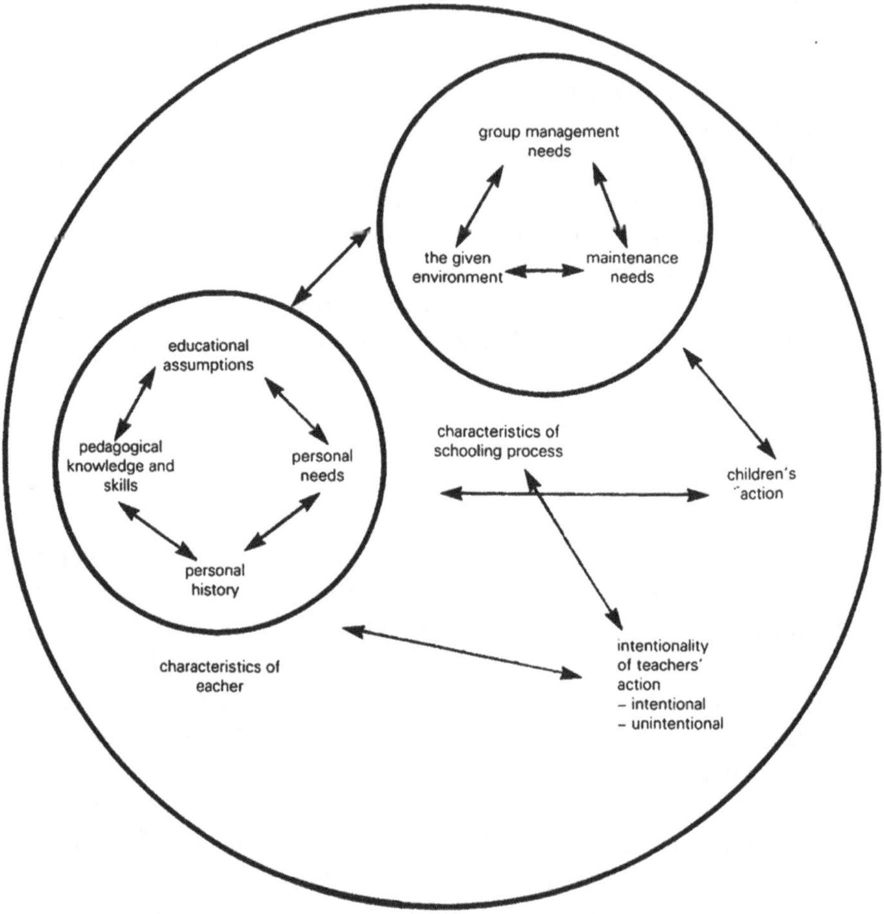

fourth, in the observed children's actions that are allowed and/or encouraged.

First, we have indicated how these teachers' use of space and time predominantly encourages children's individual task involvement. At Rosehill, there are ample space, materials and time for teachers to stimulate both individual and social learning experiences. However, during the six hours of early and late care, teachers choose to have many socially oriented materials and spatial areas closed to the children. When socially oriented materials are available but adults are distant from the area, materials alone do not seem sufficient to enable these children to engage in sustained sequences of social interaction.

Second, we have indicated how these teachers' interactions with children predominantly emphasize individual learning experiences. The two frequent pro-active teacher interaction patterns — *assistance* and *praise* — involve children's individual task mastery and skill in independent functioning. A large proportion of teacher-child interaction is reactive, in response to children's misbehavior. And in their redirection of children's misbehavior, teachers ignore the context of children's misbehavior and focus on children's learning to function independently through internalization of adult directives. Given these teachers' lack of focused involvement during early and late care, teachers miss many opportunities to facilitate children's social learning. They are a *stabilizing presence* only during the one-hour activity period. Only Pam is skilled in shared *participation* and *facilitative intervention* — two effective teaching strategies to guide children's social learning. When children spontaneously engage in pro-social interaction, teachers most frequently are not directly observing these activities, and thus are not available to reinforce or guide the children's social experience.

Third, we have seen how these teachers relate to each other as peers yet teach the children as individuals, even when they work in the same space and activity period with the same children. As a result of this individualistic stance, these teachers miss many opportunities to coordinate their teaching, to give each other feedback and/or assistance, and to review and evaluate daily events at Rosehill. This lack of effective team teaching inhibits children's individual and social learning opportunities.

Fourth, we have described the children's actions that these teachers allow and/or encourage. Most of the children are involved in individual activities during early and late care, and at least half are involved in individual tasks during activity period. Pro-social activities that do occur usually are child initiated. Further, most pro-social activities involve at least one of the sixteen children who have spontaneously developed special friendships. It seems as if the children who have special friends also have more mature social skills than their peers. Since these friendships developed independent of teacher action, the outsider wonders if these sixteen children's social maturity is unrelated to teacher action.

In this chapter, I have tentatively suggested several possible reasons for these teachers' emphasis on individual learning experiences. These explanations are based on my six months of participant observation at Rosehill. They include: (i) teachers' educational assumptions; (ii) teachers' management needs; (iii) teachers' maintenance needs; (iv) the given environment at Rosehill; (v) teachers' personal needs; (vi) teachers' personal histories; (vii) the level of teachers' pedagogical skill and/or knowledge; and (viii) children's actions. In the next chapter I will move beyond the context of Rosehill to ask whether these teachers' actions also are reflective of issues beyond the context of one day care center — issues reflective of the broader American society.

Notes

1 Currently I direct an early prevention/treatment program, the Therapeutic Family Day Care Project, for young children at risk of maltreatment. In my attempt to conceptualize the family day care provider's daily childrearing interactions that make possible quality developmental child care, I began with the nine interaction patterns developed from the field study reported in this book. I have reconceptualized this initial model by separating those interaction patterns that most clearly designate levels of adult involvement and degree of interaction with children. Three levels, different in the amount of adult involvement are possible in competent child care. First, the adult can be in the vicinity of the children but not directly relating to them. This role is termed *stabilizing presence*. Second, an adult can enter the children's activity, interact with them and then leave. This moving in and out of children's experience is termed *facilitative intervention*. And finally, an adult can be a total participant in children's activity, termed *shared participation*. Within these varying levels of involvement are six distinct patterns of adult child interaction, six patterns identified in the Rosehill field study: *physical intimacy*, *spontaneous conversation*, *praise*, *assistance*, *structured turntaking*, and *redirection*.

2 William Damon's (1977) studies are an attempt to obtain an understanding of children's social world on their own terms. He is interested in the changing nature of both children's social behavior (practical knowledge) and children's social conceptions (reflective knowledge). Damon considers conception and action inseparable. He instituted real life situations for children ages four

through twelve years and then, through clinical interviews, he probed what the subjective meaning of the child's overt conduct was. More specifically, he studied two relational concepts, friendship and authority, and two regulational concepts, positive justice of fair distribution and sharing and social regulation (adherence to rules). In his work, Damon depicts the regularity of progressive developmental reorganizations of social behavior and knowledge. Damon reports that children under six years understand friends as '... associates with whom one plays or comes into frequent contact ... there is no sense of liking or disliking the stable traits of another' (p. 153). With increasing age there is movement in children's understanding from an understanding of a material basis for friendship to an understanding of a psychological basis, and an increasing appreciation of the mutuality of friendship.

5 *From Situation to Structure: Relating Field Study Findings to America's Value Tradition of Individualism*

We have seen that Rosehill teachers' schooling acts involve characteristics of the specific teachers, their intentionality, the characteristics of the Rosehill schooling process, and the ongoing children's action. In this chapter, I will move beyond the daily life at Rosehill to examine how these teachers' actions reflect patterns within the larger culture, specifically patterns within America's dominant value tradition of individualism.

Over twenty-five years ago, C. Wright Mills (1959) wrote:

> To formulate any problem requires that we state the values involved and the threat to those values. For it is the felt threat to cherished values — such as those of freedom and reason — that is the necessary moral substance of all significant problems of social inquiry, and as well of all public issues and private troubles. (p. 175)

In the following, America's dominant value tradition of individualism is depicted from an historical perspective in order to ask whether children's experiences in contemporary day care centers are congruent with this value orientation. Using my field study's data and interpretations, I will discuss how Rosehill teachers' actions reflect the dominant value tradition of individualism.

America's Value Tradition of Individualism

The American tradition of individualism encompasses a complex dynamic of behavior, belief, attitudes and values which often are taken for granted aspects of American everyday life, and which encompasses multiple meanings, some of which are contradictory. In describing this tradition, I will propose that individualism is rooted in the interplay of the material conditions of a new nation, in Lockean philosophical perspective, and in the religious, economic and political system of the national social structure. In order to adequately understand the complexity of this value tradition, the evolution it has gone through in different eras of our history is traced. In the following, I will describe how basic themes of individualism became manifest in different historical periods of our nation, beginning with the seventeenth-century settlers and continuing to our present society. In this discussion I will argue that the multiple meanings of individualism are both complementary and contradictory.

My intention here is to provide a brief overview of the changing manifestations of individualism as related to changing social contexts. I assume that understanding any social patterns of society must be done within the specific period in which it exists. Yet at the same time, each specific historical period of a society entails salient trends of past social arrangements; therefore, an understanding of the present demands an historical perspective. This dynamic unity of sociological and historical understanding is clarified by the political scientists, Wood and Wood (1978) in the following statement:

> . . . Historical social contexts are not separate isolated, watertight compartments. Despite fundamental changes and disjunctions, there is always continuity in the form of a residue of the past in the present, of persistent social structures and arrangements and patterns of human conduct. Social history of which ideas, values, and attitudes are an integral part reveals a complex dialectic of continuity and change, of permanence and flux. The Heraclitean river both changes and remains the same. (p. 7)

Seventeenth-Century Beginnings of American Individualism

Americans always have had a more objective basis for individual freedom than any other group of people. After their arrival in America, the Puritans and Pilgrims had a degree of freedom both from the tutelage of the Catholic Church and from feudalism unknown to other seventeenth-century people. Within their struggle for survival, rugged individualism, specifically hard work, self-reliance, and self-determination were nourished by the material conditions of a newly 'undeveloped' frontier country. The exercise of this frontier independence was an integral aspect of settling new land until the end of the nineteenth century.

The first settlers were men and women who came to America to escape religious persecution. As Weber (1958) demonstrates, their Protestant ethic was a key factor in their ability to succeed. For salvation was no longer found in the Catholic Church. Rather, the Calvinist oriented settler believed that an individual's work expressed salvation — that God's grace was to be experienced through an individual's good works. If the settler experienced material success, that success was a 'sign of God's election' (Weber, 1958, p. 115). As Weber notes, 'The faithful then must follow the call by taking advantage of the opportunity' (p. 162). And the vast wilderness of America offered the individual unlimited opportunity to follow God's 'calling'.

Just as the settlers' rugged self-determination was rooted in religious conviction, so too this individualistic orientation stems from their emerging economy and polity, a polity in which economic development often became the governing principle of decision making. When the Puritans sailed to America, they were accompanied by a group of men coming to seek their fortune in a new land. Before landing in America, the Puritans gained the consent of these economic opportunists that together the two groups would establish a settlement where all men had a voice in decision-making. This Mayflower Compact was the beginning polity of a new independent people joined together through common material interests. The philosophers Boggs and Boggs (1974) note: 'The Mayflower Compact is a historic document because it represents the fruit of the first bargaining of working people for political rights in exchange for their contributions in labor' (p. 147). But ironically, these same people, as they established representative governing institutions in a new land where they had religious freedom, let economic self-interest govern their relationships with the Native Americans. In reality, the early settlers' domination and restriction of the Native Americans were not unlike the treatment which had caused the Puritans and Pilgrims to flee Europe.

The life experience of the early settlers in America expressed a valuing of freedom, self-reliance, hard work, and egalitarian political rights prior to the existence of any explicit conceptualization of individualism. The philosophical conceptualization of liberal individualism is attributed to the eighteenth century English philosopher, John Locke (Bell, 1977; DeLone, 1979; Miller, 1967; Wood, 1972). Since the architects of the American Revolution built upon a Lockean scaffold, this philosophical perspective needs to be briefly examined.

Contrary to eighteenth century continental Europe, where property and status were determined by birth, Locke claimed that all individuals are of equal privilege in pursuit of achievement. According to Locke, a person's identity rests on her/his irreducible egoism. His famous tabula rasa tenet — that a person is born a blank slate, upon which sensory impressions are received — became the foundation for empiricist philosophy and later empiricist psychology.

Locke claims that freedom is a function of rational thought; and it is this reason that binds individuals into community. That is, through rational contract — Locke's principle of freedom of contract — civil society exists to enforce individual freedom. This moral primacy of the individual is articulated by the twentieth century economist Daniel Bell (1977), in his explanation of equality of opportunity.

> The principle of equality of opportunity derives from a fundamental tenet of classic liberalism that the individual — not the family, community, or the state — is the singular unit of society, and that the purpose of societal arrangements is to allow the individual the freedom to fulfill his own purposes — by his labor to gain property, by exchange to satisfy wants, by upward mobility to achieve a place commensurate with his talents. (p. 616)

Basic to this understanding of the individual is the question of property. Locke is seen as the earliest and foremost exponent of the liberal conception of property (Hall, 1956; Lukes, 1973; Miller, 1967; Wood, 1972). Locke used the term property both in its original meaning, to designate that which is characteristic to something, and to designate that which one acquires through one's labor. Locke claims that persons have natural rights to private property, and these rights can be traced to the right each person has to her/his own body and thus to the fruits of her/his own labor. As explained by Hall (1956):

> Locke reasoned: In the state of nature each man has an exclusive right to his own body and its free activity. Therefore, he has a right to his own productive labor and its fruit. So far as labor takes something not wanted and makes of it something desirable, it is the laborer's own; he has mixed himself with it. (p. 348)

For Locke, civil society exists to preserve each individual's life, liberty, and property. Individuals are essentially egoistic and private. Reason, or freedom of contract, becomes the bond that unites individuals into a civil society. And the government of this civil society — the public — exists to represent the private interests of the individual. This Lockean philosophical perspective can be seen in the following overview of historical and current manifestations of American individualism.

Manifestations of Individualism in the Eighteenth Century

Whereas the early settlers of the seventeenth century stressed an ethic of personal survival, the eighteenth century Yankee stressed self improvement, an ethic best represented in the writings of Benjamin Franklin. Franklin (1791) emphasized self-discipline, industry, thrift, and the cultivation of reason. Just as Franklin so clearly articulated the American 'protestant ethic', so too his contemporary, Thomas Jefferson, articulated the American 'revolutionary ethic' in the Declaration of Independence, that '... all men are created equal, and possess the inalienable right to life, liberty, and the pursuit of happiness'. This emphasis on egalitarianism became a significant component of individualism. Equal political rights are best exemplified in the equal representation of New England town meetings. But Jeffersonian equality also encompassed equal rights of individuals in pursuit of self-interest, a liberal economic ethic that can in fact contradict the Jeffersonian political ethic, which presupposes a collaborative effort of decision making. DeLone (1979) comments on this inherent contradiction between America's polity and economy: 'The political tradition of rights embraces equality while the economic tradition of prerogatives leads to inequality' (p. 28). Attempts to resolve this political and economic tension can be seen in the equal opportunity movement of the nineteenth century.

Development of Individualism in the Nineteenth Century

In America, equality has been translated into an ethic of equality of opportunity, an ethic which seems to lessen or even obscure the tension between our society's political tradition of equal rights for all individuals and our economic tradition of the individual's right to pursue self-interest, like the accumulation of wealth. Through equality of opportunity, inequities in material conditions of individuals are said to be transformed through equal opportunities for 'fame and fortune'. Yet from the outset, this egalitarian ethic has had dual objectives. In the 1820s and 1830s, Horace Mann seized upon education as the great equalizer of unequal material conditions. Free and universal education was instituted in Massachusetts, and the tradition of our society's focus on both the child as the avenue to resolve social inequities, and on development of the individual through education was initiated. But this was also the time of increased immigration and the increasing need for laborers in the textile and other rapidly growing industries in New England. Universal education offered not only equality of opportunity but an avenue for socialization and control of the 'foreign element', needed as laborers in industry. The timing was propitious for the acceptance of this new ethic of equal opportunity embodied in universal education. Just as the frontier experience within westward expansion was the embodiment of equal opportunity, so too Andrew Jackson, who though orphaned at 13, could become President.

As depicted thus far, the American tradition of individualism embraces the valuing of self-reliance, hard work, and self-improvement, an egalitarian democratic polity, an economy based on the pursuit of self-interest, and an ethic of equality of opportunity. Both the multiplicity of meaning and the internal tensions within this tradition can be seen in patterns of conformity of American citizens in the nineteenth century. America was the first Western nation where social status was not automatically determined by birth. This ambiguity of the status system and the egalitarian value system invited conformity, a conformity that was frequently noted by English and European visitors before and after the Civil War (Lipset, 1967). The sociologist Lipset observes:

> While some Europeans explained American behavior that they found strange — the sensitivity, kindliness, concern for others' feelings, and moral meekness — by reference to the nature of political democracy or the overbearing desire to make money, others saw these traits as consequences of the extreme emphasis on equality of opportunity, the basic American value which they properly regarded as unique. Many argued that this very emphasis on equality, and the constant challenging of any pretensions to permanent high status, has made Americans in all social positions extremely sensitive to opinions of others, and causes status aspirants greater anxiety about the behavior and characteristics indicative of rank than is the counterpart in more aristocratic societies. (p. 90)

Conformity is not necessarily the antithesis of individualism; rather, conformity is one of its many dynamics, dynamics which can be both complementary and contradictory.

The power and complexity of individualism also is seen in the events leading to the Civil War. At the end of the eighteenth century,

Americans were able to win a revolution for independence in the name of egalitarian principles of '... life, liberty, and the pursuit of happiness'. Yet one-quarter of the American population was black, and human rights were denied to this population. As early as in the 1830s, New England intellectuals decried this contradiction and stood for egalitarianism in the Abolition Movement, a primary force bringing the Civil War. Within the Western expansion movement of the mid-nineteenth century, this humanitarian force became linked with economic individualism over the question of who should control Kansas and Nebraska, the small independent farmers or the Southern plantation owners. Just as economic and political interests united in the formation of the Mayflower Compact, these same interests united in the initiation of the Civil War.

As indicated previously, the exercise of may aspects of the value orientation of individualism existed prior to any explicit conceptualization. The term individualism apparently was coined by de Tocqueville to describe America in the 1840s (Rapson, 1967; Wood, 1972). De Tocqueville (1835) claims that democracy breeds individualism:

> Individualism is a mature and calm feeling which disposes each member of the community to sever himself from the mass of his fellows and to draw apart with his family and his friends, so that after he has thus formed a little circle of his own, he willingly leaves society at large to itself ... Egotism blights the germ of all virtue; individualism, at first, only saps the virtues of public life; but in the long run, it attacks and destroys all others and is at length absorbed in downright selfishness. (p. 293)

De Tocqueville and other Europeans used the term individualism with a note of censure, to signify American's emphasis on the individual, defining self as separate and in pursuit of self-interest. By the end of the Civil War, this term individualism had become a common part of American vocabulary but in American popular usage the term usually denoted positive moral sanction. The political scientist Wood (1972) comments on these differences in valuing:

> What has happened, in one sense, is that the popular conception of individualism has transformed de Tocqueville's atomistic society into a moral norm and his concept of privatization into the model of individual liberty. (p. 128)

The moral primacy of the individual is congruent with the laissez-faire capitalism and the burgeoning industrialization of the late nineteenth century. The frontier ethic of hard work and self improvement developed into an ethic of success for many entrepreneurs. The art of making money was mastered by businessmen like Vanderbilt, Swift, and Armour. Given the country's rich resources, the availability of cheap immigrant labor, and the expanding economy, the free enterprise system flourished. Americans embraced the economic theory of Adam Smith, the eighteenth century Scottish professor of moral philosophy. For Smith (1776), liberty rests on one's individual right to enjoy the free play of market forces. Society consists of the interaction of private interests; therefore, self-interests become the principle of cohesion. This market model of society, where relations are based on exchange of interests, and interests are defined in terms of property, was a logical extension of Lockean political theory.

The Development of Individualism in the Twentieth Century

In the twentieth century, the industrial growth of nineteenth century laissez-faire capitalism developed into large competitive corporate bureaucracies. Whereas material success had reflected the Protestant ethic of hard work, thrift, and self-reliance in the eighteenth and nineteenth centuries, success and the competitive pursuit of profit became ends in themselves in the twentieth century. The modern historian Christopher Lasch (1979) observes:

> The nineteenth century cult of success placed surprisingly little emphasis on competition. It measured achievement not against the achievements of others but against the abstract ideal of discipline and self-denial. At the turn of the century, however, preachments on success began to stress the will to win. The bureaucratization of the corporate career changed the conditions of self-advancement. The captain of industry gave way to the confidence man, the master of impressions . . . The pursuit of wealth lost the few shreds of moral meaning that still clung to it . . . the victory over your competitors, that alone retained the capacity to instill a sense of self-approval. (pp. 57–9)

Lasch is describing characteristics of the management level of the corporate enterprise. The realm of corporate management was initiated by Taylor in order to gain control and organization of labor through the use of scientific methods in order to maximize profits (Braverman, 1974). With 'Taylorism', decision-making and conception of the labor process was given to a new coterie of managers and engineers. Now conception was separated from implementation and increasingly, work became alienated labor. As early as 1929, Dewey articulated the contradiction embedded in the tradition of individualism and a competitive corporate bureaucracy.

> It is not too much to say that the whole significance of the older individualism has now shrunk to a pecuniary scale and measure . . . The virtues that are supposed to attend rugged individualism may be vocally proclaimed, but it takes no great insight to see that what is cherished is measured by its connection with those activities that make for success in business conducted for personal gain. Hence, the irony of the gospel of 'individualism' in business conjoined with suppression of individuality in thought and speech. One cannot imagine a bitterer comment on any professed individualism than that it subordinates the only creative individuality — that of mind — to the maintenance of a regime which gives the few an opportunity for being shrewd in the management of monetary business. (pp. 90–1)

For workers in the twentieth century, the self-determination and self-improvement of individualism were possible only through one's family life. Increasingly men began to conceive of work as merely a means to an end — a satisfying personal life within the family. The negative opposite of man's work place became the home, the prized refuge separate from the sphere of production. Within the private sphere of the family, workers, especially the unskilled and semi-skilled, began seeking personal identity and fulfillment that was no longer available in their work within their homes. Zaretsky (1973) observes: 'The family became the major sphere of society in which the individual could be foremost — it was the only space that proletarians "owned"' (p. 61). Women became the guardians of the home. As previously discussed in chapter 2, the romanticized role of women as homemaker continues to be central to our society's lack of support for day care.

Emerging from the affluent women's clubs of the nineteenth century, the home economics field was formally organized in 1899 and added impetus to the growth of 'domesticity'. Laslett (1974) notes:

> The home economics movement can be seen as developing a modern ideology for the American family in general and for the women in it in particular. The goal of scientific home management and efficiency and use of educational institutions to achieve this end through the training of girls to be modern

> homemakers, emphasized traditional views of women's place in the home and reinforced the sanctity and privacy of the individual family. (p. 108)

The popular woman's magazine *Good Housekeeping* focused on housekeeping as a science, and was the unofficial arm of the home economics movement (Lasch, 1976). State universities instituted home economics departments, which in later decades, developed training programs for nursery school teachers (for example, the University of Iowa and the University of Missouri).

The pre-World War I Progressive Era, with its mushrooming corporate bureaucracies and its idealization of the family, added new meaning to individualism. The egalitarian pattern of social reform established in the Jacksonian period became institutionalized and professionalized in this period. The 1880s and 1890s were decades characterized by a huge wave of immigrants who expanded the ranks of the poor in large urban slums. Progressive social reformers developed an array of services for these impoverished immigrant families. A new coterie of professional experts — social workers, probation officers, and teachers — and new institutions, the juvenile court system and neighborhood houses — emerged to offer equal opportunity to impoverished children. Social inequities were to be reduced through assistance to individual children in order to improve their chances for the future. DeLone (1979) observes: 'The actual achievement of equality was deferred to the next generation through the focus on children and equal opportunity' (p. 36).

The institution where many of the beliefs and practices of twentieth century individualism were expressed was the public school, which expanded tremendously during this time. Reformers claimed that social progress in the urban slums could be achieved through Americanization of poor immigrant children in the schools. Schools adopted the new discoveries of psychology and the scientific management of the business world. Now intelligence testing offered explanations of individual differences. With instruments to measure individual differences, new efficiency could be brought into the schools. The curriculum was standardized and divided into small sequential units. Through testing, children's potential was measured, they were tracked by ability, and their achievement was measured. Modern management techniques led to the creation of new school specialists: school nurses, school counselors, school social workers, industrial arts teachers, and home economics teachers. The science of instructional management brought about a differentiated curriculum allowing for individualized instruction. With tracking by ability and achievement tests, motivation for learning commonly was based on competition, or as Henry (1963) describes 'the wringing of success from somebody's failure' (p. 296). Increasingly, this competitiveness, standardization, differentiation and individualization in schools mirrored the hierarchically organized business world. DeLone (1979) argues that even cooperation took on new meaning in schools, a meaning that directly related to the work world.

> Cooperating no longer meant mutual relationships of equals but complementary interdependency of differentially ranked individuals in a hierarchy. Individuality was to be achieved through cooperation, and an individual's 'uniqueness' was increasingly defined by the role one played in the productive system. (p. 60)

Americans have viewed education as the great equalizer of differences in material wealth. All children may attend school to get an equal start for achieving personal success. Yet recent observational studies of everyday classroom happenings give evidence that education may *not* be the great equalizer (Keddie, 1971; Nash, 1973; Sharp and Green, 1975). These studies indicate that children's social origins have tremendous influence on their schooling experience, and as a result, on their ability to get needed credentials for economic success. The data in these studies show how teachers' expectations, teacher-child communication patterns, and teachers' arrangements of knowledge vary according to the social class of the children. Rather than serve as an equalizer, schooling also operates as a sifter in sending students into an already stratified work world (Bowles and Gintis, 1976). Levin (1983) comments on these contradictory elements of schooling:

> . . . The schools are situated within the state and are characterized by the same internal contradictions between the demands for popular and egalitarian reforms and the pressures of capital accumulation. That is, the schools are in opposition to themselves in being organized to satisfy the needs of two masters with conflicting goals. This internal contradiction is mediated by school policies which represent an attempt to meet the needs of both the democratic and egalitarian aspects of schooling and the authoritarian and hierarchical ones that are needed for reproducing labor for capitalist firms. (pp. 19–20)

Levin notes that within this internal contradiction schools remain far more equal and provide far more opportunities for advancement than does the workplace.[1]

The above discussion examines the ways in which business and education have given new meaning to America's value tradition of individualism since the beginning of the twentieth century. The following discussion will focus on changes in the exercise of individualism since World War II. This overview is not meant to include all cultural expressions of individualism but manifestations that seem most directly relevant to the lives of young children and their caretakers.

Individual freedom always has been a central component of American individualism. And since the Enlightenment, the discovery and control of this freedom is viewed to be through reason. Within the tradition of individualism, this unity of freedom and reason can be seen in the rational conduct of the Calvinist pioneers, the rational contract of the Lockean political franchise, the utilitarian virtues of Benjamin Franklin, or the therapeutic process of psychoanalysis. Since World War II, social analysts have agreed that, in spite of the celebration of individual freedom in popular psychology, in the literature and arts, in the mass media, and in consumer products, the most notable characteristic of this period is ironically, the lack of individual freedom (Mills, 1959; Fromm, 1955; Riesman, 1950; Lasch, 1979; Zaretsky, 1973). A brief overview of major post World War II trends can clarify this irony.

The post-war years through the 1950s were characterized by a baby boom, increased prosperity, and a housing expansion into sprawling suburbs. There was tremendous popularization of psychology, a psychology stressing individual development, and the crucial importance of the mother-infant bonding and the family in early development. The wide circulation of child rearing manuals and parenting articles in the numerous women's magazines gives evidence of an increased concern over childrearing. Proliferation of the mass media was also characteristic, and the pastime in most homes was watching television. With the growth of the mass media and the advertising industry, appetites became standardized. This standardization was dependent on industrial growth, a growth increasingly dependent upon consumerism of prescribed needs, whether of dishwashers in the 1950s, microwaves of the 1970s or home computers and video recorders of the 1980s.[2] Mills (1959) describes this collapse of individual freedom and reason:

> . . . social, technological, or bureaucratic rationality is not merely a grand summation of the individual will and capacity to reason. The very chance to acquire that will and that capacity seems in fact often to be decreased by it. Rationally organized social arrangements are not necessarily a means of increased freedom — for the individual or for the society. In fact, often they are a means of tyranny and manipulation, a means of

> expropriating the very chance to reason, the very capacity to act as a free man. (pp. 168–9)

Just as earlier English and European visitors called attention to conformity they observed in nineteenth century America, American social scientists of the 1950s warned against the emergence of a new standardized mass conformity (Fromm, 1955; Riesman, 1950).

The pluralism of America's tradition of individualism is evident in the collective efforts within the civil rights and peace movement of the 1960s. In demonstrations in all parts of the country, the egalitarian democratic ethic of equal political rights and equal opportunity, reminiscent of eighteenth century Jeffersonian democracy, was espoused by individuals representing diversity in age, religion and social class. In this decade social legislation created new opportunities for disenfranchized minorities and poor Americans.

The 1960s was a decade of economic prosperity, which allowed politicians to initiate massive federal social programs. Once again the complementary, sometimes contradictory nature of individualism was expressed as prosperity was reflected in new manifestations of individualism. In the late 1960s and 1970s the Human Potential Movement, characterized by the search for self-awareness and personal meaning emerged, celebrating the self. Psychotherapy replaced religion. A 'now' divorced from either the historical past or any concern for the future was emphasized (Jacoby, 1975). Lasch (1979) terms this preoccupation with the self narcissism: 'For the narcissist, the world is a mirror, whereas the rugged individualist say it as an empty wilderness to be shaped to his own design' (p. 10).

In the 1980s, President Reagan, in his sweeping economic reform and dismantling of many social programs from the Roosevelt era of the 1930s to the Kennedy-Johnson period of the 1960s, espoused a return to rugged individualism and the Calvinist work ethic. As many experienced economic decline and embraced the rebirth of an evangelical religion which offered them personal salvation, Reagan's 1984 presidential re-election was a sweeping affirmation of his Lockean understanding of the individual and society. Yet this celebration of the individual once again was accompanied by complementary social reform movements. For example, the 1980s also was a decade marked by a growing anti-nuclear movement. Programs such as quality circles imported from Japanese management stressed the quality of the work environment and undercut the individualistic Taylorism of the early twentieth century. In July of 1985, legions of American and English youth joined the rock stars of the 1960s, 1970s and 1980s, in the 'Live Aid' sixteen-hour benefit concert. Rock stars, many of whom had gained fame with songs exhalting hedonistic exploration and celebration of self, preached 'We are the world . . . we are the children . . .' in their collective effort to raise millions for the famine in Africa.

Conclusion

As indicated earlier, the American tradition of individualism is a complex dynamic of behavior, belief, attitudes and values, encompassing multiple meanings some of which are contradictory. I have attempted to sketch dominant expressions of this tradition within America's society's changing historical contexts. The complexity of this tradition is staggering; yet if individualism is central to much of our society's ideas, knowledge, social practices, and relationships, an attempt to unravel this complexity is warranted. Figure 12 attempts to depict major themes within this tradition. These themes are the psychological dimension, the economic dimension, and the political dimension of America's value tradition of individualism.

Figure 12 provides a framework to summarize some of the strands within this tradition. From our nation's beginning, contradictions have been embedded with the tradition. The seventeenth-century egalitarian polity of the white settlers begun with the Mayflower Compact coexisted with the exploitation of Native Americans in the expropriation of their land. The eighteenth century constitution embraced equality and the balance of power within government as the economic tradition promoted private control and personal gain. In the first half of the nineteenth century, the universal education movement served contradictory goals — to simultaneously socialize laborers to the workplace that maintained inequities and to provide equal opportunity for the self improvement of each citizen. During the latter half of the nineteenth century, the Abolitionists sought freedom for the slaves but could only obtain a united northern force by using the economic interests of northern independent farmers, who were seeking the same land as the southern plantation owners. During this time emerged social reforms focused on the individual; yet the inequities were enlarging as industrialization grew. This same irony is seen in the social reform of the twentieth century Progressive Era, in which reformers focused on individual betterment rather than the combating structural inequities created by the growing corporate pursuit of profit. As the twentieth century progressed, the popular search for personal meaning and individualistic striving was standardized by the advertising industry,

	Psychological Dimension		Economic Dimension		Political Dimension	
	Valuing/Ethics	*Events/Manifestations*	*Valuing/Ethics*	*Events/ Manifestations*	*Valuing/ Ethics*	*Events/ Manifestations*
17th century	rugged individualism — hard work — self reliance — self determination	1.1 material conditions of the frontier Calvinist Protestant ethic Locke's philosophical conception	economic prerogativc to pursue self interests	1.2 forces joined in creating Mayflower Compact expansion of frontier and exploitation of native Americans	democratic ethic of equal political rights	1.3 Mayflower Compact
18th century	self improvement	2.1 writings of Benjamin Franklin	economic tradition of pursuit of self interests	2.2 economic theory of Adam Smith westward expansion	democratic ethic of equal political rights	2.3 writings and polity of Thomas Jefferson American Revolution American Constitution
19th century	reforming the individual	3.1 prison reforms, mental health movement, foundling homes, temperance movement writings of Emerson and Thoreau	economic tradition of pursuit of self interests — increasing competition — increasing profit motive	3.2 laissez-faire capitalism and the emergence of robber barons popularization of Newtonian scientific revolution conflict of independent farmers and So. plantations	democratic ethic ambiguity of the status system ethic of equal opportunity	3.3 immigration and growing industralization Horace Mann-universal education Civil War-freedom of slaves conformity of individuals
20th century	reforming the individual self actualization search for pleasure and personal meaning	4.1 juvenile court system, social work profession, day nurseries, neighborhood houses psychology of Freud and followers, behaviorism, humanistic psychology movement, human potential movement glorification of mother and the family — childhood determinism	success, competition, and the valuing of efficiency economic self interest and the pursuit of profit	4.2 large corporate bureaucracies/ Taylorism standardized mass conformity via consumerism Reagonomics	democratic ethic ambiguity of the status system ethic of equal opportunity	4.3 increased immigration and burgeoning industrialization pragmatism and progressive social reform movement standardized mass conformity, democratization of pursuit of pleasure increased educational institutions extending political franchise to blacks and women

mass media, and increased consumerism.

Within each of the three dimensions depicted in figure 12, themes can be identified that are central to contemporary manifestations of individualism and are continuous with our society's past. These themes include the valuing of individual uniqueness, self reliance and self actualization within the psychological dimension; the ethic of work, success and competition within the economic dimension; and the egalitarian democratic ethic of equal political rights and equal opportunity within the political dimension.

The Relation of this Field Study's Findings to America's Value Tradition of Individualism

If individualism is a dominant social value, can that value tradition be transmitted to very young children in the social childrearing context of day care? In the following discussion, I will present findings from my field study at Rosehill which show that within a social context, day care teacher's emphasis of individual experiences perpetuates the value tradition of individualism. At the same time however, just as our society's value orientation has complex multiple meanings, this pluralism can be seen in these teachers' actions.

Teachers' Emphasis of Individual Experiences

Rosehill teachers' emphasis of individual experiences are related to dominant strands of America's value tradition of individualism. More specifically, these teachers' actions are congruent with the values and ethics of the psychological dimensions of individualism, as presented in figure 12.

Self-reliance and self-determination

Since the time of the seventeenth century early settlers in America, self-reliance and self-determination have been dominant values of our society. Much of Rosehill teachers' arrangement of environment and interaction patterns with children foster the children's development of independence, an emphasis affirming America's valuing of self reliance and self determination. For six hours during early and late care, children primarily are on their own, to 'do what they want in their own way'. The preponderance of individually-focused materials available reinforces this orientation toward independent functioning. This independent functioning is reinforced in teachers' interactions with children. For teachers are quick to assist the children's mastery of routine self care habits and self-selection of play activities, actions teachers frequently praise. Teachers' consistent use of slogans in redirecting the children's misbehavior effectively facilitates children's ability to function independently through internalization of these adult directives. And in fact, these children often are playing on their own, even ending disputes with each other on their own, as adults are either physically or psychologically not focused on the children.

Respecting individual rights

From the architects of the American Revolution to proponents of Reagonomics in the 1980s, Americans have embraced the eighteenth century Lockean philosophical perspective, that a primary rationale of civil society is to preserve the private interests of individuals. This respect for individual rights is reinforced by Rosehill teachers' action. Though classroom space is very limited, children do have their own area ('cubbies') for storage of their toys from home, art papers and clothing. The clearest expression of this valuing of individual rights is the center's first choice policy, which teachers view as giving children the 'right to use materials in their own way' without the need to share with others. Frequently teachers redirect the children's conflicts with the slogan 'play in your own area'. When Pam and Barb describe why they think day care is a good experience for young children, they comment that day care children learn to 'get along with other children'. A central aspect of 'getting along' that is observed in this center is respect of the private interests of each individual.

Self-improvement and self-actualization

Since the colonial period, America's ambiguous status system has been accompanied by the ethic of self improvement, an ethic most clearly articulated in the writings of Ben Franklin and embodied in American heroes like Presidents Andrew Jackson and Abraham Lincoln. With the popularization of psychology in the twentieth century, this ethic often is termed self actualization or self fulfillment.

A large proportion of Rosehill teachers' action fosters children's individual accomplishment and individual achievement, an emphasis affirming America's ethic of self-improvement and self-actualization. As previously noted, teachers provide an abundant supply of individually focused materials that not only foster independence but individual skill mastery. Teachers also provide many materials for individual creative art projects throughout the day, and displays of these art projects are hung on walls and from ceilings throughout the center. Through these art projects, children's self expression is highlighted. The teachers speak of the significance of this art in terms of enhancing the children's sense of self esteem and personal meaning, of '. . . doing your own thing in your own way'.

In their interactions with the children, teachers frequently praise these creative art projects and individual accomplishments in tasks; at the same time however, they do not seem to focus on spontaneously formed group projects. Similarly, teachers are observed assisting children in skill mastery rather than enabling children to help one another. Pam is very skilled in shared participation in activities with the children, and as an observer, I sense that the children experience social learning in these experiences with Pam. Interestingly, when Pam speaks of her purpose in these experiences of shared participation, she stresses her interest in helping individuals learn to focus during early care, and to learn skill mastery during activity period. Dana structures games involving turntaking during group time. Dana speaks of her intent in making certain that individual children develop the basic skills needed for kindergarten. In their interactions, these teachers recurrently stress individual accomplishment, achievement and self-esteem.

Teachers' Emphasis on Social Experiences

Just as the complexities of American individualism encompass social reform movements and democratic egalitarianism, so too these teachers' dominant pull toward individual experiences exists within their alternative, albeit less frequent emphasis on social experiences. This pluralism of teacher action can be seen in the following brief overview of these teachers' orientation to social experiences.

Though ordinarily Rosehill teachers do not focus on or become involved in children's social play experiences, nevertheless, their classroom arrangements do allow children to choose to play together (for example, the housekeeping and unit block area occasionally are available). Further, when Pam, Barb, and Anne describe the purposes of housekeeping and unit blocks, they express their valuing of social learning (for example, 'sharing materials', 'working together to make something'). However, no teacher has the pedagogical skill to enhance children's play in the housekeeping area, and only Pam gives evidence of this skill in the unit block area. Given the lack of teacher facilitation, extended pro-social play in these two areas seldom occurs. Similarly, all teachers have a teacher-directed group time, and speak of this activity period as offering children an opportunity to develop a 'sense of belonging'. Yet only Pam is skilled in directing varied group experiences in which children experience shared enjoyment.

Beyond their use of time and space, Rosehill teachers influence children's social learning through several of their interaction patterns. First, these teachers model mutual respect and companionship in their frequent informal conversations with each other. Second, these teachers engage in many friendly spontaneous conversations with the children, who also are free to engage in spontaneous 'small talk' with their peers throughout most of the day. In these many spontaneous conversations, children gain a sense of companionship and belonging. A final illustration of these teachers' alternative orientation toward social experiences is their frequent giving and receiving of physical affection with the children, for in these experiences, children can develop trust in others and a sense of self-in-relation. These three socially oriented interaction patterns however, are not unique to the teaching profession, but rather are basic components of informal human relationships. And in fact, only one of these patterns — physical intimacy — is an intentional teacher action. The other two, teachers' conversations with each other and with the children, are rooted in the very nature of the day care context. That is, they are basic to humane non-authoritarian relationships and allow a large number of children and adults to get along in a limited amount of space for long periods of time each day.

Conclusion

In this chapter, arrangements within American society that impact the lived experiences of day care teachers and children are discussed in order to explore how day care teachers' actions are connected to these arrangements. I have examined the complexity of America's value tradition of individualism, and have tried to demonstrate its pervasiveness in many areas of Americans' everyday life. Day care critics, most notably President Nixon in his 1971 veto of the Child Development Act, claim that day care will weaken America's individualistic value tradition. However, the findings from this field study point to the myriad ways in which day care teachers perpetuate the value tradition of individualism in their daily childrearing acts.

In the first section of this chapter we have seen that, in the early nineteenth century, Horace Mann and the Massachusetts legislature seized upon education as the vehicle to resolve social inequities through focus on the development of the child, and at the same time, to socialize and control prospective laborers needed for industry. Day care's root and current practices continue this egalitarian tradition that embraces dual objectives. At the turn of the century, Jeffersonian egalitarianism was continued as wealthy women of leisure offered help to poor immigrant families through establishing day cares. And this tradition of social reform continued in the community of Elton, as churches cooperated in the establishment of Rosehill in the early 1970s. During the center's intial years, donations and varied volunteers helped sustain its operations. Currently, the Rosehill Director and Board of Directors continue the center's egalitarian commitment as they enroll equal numbers of low income and middle income children, in spite of the ease with which they could fill enrollment with children from middle income families. As Horace Mann promoted public education as a vehicle to socialize immigrant children to American values, so too, day care teachers at Rosehill are socializing young children to America's value tradition of individualism.

Notes

1 In their interview study of working class men, Sennett and Cobb (1972) illustrate the insidious effect of this ethic of personal achievement through educational credentialing and accompanying economic success. Given the equal opportunity ethic, workers assume that each person has the right to transcend one's social origins through personal ability. If the worker is not economically successful, he accepts personal responsibility for his social position, a position he assumes must be due to his own inadequacy. If a worker does in fact achieve some success, his success costs him the loss of fraternity of his fellow workers, for his success signifies the failures of his friends.

2 The book, *Habits of the Heart Individualism and Commitment in American Life* (1985) documents the valuing and manifestations of American individualism in recent times. *Habits of the Heart* is a sociological study in which more than 200 middle class Americans were interviewed between 1979 and 1984 about their private lives and community and political activities. After reviewing the sources of individualism, the authors look at how individualism affects four spheres of American life: the private realms of love and marriage, and of therapy and counseling; and the public realms of politics, and of voluntary associations. The authors argue that the individualism that Tocqueville described 'may have grown cancerous — that it may be destroying those social integuments that Tocqueville saw as moderating its more destructive potentialities, that it may be threatening the survival of freedom itself' (p. viii).

6 *A Concluding Note*

In this concluding note, I will draw upon C. Wright Mills' *Sociological Imagination* (1959) to summarize my enquiry process within this book. At the outset, I referred to the attempt to follow Mills' (1959) challenge that 'No social study that does not come back to the problems of biography, of history and of their intersections within a society has completed its intellectual journey' (p. 6). Mills claims that every social study requires history in order to discover the historical development of social practices, the historical specificity of social practices — what Dilthey (1961) speaks of as '. . . unearthing the temporal structures of life for the understanding of meaning' (p. 30). In uncovering the historical specificity of social practices, the researcher discovers relationships of elements of a social structure and meaningfulness is to be found in the discovery of these relationships. Mills claims that it is the historical perspective which provides variety and the discovery of alternatives to the present.

In our review of history, we have seen how the nature of day care and the family are interconnected, how the family structure and functioning have changed and, with these changes, how conceptions of childhood evolved as a separate developmental realm, and how the role of women as guardian of the home and caretaker of young children evolved. Understanding the ideal of maternal childrearing helps to understand America's ambivalence toward day care, and the public's choice of no national policy or commitment for quality day care. We have seen that day care critics, most notably President Nixon in his 1971 veto of the Child Development Act, claim that day care would weaken the traditional American family and threaten America's tradition of individualism. In the last two decades, tremendous increases in the divorce rate and maternal employment have led to dramatic increases in the American family's need for out-of-home child care; and day care centers are burgeoning throughout the nation. Yet in the 1980s,

President Reagan's drastic cuts in social spending and block grants to states have reduced government spending on day care by at least 25 per cent.

The central focus of my field study is day care teachers' emphasis of children's individual and social experiences in order to learn whether in fact, day care critics have reason to think that this social childrearing context will threaten America's tradition of individualism. In order to penetrate the meaning of events within this day care study beyond the observed happenings and connect research findings to arrangements within the broader society, America's dominant value tradition of individualism has been examined from an historical perspective. We have seen that this value tradition is a complex dynamic of behavior, belief, attitudes and values, which often are taken for granted aspects of American everyday life and which have been manifest in multiple ways over the past 250 years. The seventeenth century ethic of rugged individualism encompassed hard work, self-reliance and self-determination. The eighteenth century ethic of self improvement existed alongside the increased economic tradition of pursuit of self interest and the democratic ethic of equal political rights. The nineteenth century rise of capitalism was accompanied by the ethic of equal opportunity and social reform of the individual. And in the twentieth century, self-actualization and search for personal meaning emerges alongside the corporate stress on competition and standardized mass conformity.

We have outlined from an historical perspective the broader social arrangements of America, specifically the two social institutions of family and day care and the dominant value tradition of individualism in America as they relate to my field study of day care. Chapter 3's brief discussion of Rosehill as an organization, its history, structure and philosophy, is a 'bridge' between observed individual teacher action and discussion of the broader social arrangements of day care, family and America's tradition of individualism.[1] When we look at Rosehill as an organization, we see that its' emphasis on multi-racial enrollment with equal numbers of low income and middle income children reflects America's tradition of egalitarianism. At the same time its' stated philosophy and goals which stress encouraging children's realization of their 'full potential individually' and fostering children's 'development as an individual' clearly reflect America's individualistic orientation.

As an organization, Rosehill's Board of Directors support their teachers' growth through providing release time and monetary help for teachers' schooling. At the same time however, the organizational structure does not have on-site teacher facilitation. Several teachers lack pedagogical skill in crucial areas such as children's conflict resolution and facilitative intervention; but the Rosehill Director, Kate, does not enter into the teachers' experiences as a facilitator. As a result, Kate seems unaware of teachers' need for pedagogical guidance in important areas of teaching. Rosehill's organizational structure has also helped us to understand the reasons for some of Rosehill's teachers' actions. For example, we have seen teachers often are not directly observing and supervising the children outdoors, and during early and late care. Understanding these teachers' need to complete maintenance tasks such as sweeping after meals, and these teachers' lack of any official 'break times' during a long work day, gives insight into understanding their lack of active observation and supervision during portions of the day.

Mills urges that social science enquiry needs not only to grasp the meaning of history and social structure as they interpenetrate social practices under study, but also the social scientist needs to grasp the role of biography as individuals' life history intersects with social practices. Mills' use of personal biography and history implies a specific view of temporality — that the present, future and past always intersect in the act; that is, the present is in constant flux, continuous with past and future. In understanding events at Rosehill, I attempted to learn how these teacher's personal biography influenced their observed action. In frequent spontaneous conversations and more formal taped interviews, teachers spoke of their personal histories and of their views of observed events. The meaning of Anne's schooling action becomes clearer when we know her personal history. Anne's understanding of self as teacher is rooted in her teaching in Poland in a state sponsored day care whose structured philosophy and practice conflict with that of Rosehill and with her recent Child Development Associate training and credentialing experiences. Anne tells me that though she thinks methods in Poland are more effective, 'I'm getting used to it here now. And it's okay'. The outside observer sees Anne's lack of enthusiasm and focus, and could argue that her lack of congruence between self as teacher and Rosehill philosophy and practice is not 'okay' in terms of effective teaching. Listening to Anne speak of her experiences in Poland and observing her schooling actions over time at Rosehill illustrates how one's present actions are continuous and interdependent with one's personal history.

Against this background of historical and current social practices and valuing, we can connect findings from my field study at Rosehill. We have seen that these research findings indicate that Rosehill teachers' emphasis on children's individual learning experiences perpetuates this dominant value tradition. For example, the preponderance of individually focused activity choices, in which children 'do what they want in their own way' promotes independent functioning which is reinforced by teachers' praise. Individual achievement and self improvement are emphasized as teachers focus on assisting children in mastery of self-care habits and success in individual task completion. Yet just as the complexities of American individualism includes social reform and equal opportunity, so too a pluralism in Rosehill teachers' action can be seen in their alternative though less frequent emphasis on social experiences. For example, daily children experience shared enjoyment in singing, story reading, and many conversations. Acknowledging this pluralism at Rosehill, as independence takes precedence over interdependence, self-responsibility over social responsibility, individual achievement over group collaboration, these teachers are promoting values congruent with America's dominant tradition of individualism.

Findings from my field study indicate that Nixon and day care critics may not need to worry; day care in America seems to foster the development of autonomous children. At the same time however, we can ask if autonomy as depicted in Rosehill — autonomous children capable of being left on their own without multiple interactions with authority and without a meaningful sense of community — is the individualism Americans want? Approaching this question the early childhood educator must focus on moral and value principles. As John Codd (1982) argues in discussing special education '. . . education is an inescapably moral endeavour' (p. 8). It is hoped that by unveiling the complexity of the daily life of young children and teachers in a day care center, this book can provide some conceptual models for understanding day care teachers' promoting of the individual and the social that can be useful when parents, early childhood educators and policy makers question what values and practices we give or want to give to our young children.

Note

1 Thirty years ago, Robert Redfield presaged this approach when he wrote of 'an ecological system' in *The Little Community* (1955). Smith (1983) speaks of this approach as a longitudinal nested systems model which can indicate '. . . the chronicle of multiple systems treated as interdependent strands' (p. 59). Urie Bronfenbrenner (1979) speaks of an ecological environment '. . . conceived as a set of nested structures, each inside the next, like a set of Russian dolls'. (p. 3).

Appendix A: Activity Scans

10/29 — end of early care —

9.15–9.30 a.m. There are ten-twelve children outdoors with two teachers supervising. Both teachers stand by the railroad ties and chat together. An elaborate role playing sequence between Rebecca, Nikki, and Jennifer continues on the far climber for the entire fifteen minutes; however no teacher observes this.

9.35 a.m. Four teachers are indoors; however for five minutes, no teacher is focused on observing the twenty-five children. Two teachers are in the kitchen and two prepare art materials in the art area.

— four children roam about the room
— two build with Tinker Toys on the checkered rug area
— four sit on bean bag chairs and look at books
— two build structures with A blocks at table (independently)
— two build with small block city pieces on the checkered rug. (independently)
— six have made a train with chairs under the 'tree climber' in housekeeping
— three use puzzles at the center table
— three eat snack

Late care —

4.00 p.m. Dana is washing items used during snack, and cleaning kitchen area.

— twenty-seven children are in the Big Room, as is Gary. The only interaction observed between Gary and children involves redirection of inappropriate child action.
— five children are in the rocking boat, where they are singing together
— six children are in the playhouse. Their play seems very

erratic and surface in quality, i.e., manipulating materials.
— eight children make pictures with markers at a table
— four children play with Fisher Price play people and vehicles on the checkered rug
— five children use table toys at front tables

11/10 — Late care — 4.10 p.m.
— five children use markers at the art table
— two children play together with Fisher Price play people and house
— four children 'mess about' with dishes and pots and pans in housekeeping area
— two children snap together train track
— All other children are outdoors. Children in Big Room are playing with no adult in the room. Dana washes dishes in the adjoining kitchen

12/17 — Early care —
7.45 a.m. — present: nineteen children, two teachers
— one child builds with crystal climbers. Pam sits next to him and assists
— four children rock on the rocking boat
— six children eat breakfast
— four children help Barb move the large hollow blocks from the unit block area to housekeeping
— four children play with Fisher Price play people, vehicles, and doll house on the checkered rug

8.45 a.m. — Present: forty children, three teachers
— one child builds with Lego, on block area rug
— one child sorts one inch cubes by color on block area rug
— two children build a simple unit block tower together
— one child builds with unit blocks while a second watches him
— eight children listen to volunteer read in quiet area
— sixteen children sit at front tables and complete independent tasks
— six children explore materials and engage in brief sequences in housekeeping
— five children make pictures at the art table
(interpretative aside: There is more shared participation today with the unit blocks available than during most early care periods.)

Barb sits at the art table with children, Anne sits at the front table and Pam chats with Kate in the kitchen area.

Activity Period (Big Room) —

10.40 a.m. — art area:
— two children paint at the easel
— five children make paper chains at the table, with Barb's assistance
Manipulative area:
— six children complete individual tasks: ringing tone bells, matching caps and bottles, looking through viewfinder, completing puzzles, and sorting cubes by color with Pam's assistance.
Block area:
— four children build a structure with Lisa's assistance
Cooking area:
— seven children take turns in making holiday cookies with Gary for the parent open house next week
Late care — It is raining outside, therefore Tina has opened the Yellow Room
3.25 p.m. — Yellow Room (eleven children and Tina)
— four children make individual pictures with markers at a table
— two children play with play dough at a small table
— two children work individual puzzles at another table, where Tina sits and watches
— three children listen to a record in the quiet room
3.30 p.m. — Big Room (four teachers and thirty children)
— Gary is folding cot covers in the back of the room
— Dana washes dishes in the kitchen
— Lisa sits at the table where five children use markers, scissors, and paper
— Barb 'floats' about the different areas
— fifteen children use individual choice activities at the front table
— five children play with Fisher Price vehicles and play people on the unit block rug area
— five children engage in simple non-sequitur play in housekeeping

1/21 — Early care, 7.45 a.m. — two adults and twenty-one children
— five children are aimlessly manipulating objects around the stove/sink area in housekeeping
— five children eat breakfast
— two boys play the game Candyland Bingo together, and a third boy watches next to them
— eight children complete individual table tasks at the front choice table area

Pam places not covers on cots in the center of the room. Anne, with Andrew on her lap sits with children at the front choice table, her back to the housekeeping area
8.45 a.m. — forty-four children present
— seven children make individual pictures at the art table
— five children build individual structures with unifex cubes at a front choice table
— six children play with Fisher Price vehicles, play people, and playhouse on checkered rug where Pam is seated, and observing the children as they play
— seven children sit at front tables with puzzles and other manipulative toys — each works individually
— remainder of the children are outdoors with Anne and Barb
Activity Period — Big Room, 10.15 a.m. — twenty-eight children and three teachers
— eight children complete individual tasks on the manipulative rug with Barb
— eight children make collages with corn, various bean seeds and noodles in the art area with Tina
— three children make calendars with Ellen on a front circle table
— five children cut up carrots and tear lettuce with Gary. They are making a salad for lunch.
Late care — It is raining outside, therefore Tina has opened the Yellow Room
3.30 p.m. — Yellow Room
— four children make pictures with markers at circle table
— four children mold with play dough at small table
— three children complete puzzles, Tina sits with them
— three children listen to a record in the Quiet Room
Big Room:
— six children play side by side with Fisher Price toys on use markers
— four children look through books in the Quiet Area
— sixteen children use assorted manipulative toys on the front area tables
— ten children are in the art area with Lisa, eight use play dough and seven use markers
— Dana washes dishes and cleans kitchen area
— Barb walks about the room as she observes the children
— Gary sorts cot covers and places them on cots in the back room

Appendix B: Theoretical Orientation

In recent decades debate on the theoretical foundations of educational and social science research has increased at an accelerated rate. Criticism against mainstream social science has been launched not only by researchers following the interpretive and critical perspective but also by individuals who have devoted their professional life working in the positivist mode of the scientific method of the natural sciences (Cronbach, 1975; Koch, 1981). Concurrently, several scholars have analyzed the belief systems and relation of theory to practice of the three main domains of educational and social science — the positivist, interpretive and critical tradition (Bernstein, 1971 and 1976; Bredo and Feinberg, 1983; Fay, 1975).

The use of participant observation is not a theoretical position in and of itself and can be implemented from varying theoretical orientations — positivist (for example, Glaser and Strauss, 1967; Homans, 1950), interpretive (for example, Geertz, 1973; Jackson, 1978), or critical (for example, Berlak and Berlak, 1981; Willis, 1977). The research approach of my field study of day care primarily follows the interpretive tradition; however, I have attempted to integrate aspects of the positivist and critical social perspective. In this process I am following Bernstein's (1976) claim that '... empirical research, interpretation, and critical evaluation dialectically involve each other.... An adequate, comprehensive political and social theory must be at once empirical, interpretative, and critical' (p. xiv). Figure 13 depicts an overview of the basic assumptions within these three intellectual traditions. The positions portrayed in this figure reflect my attempt to synthesize my reading of both researchers and theorists in each tradition and those scholars who have analyzed these three major domains of research (for example, Bernstein, 1976; Bredo and Feinberg, 1982; Fay, 1975; Karabel and Halsey, 1977).

Figure 13: Basic Assumptions Within the Research Process Emerging from Three Intellectual Traditions

Positivist	Interpretive	Critical
. . . maintains a dualistic view of mind and body, subject and object	. . . maintains the unity of thinking and experience, subject and object	. . . maintains the unity of thinking and experience, subject and object
. . . assumes that objective reality is known independent of self	. . . assumes that reality and the self interpenetrate	. . . assumes that reality and the self interpenetrate
. . . separates past, present and future	. . . assumes the unity of past, present and future	. . . assumes the unity past, present and future
. . . seeks objective, impersonal, exclusive knowledge — 'How do I know what I know?'	. . . seeks intersubjective, interpersonal, inclusive knowledge — 'How do I know what I do?'	. . . seeks intersubjective, interpersonal, inclusive knowledge — 'How should I do?'
. . . uses a preordained research design that is reductionistic and deductive	. . . uses a research design that is emergent and the process is inductive	. . . uses a research design that is emergent and the process is dialectic
. . . aims to verify hypotheses for the purpose of prediction and control	. . . aim is to capture the process as it naturally occurs	. . . aim is to raise consciousness of actors to empower them for self-emancipation
. . . strives to screen out all confounding variables in the research process	. . . remains open to all factors within the given context	. . . remains open to all factors within the given context and searches for historical and structural connections
. . . maintains a clear distinction between subjects and researcher	. . . attempts to capture the subjects' meaning and intentionality via an intersubjective process	. . . actively involves subjects in all aspects of the research process
. . . conducts research that is context stripping	. . . focuses research on situational contextual issues embedded in actions and meanings of those being observed	. . . searches beyond the situational to uncover broader social/structural elements embedded within the situational events
. . . studies only overt aspects of behavior	. . . studies covert as well as overt aspects of behavior	. . . studies covert as well as overt aspects of behavior
. . . seeks explanations giving probability of proof via mathematical/statistical procedures	. . . seeks explanations concerned with understanding meaning and purposes of actions embedded within specific situations	. . . seeks explanations concerned with understanding meaning and purposes of actions as they relate to historical and social structural elements of larger society
. . . claims that theory and research are value free	. . . claims that theory and research are embedded with values which need to be uncovered and examined	. . . claims that 'ought' question and the value of self-empowerment and accompanying emancipation is central to the research process
. . . separates theory and practice	. . . separates theory and practice	. . . unifies theory and practice
. . . is concerned with validity that is measurement oriented	. . . is concerned with validity based on internal consistency, experiential consensus and theoretical coherence	. . . views validity as tied to the subject's self empowerment and emancipation

The Positivist Tradition

Some aspects of this enquiry take its direction from the positivist tradition of case study research, such as the work of Homans (1950) and Glaser and Strauss (1967). Four features of my field study emerge from the positivist tradition. First, I accept their argument that the underpinning of all concepts is the concrete description of observed events. All generalizations regarding the four teachers in this study are 'grounded' in the daily events at Rosehill. Second, in data collection, I attempted to record ongoing events as objectively as possible, and to separate interpretative comments from observations of actions and activities. Admittedly the decision of what to observe always is somewhat subjective, but I tried to keep the actual recording as true to the events in process as was possible for one person to do. Third, from this tradition of field research, I have utilized specific indices initially to guide but also to ensure credibility of my research process. Glaser and Strauss's (1967) discussion of 'theoretical sampling' was a significant guide in my generating categories or themes, and in my judging the adequacy of my data gathering process. Bruyn's (1966) discussion of 'subjective adequacy' and Becker's (1970) discussion of 'field work evidence' was integrated into Smith's (1979) discussion of 'major conditions assuring valid data'. Fourth, this qualitative study does utilize some quantitative indices to communicate both research process and findings. For example, in judging credibility of method, the number of days in the field, of variety of situations observed, of methods used in data collection were significant criteria. Comparative analysis of the proportion of one type of event versus another also assisted in analyzing my findings. Obviously my use of quantitative data is markedly different from the usual mathematical and statistical methods of verification research. But my point is that mere use of qualitative case study methods does not negate the value of quantitative indices.

The Interpretive Tradition

Following the interpretive tradition, a central mode of this enquiry is the intent to capture the meaning of events from the perspective of the actors, that is, the teachers. Hence, recurrently I asked teachers 'What do you make of this? — What do you see as the meaning/purpose of that?'. I attempted to keep teachers' interpretation of meaning close to the observational data. As Geertz (1973) speaks of this process, he notes:

> This is the first condition for cultural theory; it is not its own

master. As it is unseverable from the immediacies thick description presents, its freedom to shape itself in terms of its internal logic is rather limited. What generally it contrives to achieve grows out of the delicacy of its distinctions, not the sweep of its abstractions. (pp. 24–5)

Fay (1975) sees this understanding of actors from their own perspective to be the first step in both interpretive and critical enquiry. Historically, this process has been called *verstehen*. A basic assumption underlying this type of explanation is that intentionality is contained within the person's action. Understanding focuses on covert as well as overt aspects of a person's action; and thus, the dualistic separation of behavior and intentionality common in the positivist tradition is rejected. In his now classic essay on 'The operation called verstehen', Abel (1948) distinguishes this verstehen explanation that uncovers *possible* understanding with the positivists' focus on verification and prediction. In other words, explanation following the interpretive approach does not provide certainty; rather, it provides an understanding that can be considered *adequate* if the reader considers it *possible*. On this issue of certainty Geertz (1973) comments:

The fact is that to commit oneself to a semiotic concept of culture and an interpretive approach to the study of it is to commit oneself to a view of ethnographic assertion as, to borrow W.B. Gallie's by now famous phrase, 'essentially contestable'. Anthropology, or at least interpretive anthropology, is a science whose progress is marked less by a perfection of consensus than by a refinement of debate. What gets better is the precision with which we vex each other. (p. 29)

Locating this approach in a broader stream of knowledge and philosophy, this study's interpretative process takes its direction from the nineteenth century historian and mentor of George Herbert Mead — William Dilthey. Dilthey (1961) claims that the use of *understanding* provides the social sciences with a method distinct from those of the physical sciences. Pivotal to Dilthey's argument is the concept of *meaning*. 'A story is meaningful we may say, if some relevant connections between facts or events can be made intelligible' (p. 24). Dilthey differentiates meaningful relations from causal relations. He claims that we understand meaning through *expression*. We recognize expressions or signs from our own experiences; that is, we understand conventional signs from having learned conventional accepted ways of doing things. We also understand by relating a sign to a wider context — what Dilthey calls the hermeneutic process.

> The goal of this understanding is always penetration to the mental states or processes which lie behind outer manifestations and we are helped towards this not merely by purely intellectual processes but by the wealth of our own experience of life. Understanding is the rediscovery of the I in the Thou; the mind rediscovers itself at every higher level of connectedness; this sameness of the mind in the I and the Thou and in every subject of a community, in every system of culture and, finally, in the totality of mind and universal history, makes the working together of the different processes in the human studies possible . . . (pp. 67–8)

Dilthey links experience, expression, and understanding. Central to this hermeneutic process is the shared language of people. In presenting Dilthey's perspective, Habermas (1971) notes:

> . . . every form of interaction and mutual understanding between individuals is mediated by an intersubjectively valid employment of symbols that refer in the last instance to ordinary language. Language is the ground of intersubjectivity . . . (p. 157)

Experience and understanding of expression are reciprocally related.

> . . . From the fullness of our own experience, experience outside of us is reproduced and understood through transposition. And even in the most abstract sentences of the cultural sciences the factual element that is represented in thought is experience and understanding. (Dilthey quoted in Habermas, 1971, p. 146)

In this study, I have tried to describe teachers' actions and to present an understanding of their aims and cognitions within the specific situational characteristics of Rosehill Child Care Center. As I have analyzed my data, I have searched for themes and connections among the many observed events. My understanding is achieved through an intersubjective process, as my own personal and professional experience interpenetrates the behavioral and verbal expressions of these teachers and their children. When collecting data, though I tried to let the teachers' perspective dominate, no doubt my choice of questions to them as well as my choice of which events I would observe also reflect my own experience and understanding of them, of the child care field, and of the research process. I present this study's explanations as tentative possible means of understanding events at Rosehill through a similar intersubjective process. If valid, my understandings will have meaning to the reader via a new hermeneutic process, that is, interpretation of meaning through the reader's intersubjective understanding.

My use of this interpretive process in this field study is grounded in the American tradition of pragmatism, and more specifically, the work of William James, John Dewey and George Herbert Mead. In particular, I accept their claim that language, self and social experiencing are intertwined. This position is articulated most fully by Mead (1962 and 1964). Mead claims that the development of self arises from the developing ability to take on roles, arising out of social experience and made possible through language. Mead, Dewey and James argue that thinking and experience are a unity; one does not have meaning without the other. A person's action entails intentionality for the act is always selective, selective to aspects of the environment and to the self as object. As James argues: 'My experience is what I agree to attend to' (quoted in Barzun, 1983, p. 47). James argues further that this selectivity is the central characteristic of mind.

> 'The human mind is essentially partial', but its success comes from the very 'necessity of limiting our view'. For there are 'different cycles of operation in nature that are relatively independent of one another. The mould on the biscuit in the store-room of a man of war vegetates in absolute indifference to the nationality of the flag'. And the 'captain who in manoeuvering the vessel through a naval fight should think it necessary to bring the mouldy biscuit to his calculations would very likely lose the battle by reason of the excessive thoroughness of his mind'. (p. 53)

In the act, the past, present and future intersect; that is, the present always is in constant flux, continuous with the past and future. This view of temporality has implications for participant observation research. In embracing this view of temporality, I am assuming that to understand the present one must have an historical perspective. Hence in understanding ongoing events at Rosehill, I strove to learn how each teacher's personal biography intersected with observed action. As Mead (1964) notes: 'Each person slices the world from a different time system' (p. 341). At a broader level, I assume that characteristics of social institutions contain salient trends of past social arrangements. Hence, I examined day care and the family in America, two social institutions central to my study, from an historical perspective. In this unity of historical and sociological I am following Mills' (1959) challenge:

> The sociological imagination enables us to grasp history and

> biography and the relations between the two within society. That is its task and its promise. (p. 6)

Although I strove to understand through this intersubjective process of meaning, I also tried to refrain from *total* immersion in the teachers' perspective. Geertz (1975) argues that the participant observer simultaneously utilizes experience-near and experience-distant concepts.

> Confinement to experience-near concepts leaves an ethnographer awash in the immediacies as well as entangled in vernacular. Confinement to experience-distant ones leaves him stranded in abstractions and smothered in jargon . . . to produce an interpretation of the way a people live which is neither imprisoned within their mental horizons, an ethnography of witchcraft as written by a witch, nor systematically deaf to the distinctive tonalities of their existence, an ethnography of witchcraft as written by a geometer. (p. 48)

I found this balance of distance and proximity to be an ongoing challenge both in data collection and in the writing process. At the center I ordinarily remained distant as an observer, with pen and clipboard in hand, silently moving about the given space and recording events. As I wrote neither adults nor children initiated much conversation with me; I seemed to be merely a 'familiar fixture'. Yet I occasionally participated as teacher whenever there was an obvious staff shortage and accompanying need. On these occasions, when I was without pen and clipboard in hand, teachers initiated many conversation with me and often asked me questions regarding my views. Like a 'scratched record', I recurrently refrained from giving my specific perspective, returned to my earlier statements of my research intent, and occasionally shifted the dialogue to 'brainstorming' with the teacher about the many possible understandings of the teacher's initial question. In writing, this balance between distance and proximity has been an even greater challenge. Being a teacher myself, and becoming quite familiar with Rosehill teachers, I find it difficult to collapse or omit the many 'distinctive tonalities of their existence'. At the same time however, I find it difficult to avoid falling victim to abstractions that can conceal rather than clarify observed events. As Barzun (1983) warns:

> The ladder of increasing generality is traveled up and down by the mind a dozen times an hour without one's noticing it. If from love of abstraction new conceptual terms are substituted for common ones, it so happens that the power of words to direct

> thought approaches zero. 'Serious love affair' used to be a good enough phrase to indicate a whole range of feelings and actions. We have substituted 'meaningful relationship', which is so indefinite that it could cover the association of a hunter and his dog — or even that of oxygen and hydrogen in water. (p. 60)

In the day to day data collection process, I followed Glaser and Strauss (1967), Smith (1979), Berlak and Berlak (1981), and the 'new' sociology of education. Following Smith and Glaser and Strauss, I attempted to immerse myself in the ongoing events at Rosehill, and at the same time search for interpretive meaning of these events, for patterns, connections, and themes. During my months in the field, I moved from the particular (events at Rosehill), to the general, in terms of reading case studies (for example, Kanter, 1972; Keddie, 1971; King, 1978; Nash, 1973; Willis, 1977) — reading different positions on field study (for example, Apple, 1979; Geertz, 1973; Mills, 1959; Reinharz, 1979) — and reading on child care in other countries (for example, Israel, Russia and China). These readings recurrently sparked new awarenesses and questions regarding my observations in the field as I tried to see the familiar as strange and the strange as familiar. For example, Keddie's (1971) essay sensitized me to the contradictions between teachers' practice and their espoused 'educationeze'. Young's (1971) work challenged me to take as problematic several taken for granted priorities in early education, such as the standard independence training, to search out individual teachers' underlying assumptions, such as their priority in making certain that children learn to respect each other's property, and to be sensitive to teacher omissions, such as not praising group endeavors, only individual projects.

Toward a Critical Approach

Several strands of critical social science have been incorporated into this study's central interpretive approach. Specifically, the Berlaks' understanding of thought, action and social context in the schooling process, plus my reading of social theorists such as Giddens (1976 and 1979), Habermas (1971) and readings in the 'new' sociology of education such as Bernstein (1971 and 1977), Bourdieu (1971), and Young (1971) offered me challenges to direct my own enquiry process.

The Berlak's perspective provided a significant framework during data collection and formulation of my enquiry problem. I accepted their dialectical understanding of schooling, where relations between persons and their environment are dialectic in three senses: dialectic within the person as actor and reactor in action; dialectic among persons as subjects and objects in action; and dialectic between persons and environment, persons being shaped and shaping their environment. With this dialectical frame of reference, I strove to be sensitive to the reflexive dynamics within patterns of action that emerged, for example, when children influenced teacher action and not merely teachers influencing children, or when children and teachers shaped the given environmental boundaries rather than merely acting within these boundaries. The Berlaks speak of teachers' schooling acts as containing the contradictions or paradoxes that are endemic to both their own personal histories and the larger society. Teaching is viewed as a dynamic process, where teachers experience alternative, sometimes contradictory tendencies to act, tendencies which are in continuous flux. With this understanding of teacher action, as observer I tried to be sensitive not merely to dominant patterns, but also to the exceptional acts that inevitably occur. For example, though one teacher ordinarily maintained social distance from the children, I became sensitive to her alternative pattern of receptiveness to child initiated physical intimay. Another teacher consistently refused to participate in free play activities with children indoors; yet on a few occasions, she initiated and participated in high interest involvement outdoors (for example, kickball games).

In my early work, I had accepted the Meadian understanding of language, action, mind and self, all of which are reflexively intertwined; however, I had not penetrated the meaning of acts beyond the immediate situational context. I found compelling the arguments of the Berlaks, critical theorists and the 'new' sociologists of education, that arrangements in the classroom need to be connected to arrangements within the structural elements of the social order. That is, the meaning of classroom events needs to be penetrated beyond the objective happenings to uncover assumptions underlying these happenings, whether they entail the management of knowledge, or arrangements of social relations. Critical theorists have critiqued field studies done from an interpretive perspective for their failure to relate observed action and meaning in the specific context to structural elements of the social order, and their neglect of historical change (Fay, 1975; Karabel and Halsey, 1977).

This field study attempts to move toward a critical approach in three ways: (i) by locating the observed events at Rosehill in the broader context of two social institutions in America, day care and the family; (ii) by reflecting on whether these day care teachers' emphasis of individual and social experiences is congruent with America's dominant value tradition of individualism; and (iii) by adopting an historical perspective in understanding observed events and elements of the broader society, specifically the social institutions day care and the family, and America's value tradition of individualism.

In summary, though this field study takes its primary direction from the interpretive social science tradition, the research process also incorporates aspects of positivist and critical social sciences approaches. In this attempt I am following Bernstein's (1976) argument that adequate social science needs to be empirical, interpretive and critical.

Bibliography

ABEL, T. 'The operation called Verstehen', *American Journal of Sociology*, 54, pp. 211–8, 1948.

ANDERSON, J.E. *Nursery Education: A Survey of Day Nurseries, Nursery Schools, Private Kindergartens in the United States*, Report of the Committee on the Infant and Preschool Child, The White House Conference on Child Health and Protection, New York, Century Company, 1931.

APPLE, M. *Ideology and Curriculum*, London, Routledge and Kegan Paul, 1979.

ARIES, P. *Centuries of Childhood: A Social History of the Family*, New York, Vintage Books, 1962.

AUERBACH, S. *The Child Care Crisis*, Boston, Beacon Press, 1979.

BANE, M.J. 'A profile of families in the 1980s' in BODEN, C. (Ed.), *Focus on the Family: New Images of Parents and Children in the 1980s*, Boston, Wheelock College for Parenting Studies, 1980.

BANE, M.J. *Here to Stay*, New York, Basic Books, 1976.

BARZUN, J. *A Stroll with William James*, New York, Harper and Row, 1983.

BECKER, H. *Sociological Work*. Chicago, Aldine, 1970.

BECKER, H., GEER, B., HUGHES, E.C., and STRAUSS, A.L. *Boys in White: Student Culture in Medical School*, Chicago, University of Chicago Press, 1961.

BEER, E. *The Day Nursery*, New York, E.P. Dutton & Co., Inc., 1938.

BELL, D. On meritocracy and equality. In J. Karabel & A.H. Halsey (Eds), *Power and ideology and education*. New York: Oxford University Press, 1977.

BELLAH, R.N., MADSEN, R., SULLIVAN, W.M., SWIDLER, A., TIPTON, S.M. *Habits of the Heart Individualism and Commitment in American Life*. Berkeley: University of California Press, 1985.

BERLAK, A., & BERLAK, H. *Dilemmas of Schooling, Teaching and Social Change*. London: Methuen & Co., Ltd., 1981.

BERNSTEIN, B. Class and pedagogies visible and invisible. In J. KARABLE & A.H. HALSEY (Eds), *Power and Ideology in Education*. New York: Oxford University Press, 1977.

Bernstein, R. *Praxis and Action*. Philadelphia: University of Pennsylvania Press, 1978. (First published in 1971).

Bernstein, R.J. *The Restructuring of Social and Rational Theory*. Philadelphia: University of Pennsylvania Press, 1976.

Bettleheim, B. *Children of the Dream*. London: Collier MacMillan, 1969.

Blank, H. The need to expand the dependent tax credit: An important source of assistance. *Young Children*, 1983, *38*, (5), 78–81.

Boggs, J. and Boggs, G. *Revolution and Evolution in the Twentieth Century*. New York: Monthly Review Press, 1974.

Bourdieu, P. Systems of education and systems of thought. In M.F.D. Young (Ed.), *Knowledge and Control*. London: Collier MacMillan, 1971, pp. 189–207.

Bowles, S. & Gintis, H. *Schooling in Capitalist America: Educational Reform and the Contradictions of Economic Life*. New York: Basic Books, Inc., 1976.

Braverman, H. *Labor and Monopoly Capital. The Degradation of Work in the Twentieth Century*. New York: Monthly Review Press, 1974.

Bredo, E. & Feinberg, W. *Knowledge and Values in Social and Educational Research*. Philadelphia: Temple University Press, 1982.

Bronfenbrenner, U. *Two Worlds of Childhood: U.S. and U.S.S.R.* New York: Russell Sage Foundation, 1970.

Bronfenbrenner, U. *The Ecology of Human Development Experiments by Nature and Design*. Cambridge, MA: Harvard University Press, 1979.

Bruyn, S.T. *The Human Perspective in Sociology: The Methodology of Participant Observation*. Englewood Cliffs, NJ: Prentice-Hall, 1966.

Cagan, E. Individualism, collectivism, and radical educational reform. *Harvard Educational Review*, 1978, *48*, 227–266.

Caldwell, B.M. The effects of infant care. In M.L. Hoffman & L.W. Hoffman (Eds), *Review of Child Development Research*. New York: Russell Sage Foundation, 1964.

Caldwell, B.M. How can we educate the American public about the child care profession? *Young Children*, 1983, *38*, (3), 11–17.

CDF Reports, 1985, *6*, (12), Official newsletter of the Children's Defense Fund.

Chan, I. New people in new China: As reflected through education and child rearing. Paper presented at Biennial Meeting of Society for Research in Child Development, April 10–13, 1975, Denver.

Chodorow, N. *The Reproduction of Mothering Psychoanalysis and the Sociology of Gender*. Berkeley: University of California Press, 1978.

Codd, J.A. Research and review Some ethical problems in special education. *The Australian Journal of Special Education*, 1982, *6*, (1), 8–14.

Cronbach, L.J. Beyond the two disciplines of scientific psychology. *American Psychologist*, 1975, *30*, 11–17.

Damon, W. *The Social World of the Child*. San Francisco: Jossey-Bass, 1977.

Damon, W. *Social and Personality Development*. New York: W.W. Norton &

Co., Inc., 1983.

DELONE, R.H. *Small Futures Children, Inequality, and the Limits of Liberal Reform*. New York: Harcourt Brace Jovanovich, 1979.

DETOCQUEVILLE, A. *On Democracy, Revolution and Society*. (Eds). J. Stone & S. Mennell, Chicago: University of Chicago Press, 1980. (First published in 1835).

DEWEY, J. *Individualism Old and New*. New York: Capricorn, 1929.

DEWEY, J. *Democracy and Education*. New York: Macmillan Co., 1966.

DILTHEY, W. *Patterns and Meaning in History Thoughts on History and Society*. New York: Harper & Row, 1961.

EHRENSAFT, D. When women and men mother. *Socialist Review*, 1980, *10*, #49.

ELSHTAIN, J.B. *Public Men, Private Women: Women in Social and Political Thought*. Princeton, NJ: Princeton University Press, 1981.

ERIKSON, E. *Childhood and Society*. New York: Norton, 1950.

ETAUGH, C. Effects of nonmaternal care on children: Research evidence and popular views. *American Psychologist*, 1980, *35* (4), 309–19.

FAY, B. *Social Theory and Political Practice*. Boston: George Allen & Unwin, 1975.

FISHHAUT, E.H. & PASTOR, D. Should the public schools be entrusted with preschool education: A critique of the AFT proposal. *School Review*, 1977, 38–49.

FOSTER, J.C. & ANDERSON, J.E. *The Young Child and his Parents A study of 100 Cases*. Minneapolis: University of Minnesota Press, 1930.

FRANKLIN, B. *The Autobiography of Benjamin Franklin*. L.W. LABAREE, R.L. KETCHAM, H.C. BENTFIELD, & H.H. INESMAN, (Eds). New Haven: Yale University Press, 1964. (First published in 1791).

FREUD, A. (1946) *The Psychoanalytic Treatment of Children*. New York: Schockner, (reprinted 1969)

FREUD, S. *Three Essays on the Theory of Sexuality*. New York: Basic Books, Inc., 1962. (First published in 1905).

FREUD, S. *The Ego and the Id*. New York: W.W. Norton and Co., 1960. (First published in 1923).

FRIEDAN, B. *The Second Stage*. New York: Summit Books, 1981.

FROMM, E. *The Sane Society*. New York: Rinehart, 1955.

GEERTZ, C. *The Interpretation of Cultures*. New York: Basic Books, Inc., 1973.

GEERTZ, C. On the nature of anthropological understanding. *American Scientist*, 1975, 47–53.

GIDDENS, A. *New Rules of Sociological Method: A Positive Critique of Interpretative Sociologies*. New York: Basic Books, Inc., 1976.

GILLIGAN, C. *In a Different Voice: Psychological Theory and Women's Development*. Cambridge: Harvard University Press, 1982.

GLASER, B. & STRAUSS, A.L. *The Discovery of Grounded Theory: Strategies for Qualitative Research*. Chicago: Aldine, 1967.

GORDON, T. *Parent Effectiveness Training The 'No-lose' Program for Raising*

Responsible Children. New York: Peter W. Upjohn Co., 1970.
GOULDNER, A.W. *The Coming Crisis of Western Sociology*. New York: Avon, 1971.
GREENBLATT, B. *Responsibility for Day Care*. San Francisco: Jossey-Bass, 1977.
HABERMAS, J. *Knowledge and Human Interests*. Boston: Beacon Press, 1971. (First published in 1960).
HALL, E.W. *Modern Science and Human Values A study of the History of Ideas*. New York: D. Van Nostrand Co., Inc., 1956.
HENRY, J. *Culture Against Men*. New York: Random House, 1963.
HERRON, R.E. & SUTTON-SMITH, B. *Child's Play*. New York: John Wiley & Sons, 1971.
HEWLETT, S.A. Child carelessness. *Harper's*, 1983, 20–25.
HOMANS, G. *The Human Group*. New York: Harcourt Brace, 1950.
HONIG, A.S. (1985a) Compliance, control, and discipline. *Young Childhood*, 1985, 40, 2, 50–58.
HONIG, A.S. (1985b) Compliance, control, and discipline (continued). *Young Children*, 40, 3, 47–52.
HOWARD, A.E. *The American Family: Myth and Reality*. Washington, DC: NAEYC, 1980.
HUTT, C. Exploration and play in children. In R.E. Herron & B. Sutton-Smith (Eds), *Child's Play*. New York: John Wiley & Sons, 1971.
HYMES, J.L., JR. *Teaching the Child Under Six*. Columbus, OH: Charles E. Merrill, 1968.
ISAACS, N. *Children's Way of Knowing*. New York: Teacher College, 1974.
ISAACS, S. *Intellectual Growth in Young Children*. New York: Schocken Books, 1966.
ISAACS, S. *Social Development in Young Children*. New York: Schocken Books, 1972.
JACKSON, P.W. *Life in the Classroom*. New York: Holt, Rinehart, & Winston, Inc., 1968.
JACOBY, R. *Social Amnesia*. Boston: Beacon Press, 1975.
JOFFE, C. *Friendly Intruders Childcare Professionals and Family Life*. Berkeley: University of California Press, 1977.
KAGAN, J. The child in the family. In A.S. ROSSI, J. KAGAN, T.K. HARAVEN (Eds), *The Family*. New York: W.W. Norton, 1978.
KANTER, R.M. The organization child: Experience management in a nursery school. In R. DALE, G. ESLAND, & M. MACDONALD (Eds), *School and Capitalism*. London: Routledge & Kegan Paul Ltd., 1976.
KARABEL, J., & HALSEY, A.H., (Eds). *Power and Ideology in Education*. New York: Oxford University Press, 1977.
KATZ, L. The professional early childhood teacher. *Young Children*, 1984, 39, (5), 3–23.
KEDDIE, N. Classroom knowledge. In M.F.D. Young (Ed.), *Knowledge and Control*. London: Collier MacMillan, 1971.

KENISTON, K. *All Our Children: The American Family Under Pressure*. New York: Carnegie Corporation, 1977.

KESSEN, W. (Ed.). *Childhood in China*. New Haven: Yale University Press, 1975.

KEYSERLING, M.D. *Windows on Day Care*. New York: National Council of Jewish Women, 1972.

KING, R. *All Things Bright and Beautiful? A sociological study of infants classrooms*. New York: John Wiley & Sons, 1978.

KOCH, S. The nature and limits of psychological knowledge. *American Psychologist, 36*, 257–269.

KOHLBERG, L. Stage and sequence: The cognitive-developmental approach to socialization. In D. Goslin (Ed.), *Handbook of Socialization Theory and Research*. Chicago: Rand-McNally, 1969.

KOUNIN, J.S. *Discipline and Group Management in the Classroom*. Huntington, NY: ROBERT E. Krieger Pub. Co., 1977. (First published in 1970).

KROWN, S. *Threes and Fours Go to School*. Englewood Cliffs, NJ: Prentice-Hall, 1974.

LASCH, C. Woman as alien. In J.E. FREEDMAN & W.G. SHADE (Eds), *Our American Sisters Women in American Life and Thought*. Boston: Allyn and Bacon, 1976.

LASCH, C. *Haven in a Heartless World The Family Besieged*. New York: Basic Books, 1977.

LASCH, C. *The Culture of Narcissism*. New York: W.W. Norton & Co., 1979.

LASH, J.P. *Eleanor and Franklin*. New York: W.W. Norton & Co., Inc., 1973.

LASLETT, B. The family as a public and private institution: A historical perspective. In A. Skolnick & J.H. Skolnick (Eds), *Intimacy, Family, and Society*. Boston: Little, Brown, & Co., 1974.

LASLO, E. *Individualism, Collectivism, and Political Power A Relational Analysis of Ideological Conflict*. The Hague: Martinus Nijhoff, 1963.

LEVIN, H.M. Education and work. Unpublished paper, 1983.

LIPSET, S.M. The unchanging American character. In R.L. RAPSON (Ed.), *Individualism and Conformity in the American Character*. Boston: D.C. Heath and Co., 1967.

LOEVINGER, J. *Ego Development*. San Francisco: Jossey-Bass, 1977.

LUKES, S. *Individualism*. New York: Harper & Row, 1973.

MACCOBY, E.E. *Social Development Psychological Growth and Parentchild Relationship*. New York: Harcourt Brace Jovanovich, Inc., 1980.

MALINOWSKL, B. *The Argonauts of the Western Pacific*. London: Routledge, 1922.

MEAD, G.H. *Mind, Self, and Society from the Standpoint of a Social Behaviorist*. (C.W. Morns, Ed.). Chicago: University of Chicago Press, 1962.

MEAD, G.H. *On Social Psychology*. In STRAUSS, A. (Ed.). Chicago: University of Chicago Press, 1964.

Miller, D. *Individualism, Personal Achievement and the Open Society.* Austin: University of Texas, 1967.

Mills, C.W. *The Sociological Imagination.* New York: Oxford University Press, 1959.

Nash, R. *Classrooms Observed.* London: Routledge & Kegan Paul, 1973.

Orton, R.E. & Langham, B. What is government's role in quality day care? In S. Kilmer (Ed.), *Advances in Early Education and Day Care.* Vol. 1. Greenwich, CT: Jai Press, 1980.

Piaget, J. *The Moral Judgement of the Child.* New York: Free Press, 1965.

Piaget, J. Some aspects of operations. In M.W. Piers (Ed.), *Play and Development.* New York: W.W. Norton Co., 1972.

Piaget, J., & Inhelder, B. *The Psychology of the Child.* New York: Basic Books, Inc., 1969.

Poster, M. *Critical Theory of the Family.* New York: The Seabury Press, 1978.

Potter, D.M. The quest for the national character. In R.L. Rapson (Ed.), *Individualism and Conformity in the American Character.* Boston: D.C. Heath and Co., 1967.

Powdermaker, H. *Stranger and Friend The Way of an Anthropologist.* New York: W.W. Norton & Co., Inc., 1966.

Rabinow, R. *Reflections on Field Work in Morocco.* Berkeley: University of California Press, 1977.

Rapson, R.L. *Individualism and Conformity in the American Character.* Boston: D.C. Heath and Co., 1967.

Redfield, R. *The Little Community.* Chicago: University of Chicago Press, 1955.

Reinharz, S. *On Becoming a Social Scientist.* San Francisco: Jossey-Bass, 1979.

Riesman, D., Denny, R., & Glazer, N. *The Lonely Crowd A Study of the Changing American Character.* New Haven: Yale University Press, 1950.

Royce, J.R., & Mos, L.P. *Humanistic Psychology Concepts and Criticisms.* New York: Plenum Press, 1981.

Schorr, A.L. *Explorations in Social Policy.* New York: Basic Books, 1968.

Schweinhart, L.J., & Weikart, D.P. *Young Children Grow Up: The Effects of the Perry Preschool Program on Youths Through Age 15.* Ypsilanti, MI: High Scope Press, 1980.

Sennet, R. & Cobb, J. *Hidden Injuries of Class.* New York: Random House, Inc., 1973.

Sharp, R. Self contained ethnography or a science of phenomenal forms and inner relations. *Journal of Education,* 1982 *164,* 48–63.

Sharp, R., & Green, A. *Education and Social Control.* London: Routledge & Kegan Paul, 1975.

Sidel, R. *Women and Childcare in China.* Baltimore, MD: Penguin Books, 1972.

Smilansky, S. *The Effects of Sociodramatic Play on Disadvantaged Preschool Children.* New York: John Wiley & Sons, Inc., 1968.

SMILANSKY, S. Can adults facilitate play in children? Theoretical and practical considerations. In *Play: The Child Strives Toward Self-realization.* Washington, DC: NAEYC, 1971.

SMITH, A. *The Wealth of Nations.* (E. Cennon, Ed.). New York: Modern Library, 1937. (First published in 1776).

SMITH, L.M. An evolving logic of participant observation, educational ethnography and other case studies. In L. SCHULMAN (Ed.), *Review of research in education.* Itaska, IU: Peacock Press, 1979.

SMITH, L.M., & KLEINE, P.F. Educational innovation: A life history research perspective. In I. Goodson & S. Ball (Eds), *Defining the Curriculum Histories and Ethnographies of School Subjects*, Lewes, Falmer Press, 1984.

SMITH, L., & GEOFFREY, W. *The Complexities of an Urban Classroom.* New York: Holt, Rinehart & Winston, 1968.

SMITH. T. *Revivalism and Social Reform in the Mid-nineteenth Century.* New York: Abington Press, 1957.

SNYDER, M., SNYDER, R., & SNYDER JR., R. *The Young Child as Person Toward the Development of Healthy Conscience.* New York: Human Sciences Press, 1980.

STEINER, G. *Children's Cause.* Washington, DC: The Brookings Institute, 1976.

STEINFELS, M. *Who's Minding the Children? The History and Politics of Day Care in America.* New York: Simon and Schuster, 1973.

STEINFELS, P. & STEINFELS, P. Day care: Patchwork, realization, or utopia. In A. SKOLNICK & J.H. SKOLNICK (Eds), *Intimacy, Family, and Society.* Boston: Little, Brown, & Co., 1974, pp. 415–430.

SULLIVAN, H.S. *The Interpersonal Theory of Psychiatry.* New York: Norton, 1953.

SURANSKY, V.P. *The Erosion of Childhood.* Chicago: University of Chicago Press, 1982.

SURANSKY, V.P. Tales of rebellion and resistance: The landscape of early institutional life. *Journal of Education*, 1983, *165*, 135–57.

SUTTON-SMITH, B. The playful modes of knowing. In G. ENGSTROM (Ed.), *Play The Child Strives Toward Self-realization.* Washington, D.C. National Association for the Education of Young Children, 1971, pp. 13–25.

VAN DUSEN, R.A. & SHELDON, E.B. The changing status of American women: A life cycle perspective. In Skolnick, A.S. & Skolnick, J. (Eds), *Family in Transition.* Boston: Little Brown & Co., 1977.

Voice for Children, Vol 14, Official Newsletter of the Day Care Council, 1981.

WALKER, R. Three good reasons for not doing case studies in curriculum research. *Journal of Curriculum Studies*, 1983, *15* (2), 155–65.

WASHINGTON, V. and OYEMADE, U.J. Changing family trends Head Start must respond. *Young Children*, 1985, *40*, (6), pp. 12–19.

WEBER, L. *The English Infact School and Informal Education.* New Jersey: Prentice-Hall, 1971.

WEBER, M. *The Protestant Ethic and the Spirit of Capitalism.* New York: Charles Scribner's Sons, 1958. (First published in 1904–05).

WHITE, B.L. *The First Three Years of Life.* New York: Avon Books, 1975.

WHYTE, W.F. *Street Corner Society The Structure of an Italian Slum.* Chicago: University of Chicago Press, 1943.

WILLIS, P. *Learning to Labour.* Fainborough: Saxon House, 1977.

WINN, M. *Children Without Childhood.* New York: Pantheon Books, 1981.

WINNICOTT, D.W. *Playing and Reality.* New York: Basic Books, Inc., 1971.

WIRTH, A.G. *John Dewey as Educator: His Design for Work in Education (1894–1904).* Huntington, NY: Robert, E. Kreger Publishing Co., 1979, (First published in 1966).

WOOD, E.M. *Mind and Politics: An Approach to the Meaning of Liberal and Socialist Individualism.* Berkeley: University of California Press, 1972.

WOOD, E.M., & WOOD, N. *Class, Ideology, & Ancient Political Theory: Socrates, Plato, & Aristotle in Social Context.* New York: Oxford University Press, 1978.

WOOLSEY, S.H. Pied piper politics and the child care debate. In A.S. ROSSI, J. KAGAN, & T.K. HARAVEN (Eds), *The Family.* New York: W.W. Norton & Co., 1978.

WORTIS, R.P. The acceptance of the concept of the maternal role by behavioral scientists: Its effects on women. *American Journal of Orthopsychiatry,* 1971, *41* (5), 733–45.

YOUNG, M.F.D. An approach to the study of curricula as socially organized knowledge. In M.F.D. Young (Ed.), *Knowledge and Control.* London: Collier Macmillan, 1971.

YOUNG, M., & WILMOTT, P. *The Symmetrical Family.* New York: Pantheon Books, 1973.

ZARETSKY, E. *Capitalism, the Family and Personal Life.* New York: Harper Colophon Books, 1973.

Index

For Product Safety Concerns and Information please contact our EU representative GPSR@taylorandfrancis.com Taylor & Francis Verlag GmbH, Kaufingerstraße 24, 80331 München, Germany